Nonprofessionals
in the
Human
Services

Charles Grosser
William E. Henry
James G. Kelly

Editors

nonprofessionals in the human services

 Jossey-Bass Inc., Publishers
615 Montgomery Street • San Francisco • 1969

NONPROFESSIONALS IN THE HUMAN SERVICES
Edited by Charles Grosser, William E. Henry, James G. Kelly

Jossey-Bass, Inc., Publishers
615 Montgomery Street
San Francisco, California 94111

Library of Congress Catalog Card Number 76–92887

Standard Book Number SBN 87589–041–5

Manufactured in the United States of America
    Composed and printed by York Composition Company, Inc.
    Bound by Chas. H. Bohn & Co., Inc., New York
    Jacket design by Willi Baum, San Francisco

FIRST EDITION

6912

THE JOSSEY-BASS BEHAVIORAL SCIENCE SERIES

General Editors

WILLIAM E. HENRY, *University of Chicago*

NEVITT SANFORD, *Stanford University and Wright Institute, Berkeley*

Foreword

James H. Scheuer

The use of nonprofessionals in the provision of human services has multiplied rapidly since the initial push through the special programs of the Office of Juvenile Delinquency and the Office of Manpower Development and Training and the 1966 "new careers" amendment to the Economic Opportunity Act. What started as a demonstration effort to test some fundamental concepts about human resources development has evolved into an innovative and resourceful approach to manpower utilization. It has also helped to provide an answer to the nation's staggering demands for more trained personnel and better public and human services.

Through the program, widely referred to as "new careers," has come a new opportunity structure to enable disadvantaged people to perform useful work at new entry jobs with assured remedial education and job training to allow maximum advancement opportunities. And in developing this new paraprofessional, the program has also attempted to foster an approach for reorganizing social service agencies to meet more adequately the needs of its public.

The results have been heartening. We have seen developed an almost universal acceptance of the nonprofessional–new careers concept by the public agencies. New legislation is expanding the program far beyond the initial new careers provision in the anti-poverty legislation into the fields of education, welfare, health, law enforcement, corrections, housing and urban and community development.

In the District of Columbia, thirty unemployed or under-employed youths have just been enrolled in a new careers program with the metropolitan police department. Their ultimate objectives are to become police officers. In New York, thirty-five individuals hired by the Department of Relocation as relocation aides have been promoted to relocation assistants, and another thirty-five persons are now training to be aides. Most of the trainees in both groups did not finish high school and were almost entirely from ghetto neighborhoods.

It has been estimated that since the original thrust of the program four years ago, upwards of 500,000 nonprofessional workers have been employed in various public services. This alone has given soundness to the New Careers concept: that rich, new resources of manpower can be found among the poor and the disadvantaged who are either unemployed or underemployed.

Concurrently, the employment of the paraprofessional in neighborhood health and manpower centers has also helped to provide better and more personalized services to the residents as well as to dispel those images of the "non-caring" public service agency and the "hard-to-reach" client. The paraprofessional is the neighborhood bridge, interpreting the values and particular needs of the community to the professional and providing the necessary outreach to direct the resident to the health and service program he so badly needs. Through his efforts, the paraprofessional increases the understanding of the professional working in the neighborhood, enabling him to provide quicker and better service through appropriate adaptations in his helping techniques.

With all of the success and hopeful signals, the program of utilizing nonprofessionals is not without its problems: some degree of resentment from skeptical and insecure professionals; the frequent employment of paraprofessionals in dead-end jobs, and the lingering concept of "make work" so prevalent today in many of our manpower programs.

Professionals in all fields must be convinced that the use of workers, without credentials, as their aides—far from being a threat to their status, integrity, and professional stature—enables them to dedicate their time and skills more fully to their own professional functions of healing and educating, while other persons, with less than professional training, can assume the more routine tasks. This accomplishes a double-barreled effect: better utilization of scarce professional manpower and more extensive and improved services to the community.

Obviously, increasing employment of nonprofessionals in public service is an important part of our manpower program. In the face of the degradation and despair of the unemployed in the ghettos of our nation, there is obviously a great deal of political pressure to grasp the easiest and quickest relief from the problems of large-scale underemployment and unemployment. But it is essential that paraprofessional workers not be considered as a mass of like individuals to be employed on a hit-or-miss basis at the lowest common denominator. To turn the program into an emergency manpower "numbers game" expedient with the emphasis on the number rather than the quality of the jobs will provide neither lasting relief nor a fundamental solution to the long-term problem and would subvert the real aims and potentials of the nonprofessional–new careers development.

We must provide jobs that offer promise and fulfillment. We must aim our short-term tactics and long-term strategy toward inducing the service agencies, both public and private, the professional associations, the unions and civil service systems, federal, state, and local, to accept and understand the strategy and philosophy of using new resources of nonprofessional manpower. What we need is a maximum effort by these groups in not only legitimizing entry-level jobs, but also providing successive promotion steps up the career ladder for aides and assistants.

The multiple social goals of this program—liberation of the poor from long-term, hard-core structural unemployment, the rational use of manpower, and the improvement of human services—present a sophisticated, programmatic challenge. We have reached the stage where we must document our experiences, and then put them to work to improve and expand the exciting promise of this program.

The need for this evaluation makes this volume an important and timely one. Its detailed and insightful reports, covering the role of the paraprofessional in the mental health field, provide a working compendium for the layman in the community as well as for the professional. The social implications of this development are well documented, and the volume's in-depth studies reflect the growing acceptance of the paraprofessional in the human services.

This volume provides strong evidence that the nonprofessional–new careers program has weathered its initial growing pains, and that its adherents and disciples are now determinedly going about the business of developing the technical competence to build sound curricula and workable strategies to advance its concept of self-help, self-improvement, and unlimited opportunity for all.

Our direction is right, and our timing is good. We are pressing for new jobs and new careers at precisely the time when the demand for greater scope and improved quality of public services is growing more rapidly than our traditional manpower policies and employment programs can possibly accommodate.

No single program is going to create a perfect America. But the joint efforts of professionals and nonprofessionals as co-operating colleagues can carry us toward a better America, a new society in which the disillusion and despair, so widespread today, are replaced by hope and optimism and involvement and commitment.

Preface

Nonprofessionals in the Human Services is a joint effort by the National Association of Social Workers and the American Psychological Association. Publication of this book is unique—in that to date the cooperative activity between the two professions has been limited largely to mutual declarations of intention. Interprofessional activity started when the APA-NASW Committee on the Relationship between Social Work and Psychology undertook to explore the uses of the nonprofessional in the two professions. Over the years this collaboration has expanded and deepened, resulting in cosponsored sessions at the APA annual meetings in Chicago, New York, and Washington, and the development of the joint conference on the Nonprofessional Mental Health Work held in Washington in May 1967. The

National Institute of Mental Health facilitated the work of the committee by underwriting the conference and preparation of the chapters in this book.

The authors demonstrate that the nonprofessional can help the mental health field accommodate to rapidly changing times, but in a suggestive rather than a definitive manner.

We are aware that time has already qualified a number of the statements in the book. For example: the thrust for local community control of mental health and social welfare services has rendered obsolete some of our notions on the ancillary function of the nonprofessional; and the NASW attempt to redefine membership to include practitioners of varying credentials has caused us to review our notions regarding the relationship between the professional and the nonprofessional.

We hope that the efforts of members of the two fields will demonstrate that continuous innovation is required of all who profess to serve the community, rather than simply replicating the experiences described.

New York   CHARLES GROSSER
Chicago   WILLIAM E. HENRY
Ann Arbor   JAMES G. KELLY

September 1969

Contents

Contributors

Bertram M. Beck, Executive Director, Henry Street Settlement, Mobilization for Youth

Theodore H. Blau, Adjunct Professor of Behavioral Science, University of South Florida; Chairman, Board of Professional Affairs, American Psychological Association

Louis D. Cohen, Professor and Chairman, Department of Clinical Psychology, University of Florida

Mitchell I. Ginsberg, Administrator, Human Resources Administration, City of New York

Gertrude S. Goldberg, Doctoral Student, Columbia University School of Social Work; formerly Research Associate, Information and Retrieval Center on the Disadvantaged, Yeshiva University

J. Douglas Grant, President, New Careers Development Organization

Charles Grosser, Associate Professor, School of Social Work, Columbia University

William E. Henry, Professor of Psychology and Human Development and Chairman, Committee on Human Development, University of Chicago

Joseph Kadish, Education Specialist, Division of Allied Health Manpower, Bureau of Health Manpower, United States Public Health Service

James G. Kelly, Associate Professor, Department of Psychology, University of Michigan

Henry J. Meyer, Professor of Social Work and Sociology and Chairman, Doctoral Program in Social Work and Social Science, School of Social Work, University of Michigan

Lonnie E. Mitchell, Deputy Director, Area B Community Mental Health Center, District of Columbia Department of Public Health; Assistant Professor of Psychiatry, College of Medicine, Howard University

Russell A. Nixon, Associate Professor, Graduate School of Social Work, New York University, Center for Study of the Unemployed

Robert Reiff, Director, Division of Psychology, Albert Einstein College of Medicine

Morton S. Rogers, Director of Program Planning and Review, Human Resources Administration, New York City

Beulah Rothman, Assistant Dean, Graduate School of Social Work, Adelphi University

James H. Scheuer, Representative from the Twenty-first District, New York, Congress of the United States, House of Representatives

Alvin L. Schorr, Editor *Social Work;* formerly Deputy Assistant Secretary, United States Department of Health, Education, and Welfare

Bernard Shiffman, Deputy Administrator, Human Resources Administration, New York City

Harry Specht, Acting Associate Professor, School of Social Welfare, University of California, Berkeley

Nonprofessionals
in the
Human
Services

Prologue

Charles Grosser, William E. Henry,
James G. Kelly

The development of the professional in any field rests in substantial part on forms of exclusion. As one defines the tasks and judgments to be exercised by members of a given profession, one establishes credentials which are thought to reflect the appropriate competences and training. These acts of standard setting are understood to be approximations and to define the lower limits permitting membership. Beyond these minimal standards the professions do little in a formal way to define particular competences except occasionally to reward outstanding performance and to punish, by exclusion, those infringements of the rules that are demonstrably violations of ethical canons.

One result of this process of setting minimal entry qualifi-

1

cations stems from the fact that the standards, whether high or low in some absolute professional sense, tend to be criteria of *past* performance. The candidate must have a Ph.D., a D.S.W., an M.S.W., meaning in effect that he must have spent the previous years on a particular educational route. He must have had an internship or some related supervised practical apprenticeship. And to get this he must have had certain previous educational experiences. These and other criteria tend to follow one another in an additive way. For this reason, one must make up one's mind early —during high school, for example—as to the next steps in the sequence. And while it is easy to stop this sequence of events leading to the end point of professional acceptance, it is essentially impossible to enter the sequence at some more advanced stage. One aspect of the excluding property of the professions resides in these credentials, and a second in the fact of early commitment and the great difficulty of subsequent or alternative points of entry.

There is nothing inherently wrong with this plan, so long as one remains confident that the tasks for which the accepted criteria are prerequisite can be done properly *only* by persons who hold these credentials. One must remain convinced that some forms of helping an individual—say, social work or psychotherapy, for example—*cannot* be performed to an acceptable degree of competence by someone who has not, in the years previous, followed the typical life pattern implied by the membership requirements.

As a profession develops, it tends not only to define membership but also to claim for its own province of authority more and more of the particular tasks plausibly included within its self-defined scene of action. And as it expands its boundaries, it tends to presume the competence of already admitted members to perform these new tasks, or to devise a system of additional requirements for various new tasks which become, in effect, subspecialties within the framework defined by the initial requirements. These additions do not provide alternative routes of entry that permit some to bypass the original membership rules. They do not provide entry for new people who lack the most general requirements but who might be able to perform the new tasks satisfactorily. In fact, our presumptions are that one who lacks the more general common background could not perform the new tasks for that reason.

But in at least the health and welfare professions—in particular, medicine, psychiatry, social work, and psychology—it is becoming less obvious that the tasks to be performed for the general betterment of clients are indeed tasks for which these professions are exclusively qualified. This is in part the question of whether the old tasks—let us say psychotherapy—can really be performed only by persons with the right certificate. If we apply the older standard, an M.D. with a specialty in psychiatry, it has been obvious for some time that not only can psychotherapy be performed by people with other qualifications, but these others have won the right to do it and have developed their own professional certification to represent this fact. But even admitting that the social worker and the psychologist, in addition to the psychiatrist, can now perform these arts, where does one stop? It appears that we have already conceded this right, at least in some circumstances, to others, the pastoral counselor and the marriage counselor. Practitioners of newer forms of group treatment appear to be even more loosely distributed than this—granted the presence among group treatment workers of many who are "properly qualified" within one or another professional group.

And it is also becoming apparent that professional certification itself may carry certain specific disabilities to perform the very service for which one is presumably certified; for example, psychotherapy with the black lower class or the elderly. Certification rules do not specifically exclude this talent, obviously enough; but the long, hard, socially mobile route to such certification may well incapacitate many for just such encounters.

Or is it instead the technique, psychotherapy itself, rather than particular practitioners, that is at fault? Is psychotherapy, as a method, inapplicable to certain people? If so, then it is perhaps an example of another new concern within the health and welfare field—the concern with whether there are new tasks to be performed, particularly but not exclusively with the poor, new tasks for which our professionals are, for whatever reason, not now equipped.

These questions are beginning to disturb our complacency and our orderly assignment of professional duties. This disturbance is not only, or even mainly, within the ranks. It is in significant portion from outside—first, from a group of persons who demand some role in the care of their neighbors and themselves, and, second, from developing bodies of theory and knowledge which tend to challenge our current heavily individualistic, intrapsychic orientations toward the cause and change of inadequate or distressed behavior.

The latter concern forces us to examine far more closely the role of the social environment not only in causing but also in changing inadequate social behavior. And as we do this, we must inevitably face the question of whether or not the persons who may be effective in instigating desirable changes are not more numerous than we had imagined. This question includes, but goes far beyond, the issue of manpower. It requires both a reconceptualization of the meaning of health and illness and a reconceptualization of who are the significant others employed to create and maintain useful and personally meaningful states of social adequacy.

The first of these two external influences that are challenging professionalism comprises the so-called nonprofessionals. This is a mixed group, including many with no training at all but with a willingness to enter into some helping role with the socially distressed; the poor who see in the expanding health and welfare services the possibility of jobs, and even perhaps of careers; the partially trained, those with apprentice-like experience in some welfare enterprises; and the militants, who feel that the professions have wrongfully excluded them from certain functions for which they are or could be qualified.

For complex reasons, the professions are now confronted with significant numbers of persons—"untrained" in that they are not professionals—who demand some meaningful role in realms that were formerly the exclusive province of the professional or over which the professional exercised control. The task of the professional is clear. He must now reexamine his presumptions and convictions and review in detail the question of who, with what background of personal and experiential qualifications, can indeed perform a personally meaningful and socially useful role in the welfare enterprise. It is already amply clear that the answer is in the direction of far more people of more complex backgrounds than we now admit.

In this review, it should also be realized that the professional may well have lost the initiative.

The substantial merit of using nonprofessionals in the mental health field has been established. Most professions concede that noncertified, less trained personnel can meet manpower needs, bridge gaps with clients, and provide service organizations with skills congenial to the client populations. As the papers in this volume indicate, the professions are struggling to specify their commitment in principle so that it can be implemented in professional practice and integrated in professional training. In these attempts at implementation the professions are becoming aware of some of the structural and social consequences of engaging nonprofessionals. For example: our own professional associations, which have been central to the general legitimation of the use of the nonprofessional, have been adamant in refusing to consider workers with lesser credentials for association membership. Such action is consistent with the predilection of professional associations to respond adaptively to outside stimuli. The initiation and development of substantive innovations and structural changes in practice regarding the use of the nonprofessional have yet to take place; reluctant concessions to preserve professional domains are still the rule. The professions are mindful of the fact that the exclusion of those with lesser credentials frees them from control by the standard-setting organization. In the face of this threat of loss of control they have chosen to ensure professional ascendancy over practice by limiting the nonprofessional to a surrogate role.

At this writing, it appears that events have impelled the mental health field to consider that the independence of the nonprofessional versus his inclusion in the mental health community is no longer at issue. The central issue, we submit, has become the whole concept of local citizen-client control of mental health resources and practitioners. The use of nonprofessionals over the past several years has not redressed the deep-seated grievances between service-givers and recipients of different classes, races, and ethnic character. Current imperatives for the mental health professions stem from attempts to redress these grievances through recipient participation in the planning and disbursement of services rather than through the use of the nonprofessional (particularly the indigenous nonprofessional) as a means of providing service in a manner compatible with client need.

Use of nonprofessionl personnel has been viewed as a device to accomplish professional reform; and even further, to relieve chronic unemployment, redistribute the national resources, and integrate those who are excluded from the political and social processes of the nation. This has evolved in a somewhat Parkinsonian manner from the enthusiasm and promise which have surrounded nonprofessional activity. The new careers movement, as this phenomenon has been designated, has, in our view, inflated a useful and relevant, albeit limited, strategy to the grandiose status of a social movement. The new careers hypothesis is analogous to the Horatio Alger mystique in suggesting that individual diligence and perseverance (in the current version with federal subsidies) will provide entry to the mainstream of society, ignoring the obvious fact that only social restructuring and economic reorganization will accomplish the objectives sought. In other words, change in the mainstream itself, rather than attempts to immerse the poor in it, is what is called for. The use of the nonprofessional can, if it is elevated to the status of a social movement, become a part of what Herbert Marcuse has called "repressive tolerance"—that is, a device that provides a ventilating mechanism to the excluded minority in a system yet retains intact the institutions of the dominant elites. The service professions, having a proclivity for such roles, can avoid this pitfall by retaining a reasonable perspective regarding the scope and consequences of the use of nonprofessional personnel.

Although it may not currently be politically expedient to join the issue, few would seriously dispute the contention that this nation is a highly developed welfare state. The provision of welfare services is becoming an increasingly accepted function of government, serving millions of citizens. In contrast to the notion that welfare services should be provided as a matter of noblesse to a select group of deserving poor, the welfare state model strives to provide its benefits as a matter of right available to the entire citizenry.

The provision of service by means of a small, specially trained professional elite is viable for limited programs. But this method cannot possibly be effective in programs providing massive benefits. The future of the service professions in the welfare state is therefore inevitably linked to the utilization of the nonprofessional. Narrow professional issues will eventually be set aside to meet the more significant national welfare issues which impinge upon us. The programs reviewed have indicated many possibilities. Policy makers and social planners will have to provide the contexts within which these possibilities can be exploited fully.

If the generic benefits of nonprofessional personnel are to be realized, their services cannot be restricted to the less influential or less affluent. Complementary nonprofessional services have their place in schools, hospitals, welfare departments, family agencies, and service industries serving the entire community. Manpower plans should be predicated, if anything, on redressing the professional shortages in the less affluent community. Plans for the use of nonprofessionals should certainly avoid aggravating such shortages by providing nonprofessional substitutes.

One of the major issues facing all the mental health professions is whether we can adapt to the emergence of new alliances and new constituencies created by the nonprofessionals, with varied backgrounds, skills, and motivations, who are increasingly populating our settings. Our professions can show their resiliency by moving training and resources to "where the action is," by participating actively with the nonprofessionals and behaving as though the professional and the nonprofessional have complementary, if not equivalent, competencies. An incomplete or token response to the absorption of nonprofessionals into the professional community will accelerate the development of a social movement which is open *only* to nonprofessionals. One way of evaluating a profession, then, is how well it deals with emergence of the nonprofessional.

It is our shared opinion, based upon our personal experiences, the papers presented at this conference, and the discussion that followed, that the full utilization of the nonprofessional will aid our professions in dealing with the major issues of social reform, social welfare, and social crises in our country. If we respond to and participate in these new alliances, there is a possibility that we can develop types of service that include a new synthesis of professional and nonprofessional resources.

The use of the terms *professional* and *nonprofessional* in many ways is an erroneous and pejorative dichotomy. What this conference and the papers in this volume are about are the effects of social change upon the mental health professions. Can we accommodate, can we deliver, can we develop new definitions of community service, and can we evolve a new coalition of citizens, whatever our credentials, and invest in our communities? Or do we continue our primary attachment to our guilds, our credentials, our rites of passage, and our aspirations for professional status?

The papers that follow represent one effort by two professional associations, the American Psychological Association (APA) and the National Association of Social Workers (NASW), to examine these issues. Realizing that the conceptual and practical developments in the field of the nonprofessional concern both groups, they joined in sponsoring the conference on which this volume is based.[1]

The first aim of the Conference on Nonprofessionals was to provide a setting in which a sustained dialogue could occur between a complex of individuals and institutions concerned with the use of nonprofessionals in health and welfare fields. Our conception of the experiences necessary for such a dialogue includes experiences from a wide range of settings, some narrowly defined as mental health, some more broadly defined as general welfare. This logic stems from the realization that we are dealing in part with the circumstances under which mental health can be fostered, and in part with the circumstances under which a seldom used category of worker can be utilized.

To these ends, we attempted to encourage diversity among participants, in their personal and professional backgrounds and in their current involvement with nonprofessionals. Thus participants included social workers from psychiatric, community organization, training, and public welfare settings; psychologists with direct concern for the use of indigenous personnel in welfare tasks, as well as some with specific training for mental health experiences, union officials (our closest approximation to the direct involvement of the nonprofessional himself); and government officials concerned with

[1] Funded by a grant MH 9525 from the National Institute of Mental Health.

training, with employment standards, and with the use of nonprofessionals in other, analogous contexts.

The conference itself was, we believe, highly successful in providing this setting and in arranging for a substantial amount of involved contact among persons from these various backgrounds. This was made possible in part by the range of positions adopted in the formal presentations and by the intentional admixture of participants from diverse backgrounds in the smaller group discussions. These groups were so constructed that each reflected the composition of the full conference. This provided for intense interaction and permitted each member to make a contribution from his particular background.

These smaller group sessions focused on the following five questions: What is the range of current nonprofessional activities with which participants are familiar? What has been, and what should be, the relation of the nonprofessional to the professional? What is, and what should be, the relation of the use and training of nonprofessionals to the normal university-based training program for professionals? What are, and what should be, the non-university organizational resources for the training and utilization of nonprofessionals? What should be the role of the professional associations (including but not limited to APA and NASW) in the current and inevitably growing use of nonprofessionals in areas where professionals have been the primary workers and where professional investments are involved?

The variety of persons present provided ample evidence of the broad social complexity of this concern. It is apparent that the next steps in these directions will be taken by a variety of persons, each from his own particular value or organizational stance. These stances cover a number of specific procedures, each stemming from a different value position: the powerful social movement, which is providing jobs for those who do not have them; the trend, partly social movement and partly derived from treatment logics, toward the use of indigenous workers to bridge the ideological gap between professionals and certain kinds of clients; the effort to devise treatment forms less dependent upon delimited one-to-one relations; and the sheerly mechanical effort to provide more mental health workers for more mental health problems. Each of these positions will influence the number and range of areas in which work will be available for the nonprofessional.

The second general aim of the conference was the dissemination of such observations of value as might stem from the papers and discussions. While we believe that much was accomplished at the conference in terms of new information and insights contributed by the participants, we also believe it advisable to provide a document which can be distributed on a broader basis to interested persons.

In participating in this conference, and in reviewing the papers herein reported, we have derived several recommendations which we feel should be reviewed by the professions. In summary, we believe it necessary:

1. that the NASW and the APA jointly develop a manpower policy which takes into account the growing social need for more broadly defined workers in the welfare and mental health fields. In this context, concern should be given to the complex issue of what services are needed for the appropriate delivery of mental health care, regardless of the present occupational identity of the deliverer of that service. Organizations other than these two have vital roles when the problem is given a broader definition. These include, at least, the Social Service Employees Union, the Personnel and Guidance Association, the American Public Health Association, the National Federation of Teachers, the Hospital Workers Union, and various other regional or specialized professional associations;

2. that university training programs in the welfare and mental health fields examine their responsibility for training for increased social needs and specifically consider the manner in which nonprofessionals may be defined and provided with appropriate training and supervision. This should not be limited to currently delineated university-based training programs but should include other institutions of post-high-school education, including those defined as junior colleges and community colleges;

3. that the NASW and the APA, through their present or specially constituted boards and committees, assist in the development of local and regional mechanisms for reexamining current definitions and criteria of professional and community services, to the end of clarifying the ways in which some mental health care

delivery systems unduly delimit the social groups reached; discovering the degree to which caregiving situations have diffused beyond older established professional lines of authority and practice; and reformulating the question of what services the professional can and will offer so as to inquire instead, what persons or social settings require mental-health-relevant attention, and by what procedures that concern shall be implemented;

4. that the particular capabilities of nonprofessionals be examined to increase our knowledge of how they may be used effectively and how to provide a model for the articulation of the nonprofessional and professional to the end of more broadly based and complexly conceived mental health concern;

5. that careful consideration be given to the increasing importance of continuing education for all participants in mental health services, regardless of their formerly "terminal" training. This becomes vital as new personnel enter the broad field and as professional roles in relation to them alter.

Nonprofessionals in Human Services

Gertrude S. Goldberg

The wedding of the unemployed poor to the human services can be regarded as either a felicitous natural match or a marriage of convenience. To some, notably the proponents of the "new careers for the poor" proposal,[1] this pairing is not merely a means of employing large numbers of poor people or even of coping with the ever-deepening manpower chasm in the professions. Rather, it is a technique of improving the quality of services. The employment of persons similar in economic

---

[1] This proposal is set forth in Arthur Pearl and Frank Riessman, eds., *New Careers for the Poor: The Nonprofessional in Human Service* (New York: Free Press, 1965).

and ethnic status to low-income, minority-group clientele, it is claimed, can help to make many services, particularly those of the large public welfare agencies, more responsive to these groups. Further, the creation of one million new careers for the poor, as Riessman and Pearl have proposed, not only would raise the economic status of many poor families but would, as a result of the satisfactions of the helping role, increase the image and self-worth of the new workers.[2]

Those who deem the marriage contrived or forced find themselves torn between their deep concern for alleviating unemployment among the poor and closing the gap in manpower supply and demand and their fear that the employment of the poor in sufficiently large numbers to affect these two social problems will ultimately diminish the quality of services. Some argue that many poor persons are too debilitated by the effects of poverty to assume roles that would be meaningful rather than menial.[3] Others regard the rationalization of manpower in these professions as something more complex from the point of view of quality of service than merely siphoning off from present professional tasks those activities which do not require professionals or even adding some activities which are currently neglected.[4] The well-wishers are thus involved in grooming the professions and the prospective nonprofessionals[5]

---

[2] See Frank Riessman, "The 'Helper' Therapy Principle," *Social Work*, 10 (April 1965), pp. 27–32. Grosser reports that "project employment has profound consequences for the nonprofessionals themselves," such as a rise in the standard of living and continuation of schooling. These and other salutary effects on the workers are "perhaps the clearest and least ambiguous positive consequences of nonprofessional employment." Charles Grosser, *The Role of the Nonprofessional in the Manpower Development Programs* (Washington, D. C.: U. S. Department of Labor, 1966), pp. 49–50.

[3] See, for example, Sherman Barr, *Some Observations on the Practice of Indigenous Nonprofessional Workers* (New York: Mobilization for Youth, 1966). Paper presented at the Fourteenth Annual Program Meeting of the Council on Social Work Education, January 1966. Barr makes substantially the same points in "A Professional Takes a Second Look," *American Child*, 49 (Winter 1967), pp. 14–17.

[4] See, for example, Bertram M. Beck, "Nonprofessional Social Work Personnel," Chapter Four of this book.

[5] Various definitions of the unfortunate term *nonprofessional* are given. Here it will be used to refer to persons who fail to meet the formal credentials for "professional" positions in a given social agency. Thus a

for what they hope is an impending mass marriage, while others feel that the characteristics of both partners need further investigation during a more circumspect courtship.

It is perhaps indicative of how far the nonprofessional movement has progressed that one can begin a paper by stating as accepted fact what might have been a tentative conclusion only a short time ago. It is hardly necessary today to describe the so-called demonstration programs or the reasons for which these activities were undertaken. There are, according to a recent estimate by Frank Riessman, "probably close to 75,000 . . . new nonprofessionals, most of them in jobs . . . developed by antipoverty legislation."[6] This figure includes about 25,000 employed in full-time positions established for indigenous nonprofessionals by the Office of Economic Opportunity and another 25,000 or more in part-time jobs as preschool aides in Operation Head Start. Riessman also estimates that an additional 30,000 will be employed as teacher aides through Title I of the Elementary and Secondary Education Act, and that Medicare will hire many thousands more as home health aides. Although Grosser did not estimate how many nonprofessionals, both lower- and middle-class, were employed in the manpower development programs of the Department of Labor, the number was apparently large enough to warrant his investigation of the effects of their employment.[7] Indicative of the growing public support for new careerists was the proposal of Americans for Democratic Action at their 1966 convention that five million jobs for nonprofessionals be created in public services. This figure approaches the estimate of the National Commission on Technology, Auto-

---

person with a B.A. degree might be regarded as a nonprofessional in a highly professionalized family agency but as a professional in a department of public welfare. This paper is chiefly concerned with "*new* nonprofessionals," persons who are assuming a wider range of social welfare tasks, including, in some cases, direct service, than nonprofessionals have usually performed in the past. There are middle-class new nonprofessionals as well as lower-class workers, but a special attempt has been made to employ persons similar in ethnic, racial, and economic status to the target clientele of poverty programs. When such nonprofessionals also reside in the target neighborhoods, they are called *indigenous* nonprofessionals.

[6] Frank Riessman, "The New Careers Concept," *American Child,* 49 (Winter 1967), p. 2.

[7] Grosser, *op. cit.*

mation and Economic Progress, that expanded public service employment in six categories "where social needs are now inadequately met if indeed they are met at all" would create 5.3 million new jobs for people "with relatively low skills."[8] Finally, Congress has enacted the Scheuer-Nelson Subprofessional Career Act, which will appropriate approximately $70 million to employ and train unemployed persons for jobs in public services.

Three major recent studies—the above-mentioned work of Grosser and two under the auspices of the Office of Economic Opportunity[9]—provide not only discussions of issues and future recommendations but also, particularly in the case of the two OEO studies, descriptions of programs, job designs, and employee characteristics as careful as the helter-skelter nature of these programs permits. On the basis of these surveys, analysis of some recent programs which have come to my attention, and a fairly comprehensive review of the literature undertaken late last summer, I should like to identify the major current issues in the use of the nonprofessional. To the extent that they can be discussed discretely, these issues include the capability of the poor to assume both jobs and careers in the human services; training for jobs and careers; the responses of professional groups to the employment of new nonprofessionals; and organizational factors related to the implementation of the new careers program.

Employability of the Poor

Employability must always be viewed in terms of the specific employment and training being proffered. If aides are really maids, as Edith Lynton has said of some of the new workers,[10] there is no question that the poor are employable—they have been so employed for a long time. If the result of the nonprofessional experiment is to

[8] National Commission on Technology, Automation, and Economic Progress, *Technology and the American Economy*, Vol. 1 (Washington, D. C., 1966).

[9] National Committee on the Employment of Youth, *Opportunity or Deadend: The Future for CAP Aides: Final Report of the CAP Aide Study* (New York, 1966); and Daniel Yankelovich, Inc., *A Study of the Nonprofessional in the CAP* (New York, 1966).

[10] Edith F. Lynton, "The Nonprofessional Scene," *American Child*, 49 (Winter 1967), p. 10.

be menial jobs which offer the security of public service employment, then it is misleading to speak of new careers. Some argue that permanent jobs are not to be scoffed at, that new careerists are grateful for work and do not worry about advancement. Yet, as Joan Grant points out, the experience of several projects has shown that "within a year the gratefulness vanishes and demands for upgrading, training, and definition of career lines begin to be made. . . ."[11] It is also hard to see how a teacher aide whose work is largely confined to providing housekeeping assistance is upgraded in either income or status by accepting such a job. One fears that bringing low-income parents into the classroom on such a basis would dramatize their low status to their children rather than offer models of achievement. The professionals who became supervisors of these aides might be upgraded, but the nonprofessionals only further graded.

If, in addition, we are creaming the poor—that is, hiring only the more capable and least unemployable—to employ them in such circumscribed activities would only further the current trend in the employment market of demanding higher credentials for employment than the job requires—for example, a high school diploma and a written examination for employment as a garbage collector. If, on the other hand, persons with little formal education and some pre- or on-the-job training are being thrust into professional roles, then service may indeed be downgraded. As the surveys of the nonprofessional scene indicate, however, each of these possibilities is a distorted statement of the prevailing policies toward the selection, training, and employment of most nonprofessionals in the poverty programs.

That creaming with respect to formal credentials has been a common practice among antipoverty agencies hiring nonprofessionals has been validated by both of the previously cited OEO studies. Based on a survey of Community Action Program (CAP) projects in nine major cities, the Yankelovich study reports that "most nonprofessionals are not 'hard core.' " Only 25 per cent lack

[11] Joan Grant, *A Strategy for California's Use of Training Resources in the Development of New Careers for the Poor* (Sacramento: Institute for the Study of Crime and Deliquency, New Careers Development Project, 1966), p. 16.

a high school diploma, and 20 per cent have had at least some college.[12] Edith Lynton, commenting on the National Committee on the Employment of Youth (NCEY) study, in which she was Senior Research Associate, points out that although formal educational criteria were waived or lowered in the hiring of nonprofessionals, "selection methods and criteria, often established by teachers or social workers, tended to nullify the reduced requirements through emphasis on verbal skill or attitudes."[13] It is really very difficult to transcend our middle-class biases; in Mobilization for Youth's homemaker program, we thought we were hiring the most "down home" people possible, but, as Grosser's data revealed, the homemakers and other indigenous workers in the agency were closer in social attitudes to the professional staff than to the project community.[14]

Whether creaming has been necessary is difficult to say since the answer depends once again on how people were employed and trained, and on the job's opportunity for upgrading. Unchallenging work is perhaps tolerable in an entry job, but certainly not in one's career. That only one job level was provided in the vast majority of programs under CAP sponsorship was a finding upon which both major surveys agreed. In this respect most new nonprofessional jobs are not very different, except in unfulfilled promises, from the old nonprofessional jobs, which have characteristically been dead-end drudgery.

Leaving aside the question of career mobility, it is very difficult to determine the levels of skill and knowledge demanded by most nonprofessional jobs. Most observers have found that the new workers, in general, are performing an important role, and that they are performing it well. In fact, the Yankelovich group asserts that the satisfactions which accrue from performing helpful, socially useful work have initially compensated for the low salaries and uncertain futures of these jobs—although they anticipate that morale will wane if these marginal factors persist.[15]

[12] Yankelovich, *op. cit.*, p. 12.
[13] Lynton, *op. cit.*, p. 11.
[14] Charles Grosser, *Perceptions of Professionals, Indigenous Workers, and Lower-Class Clients,* unpublished doctoral dissertation, Columbia University School of Social Work, 1965.
[15] Yankelovich, *op. cit.*, p. 26.

It is significant, in attempting to determine the competence of nonprofessionals, that neither of the groups which have conducted the most extensive surveys of current programs has been primarily concerned with the quality of professional services, or competent to determine the extent to which the antipoverty programs meet professional standards. Grosser, on the other hand, is a member of the faculty of the New York University School of Social Work and until recently was engaged in professional social work practice. His assessment of nonprofessional competence, although somewhat more guarded than those of the CAP investigators and based on the employment of both middle-class and lower-class nonprofessionals, is nonetheless positive. Grosser recognizes that the hiring of nonprofessionals has sometimes represented a cooptation of militant activists or troublemakers and is aware of the many drawbacks of nonprofessionals (to which we shall allude later). Yet he was impressed with the extent to which the target populations were engaged when nonprofessionals were employed. "Not only is the presence of nonprofessionals very much felt by neighborhood populations," but, he asserts, despite their inability and frequent disinclination to effect institutional changes, they have had a salutary effect on professional practice in their agencies.[16] "Professionals in these projects are markedly more effective with the poor than are their counterparts in ongoing agencies."[17] Most observers admit that there have been no objective performance tests of nonprofessionals and that their impact on clients has not been measured systematically. But then, *professional* practice has not often been subjected to such scrutiny.

A major obstacle in determining the level of work required of nonprofessionals in relation to their capacities is the lack of uniformity in the tasks required by jobs with the same title. The NCEY reports the futility of attempting to make such an evaluation:

> The jobs reviewed in this study generally were defined only in terms of broad guidelines. As a result, there was little standardization within programs or between programs. The same titles often had different meanings. Any attempt to assess the nonprofessional's

[16] Grosser, *Role of the Nonprofessional, op. cit.*, p. 48.
[17] *Ibid.*, p. 50.

ability to function in a given role, or the training required, therefore, became impossible.[18]

It is nevertheless possible to discern to some extent the degree of competence which the nonprofessional jobs require. Grosser found that the wide variety of tasks assigned to nonprofessionals may be subsumed under four categories.[19] *Direct service responsibilities,* which were the least common in manpower programs, are those usually performed by professionals—counseling, remediation, job development, tutoring, and teaching. Grosser asserts that such assignments, though infrequent, made the best use of nonprofessional skills and attributes, such as enthusiasm, spontaneity, ability to communicate with clients through common language or style, empathy, and ability to help clients to negotiate the complexities of the ghetto. The most common assignments were those Grosser termed *ancillary* to the provision of professional service, such as clerical, administrative, and transport functions, all of which help to bring the client and the service into productive contact. This category might also include some tasks closer to those of professionals, such as reception, intake, and vestibule services. *Recruitment and follow-up,* which require more independence than other ancillary tasks, were also frequent assignments. In fact, according to the Yankelovich study, recruitment and referral were the most common nonprofessional assignments.[20] Grosser felt that these activities also exploited nonprofessional assets, even though the client is eventually turned over to a professional for direct service. The *bridge function,* in which most observers include recruitment, referral, and follow-up, is said by Grosser to characterize those activities in which nonprofessionals help to relate the agency to the entire target population rather than to the individual client. These functions, which are akin to community organization in social work practice, include public speaking, door-to-door canvassing, and leaflet distribution.

It is perhaps significant that Grosser's findings indicate more demanding use of nonprofessionals than the CAP studies. This is

---

[18] National Committee on Employment of Youth, *op. cit.,* p. 74.
[19] Grosser, *Role of the Nonprofessional, op. cit.,* pp. 17–21.
[20] Yankelovich, *op. cit.,* p. 14.

probably because middle-class nonprofessionals were included in the manpower programs of the Department of Labor whereas CAP aides were to be drawn from target populations. And, as might be expected, the middle-class workers were more frequently given direct service assignments.

What one can glean from available evidence is that nonprofessionals, including at least some of the indigenous lower-income employees, are being used in creative and innovative ways, including their assignment to tasks formerly done by professionals and to other previously neglected tasks, particularly those related to linking low-income clientele with social agencies. There appear, however, to be a considerable number of housekeeping assignments, particularly among teacher aides, although some school systems seem to be moving toward permanent aide positions that allow for substantial upgrading.[21] What we lack are data that would provide some indication of the extent to which nonprofessionals with various levels of skill, prior experience, and formal credentials can meet the demands of the tasks which they are required to perform.

Despite our inability to offer a definite answer to the question of the employability of the poor, it is possible to identify some of the strengths and weaknesses of nonprofessionals, particularly indigenous workers. In the following discussion an attempt is made to distinguish between the capacity to perform current nonprofessional jobs and the ability to master the knowledge required to achieve upward mobility.[22] It should be noted, however, that neither those who are skeptical of the nonprofessional's competence nor those who contend that he can perform adequately or that he has special rapport with the disadvantaged are able to supply evidence beyond their own impressions.

[21] See, for example, Newark Board of Education, *A Proposal from the Newark Board of Education to the Ford Foundation,* 1966 (presented at a Conference on Training the Nonprofessional, sponsored by Scientific Resources, Inc., Washington, D. C., March 15–16, 1967). Also see National Committee on Employment of Youth, *op. cit., passim,* for a discussion of the efforts of the Philadelphia school system to incorporate nonprofessionals into the regular school staff and to provide career potential for nonprofessionals.

[22] The content of this section is based on an earlier paper by the author, "Job and Career Development for the Poor—the Human Services," *IRCD Bulletin,* 2 (September 1966), pp. 1–5.

Sherman Barr, as we have noted, found that many of the indigenous workers in the Mobilization for Youth program were too limited, as a result of the deleterious effects of poverty, to assume new roles in the human services:

> It is extremely difficult to vitiate the effects of the many years of poverty, brutalization, and discrimination endured by many poor indigenous persons. Expected limitations remain pervasive in spite of training efforts.[23]

It is Barr's corollary view that those indigenous persons who have been less disadvantaged are more valuable human service workers. "Those who were most successful had in the main experienced less poverty, were better educated, and had managed their lives with a reasonable degree of success and productivity."[24] Such a view implies that creaming has not been *un*necessary.

In contrast, the Yankelovich study observes that aides drawn from the "hard core"—that is, persons with less formal education and prior work experience—seemed to perform as well as their more employable counterparts.[25] On the other hand, the Yankelovich group observed a lack of flexibility among these aides, which might be anticipated among technicians as opposed to workers with a more dynamic understanding of problems. Nonprofessionals had difficulty in coping with the unanticipated: "If they come upon a situation that deviates from what they have been told to expect, they do not know what to do. They fall back on improvisations that are inappropriate, or they simply do nothing."[26]

> Those with confidence in the educability and trainability of the poor as a group put emphasis on their special strengths or on that common capacity which experimental evidence suggests they share with most other human beings, that is, to perform at a higher level than they currently do. Some experience does suggest that the skills of the poor can be upgraded by the manipulation of such motivating variables as meaningful employment, job-related instruction, and opportunities for higher education; and there is evidence from

[23] Barr, *op. cit.*, p. 12.
[24] *Ibid.*, p. 3.
[25] Yankelovich, *op. cit.*, pp. 16–17.
[26] *Ibid.*, p. 75.

current training experiments in industry that with some extension
of training time, a very high proportion of persons with limited intellectual performance can be prepared for positions requiring semi-
technical skills.[27]

It is also true, of course, that those who have been impressed
by the special knowledge and style of the nonprofessionals are less
likely to use professional criteria to evaluate their performance.
They are also more prone to point out that those who appear to be
poor risks in terms of social deviance and lack of formal education
perform as well as persons who appear more promising in terms of
conventional personnel standards. One might assume that some of
the interpersonal skills required for human service jobs are not
necessarily dependent upon educational attainment.[28] And while
critics may find the poor lacking in verbal skills, advocates point
to the fact that although few are well-spoken, many are articulate.
However, one limited problem reported by the Yankelovich study
is that many aides, even those who are high school graduates, have
difficulty in using on the job the skills they possess in reading and
writing.[29]

Many slum residents, including some of the very poor and
those dependent upon public assistance, know their neighborhoods
and slum life intimately and are often quite canny in managing
well in difficult circumstances. Barr appropriately warns that we
must guard against glorifying a plucky approach to deprivation and

[27] See, for example, Walter J. McNamara, "Retraining of Industrial
Personnel," *Journal of Personnel Psychology*, 16 (October 1963), pp. 233–47.
For a general treatment of intelligence in relation to employment demands,
see John B. Miner, *Intelligence in the United States: A Survey with Con-
clusions for Manpower Utilization in Education and Employment* (New
York: Springer, 1956), *passim*.

[28] Regarding educational credentials, see, for example, National
Committee on Employment of Youth, *A Demonstration On-the-Job Training
Program for Semi-Professional Personnel in Youth Employment Programs:
Final Report* (New York, 1966), pp. 19–23. Gordon and Goldberg found
that competent performance of youth worker trainees was not necessarily
related to stable personality profiles. Edmund W. Gordon and Gertrude S.
Goldberg, *Report of the Youth Worker Training Program* (New York:
Yeshiva University, Ferkauf Graduate School of Education and New York
State Division for Youth, Youth Research, 1965), pp. 71–76.

[29] Yankelovich, *op. cit.*, p. 75.

a concomitant acceptance of the status quo.[30] But with that warning in mind, the knowledge, know-how, and understanding of the indigenous nonprofessional may be a valuable asset to human service programs. Nonprofessionals can help to familiarize professionals with the problems and expectations of the clientele. Having endured poverty themselves, they may offer a perspective on behavior which enhances the professional's understanding. Their tendency to embrace external rather than intrapsychic explanations of behavior and to react strongly to material deprivations, such as lack of food, clothing, and heat, sometimes merely reflects their lack of training, but often appropriately tempers the professional's penchant to psychologize. In addition, the nonprofessional, in offering direct service, can incorporate some of the traditional self-help patterns of the poor into the professional service.

A telling criticism of many nonprofessionals is that they have and manifest negative feelings toward the poor. Although it is sometimes assumed that proximity to slum life automatically endows neighborhood workers with empathy and understanding, many persons who have lived in poverty share the prevailing middle-class attitudes toward the poor. They tend to look down on deprived persons and to be contemptuous of those who manage less well than they in what they regard as comparable circumstances. The lower classes are, as a number of studies have shown, less liberal as a group than the upper classes. And those who have themselves been the victims of social inequities may nonetheless feel that an individual is responsible for his own circumstances and that those who receive aid have no right to be critical of services for which they do not pay. Fortunately, such attitudes appear to be less damaging to worker-client relationships than might be anticipated, possibly because their roles permit many indigenous workers to provide direct and meaningful help to clients—assisting with child care, shopping, and serving as translators and escorts on client visits to schools, clinics, and other institutions. It may also be that the styles of behavior of nonprofessionals are more naturally attuned to those of the client population, and that the relationship tends to be reciprocal rather than that of donor-donee.

[30] Barr, *op. cit.*, pp. 6–7.

In the final analysis, many of the questions about the true capacity of the poor can be dealt with more systematically if we recognize that nonprofessional jobs require various levels of competence, and that there is a wide range of capability and trainability among the poor. Levinson and Schiller have recently suggested a typology for social work that may be useful in delineating the roles of professional and nonprofessional personnel in the other human services as well.[31] They propose three levels of workers—preprofessionals, semiprofessionals, and subprofessionals—each with different tasks, training, and career expectations. The preprofessionals would be geared toward professional status, while the other two groups would have mobility through nonprofessional channels or through regular significant increments. Such a classification speaks to the capability issue by allowing for a differential use of workers in terms of their present performance and their receptivity to future training. Moreover it defines differentially the workers' problems in maintaining rapport with the client group in the face of changing status.

As he gained professional knowledge and training, the preprofessional's proximity to the clientele would be decreased by his acquisition of middle-class status. But he might well maintain a commitment to them such as is possessed by many professionals, particularly if training emphasized such attitudes. The subprofessional engaged in routine tasks now performed by professionals would have little client contact, and might even perform his work outside the target community. For him the problem of losing identification with the poor would not be relevant to adequate performance. For the semiprofessional, who would be upwardly mobile as a result of his new career but whose job would require continued closeness to the community, role discrepancy would be high. His discomfort might be mitigated, however, if agency rewards were no longer, as at present, associated solely with professional status. Grosser reports varying degrees of identification with the community versus the employing agency and observes that the choice is affected by the nature of the nonprofessional's job assignment. Identification

[31] Perry Levinson and Jeffry Schiller, "Role Analysis of the Indigenous Nonprofessional," *Social Work,* 11 (July 1966), pp. 95–101.

with the community was enhanced if the worker performed direct-service activities or activities which could stand on their own. High professional identification and orientation, in contrast, ensued where the service was ancillary and "where the nonprofessional's successful performance was tied to a client's amenability to service to be provided by a professional colleague."[32]

Training

As was probably apparent from our discussion of some of the pros and cons of employing nonprofessionals in human service positions, it is impossible to assess potential or employability without specifying the training which workers will receive. In surveying current practice, one finds, on the one hand, virtual consensus among those few who have given the matter serious thought concerning both the importance of training and its appropriate style, structure, and content. Yet even those who have developed systematic training programs have seldom provided evidence of their efficacy in relation to the interrelated variables of the workers' present level of performance and the level of employment for which they are being trained. On the other hand, the vast majority of action programs, in contrast to the relatively few projects whose primary interest and mandate are in the area of training, have offered new workers little in the way of well-conceived preemployment and on-the-job training, much less education for upward mobility.[33] This pattern makes it impossible or at best premature to assess the employability of the new nonprofessionals, particularly the hard-core, who presumably require more training.

Since there is no dearth of materials suggesting training guidelines, it should suffice here merely to allude to some general characteristics of such schemes and to comment about the assumptions on which they are based.[34]

---

[32] Grosser, *Role of the Nonprofessional, op. cit.*, p. 29.

[33] See, for example, National Committee on Employment of Youth, *CAP Aide Study, op. cit., passim;* and Arnold S. Trebach, William H. Denham, and David Z. Ben-Ami, *Survey of Community Action Program Training: Final Report* (Washington, D. C.: Howard University, Center for Youth and Community Studies, 1965).

[34] For discussions of training guidelines, see Grant, *op. cit.*, Institute for Youth Studies, Howard University, *The Organizational Manual for New*

Most experts recommend a preservice program (brief, to avoid arousing undue anxiety among neophytes) to orient the worker to the particular professional discipline, the agency, and the service as well as to enough of the basic skills to enable them to begin work. Then follows a period combining supervised field work and instruction, often split between half a day in training and half a day in the field initially, but gradually leading to a full day at work with ongoing supervision and regular but less frequent training sessions. This instruction deals with the specific skills needed to perform an increasingly complex set of tasks which Riessman in particular has suggested should be phased into the job.[35] It also includes general knowledge required of all human service roles, such as understanding of human behavior and social problems, and individual and group exploration of problems encountered in the work situation.

A particularly important component of training programs, in view of problems of recording and reporting, is remediation. Speaking in terms of the types, rather than the sequence, of instruction offered, William Denham, of the Howard University Institute for Youth Studies, identifies a "basic core curriculum" for the employability aspect of training.[36] The goal is to develop understanding of the agency, satisfactory work habits, and acceptance of supervisory authority. In addition, there is a "specialty skill component" consisting of the knowledge and skills needed to perform the particular task.

The style and format of most training programs have been based on the assumed learning characteristics of the nonprofessionals and their need for phased training, the acquisition of skills functionally related to the tasks, an active style of teaching, and

---

Careers Training (Washington, D. C., 1966); Frank Riessman, "Issues in Training the Nonprofessional" (New York: New York University, New Careers Development Center, 1967); and Anatole Shaffer and Harry Specht, *Training the Poor for New Careers,* Monograph No. 5 (Walnut Creek, Calif.: Contra Costa Council of Community Services, 1966).

[35] Riessman, "Issues in Training the Nonprofessional," *op. cit.*

[36] William H. Denham, "The Nonprofessional in Social Welfare: Dimensions and Issues," working paper prepared for the Institute on the New Nonprofessional, Massachusetts State Conference on Social Welfare, Boston, Mass., December 12, 1966.

frequent reinforcement and minimization of anxiety.[37] Peer learning and such group techniques as job simulation and role play are popular. However, in view of the fact that most nonprofessionals have been creamed in terms of educational attainments, one wonders whether on the one hand the training is unnecessarily diluted or devoid of conceptual material, or whether the learning characteristics of the group which has thus far comprised the nonprofessional corps are really so special after all. An unscholastic approach may be more compatible with the learning style of most people, particularly when they are being trained for a job. On the other hand, it is a mistake to gear training to one style of learning in view of the increasing evidence that the lower classes may exhibit a greater range of behavior and of conceptual levels than the middle classes.[38] Finally, it may be important to think in terms of goals rather than learning styles, in which case the quick, nondidactic method may be appropriate for the job at hand, especially at the entry level, and the more discursive, conceptually oriented approach more compatible with subsequent education for upgrading.

Because the nonprofessional is by definition untrained, we have naturally tended to concentrate on his need for training.[39] However, we are increasingly being warned of the need for trainers, and for training these trainers. Clearly the techniques and content of the education offered to social workers and psychologists may provide basic knowledge upon which an understanding of most practice depends, but they are hardly geared to the training needs of nonprofessionals. Riessman has recently posed the problem in terms of manpower:

[37] Grant, *op. cit.*, p. 12.

[38] The diversity of behavioral patterns among the poor has been emphasized by the findings of the Child-Rearing Study of Low-Income District of Columbia Families. See, for example, the three papers of Hylan Lewis in *Culture, Class and Poverty* (Washington, D. C.: Health and Welfare Council of the National Capital, no date). The findings of a recent study of learning patterns provides evidence that mental ability scores of middle-class children from various ethnic groups resemble each other to a greater extent than do the scores of lower-class children from these ethnic groups. Susan S. Stodolsky and Gerald S. Lesser, "Learning Patterns in the Disadvantaged," unpublished study, no date. (Authors' affiliation: Harvard University, Cambridge, Mass.)

[39] Grant, *op. cit.*, p. 12.

If one million nonprofessionals were to be employed, at least 50,000 training and supervisory personnel would probably be required. It is clear that while the New Careers movement may potentially reduce certain manpower shortages in the human service fields, it is also developing new shortages of a specialized manpower, namely trainers.[40]

The two most frequently suggested sources of trainers are professionals and successful nonprofessionals, with the former being used to train and supervise the latter. The use of nonprofessionals as trainers is often recommended in terms of its effectiveness and also its potential for upgrading the nonprofessional without impinging on the professional career line. The nonprofessional would offer a form of peer learning to the trainee and would also be able to base his instruction on the experience of having performed the task himself. In terms of mobility, using nonprofessionals as trainers would obviate the need for them to obtain substantial academic credentials in order to be upgraded, as is now the case in some instances.

There is somewhat less agreement concerning the desirable auspices of training than as regards its format. In the opinion of this observer, training should be the responsibility primarily of a training institute, with the employing agency supplying the necessary supervisory instruction on the job. Hiring organizations are now called upon to make substantial commitments of staff time and money to prepare any new workers, but the employment of nonprofessionals obviously makes special demands upon an agency; this fact may negatively influence attitudes toward hiring them. The training institute would meet this criticism. There is, however, one respect in which agencies should offer educational opportunities to nonprofessionals comparable to those made available for professionals. The latter can acquire considerable education and training at agency expense, frequently remaining on staff or receiving stipends during the period of graduate study. Lest status inequities be abetted by organizational practices, educational opportunities to acquire high school equivalency, associate of arts, bachelor, and graduate degrees should be extended to nonprofessionals. Naturally,

---

[40] Riessman, "Issues in Training Nonprofessionals," *op. cit.,* p. 3.

this kind of staff development is most feasible in permanent agencies, as opposed to temporary antipoverty projects.

Perhaps the best argument for devising training resources independent of the employers is that it would make the new workers less dependent upon the organization for which they work and therefore freer to represent community concerns that may conflict with agency plans. The danger of being coopted by the organization through reliance on it not only for a job but also for training would be mitigated. Training could become more generic, less tied to a particular work situation, and therefore more conducive to job and career mobility. Preparation for upward mobility is much more likely to receive careful consideration and emphasis if training is the province of groups whose major role is training rather than direct service. For example, the California Center for the Study of New Careers, and the Howard University Institute, neither of which has primary responsibility for direct service, have made significant contributions to the analysis and development of training strategies. The Contra Costa Council for Community Services, an action agency which has given careful training to nonprofessionals, suggests a month's period of basic training to be done centrally or contracted to an outside agency, followed by in-service training and supervision conducted by the employer.[41] Perhaps a good reason for having the employer assume full training responsibility after the nonprofessional is at work is to avoid conflicting authorities and to make the instruction as job-related as possible.

Although the majority of programs have not offered opportunities for upgrading, there are some promising programs and proposals for furthering the education and development of nonprofessionals. One of these is the Institute for Urban Service Aides at Georgetown University.[42] A year's course of study including two

---

[41] Harry Specht and Robert Pruger, *Job Creation: A Means for Implementing a Public Policy of Full Employment,* Monograph No. 109 (Walnut Creek, Calif.: Contra Costa Council for Community Services, 1966), pp. 38–39, 42–43.

[42] Sara Kestenbaum, *The Institute for Urban Service Aides: A Project of Georgetown University under Title I of the Higher Education Act, 1965* (Washington, D. C.: Georgetown University, The Institute for Urban Service Aides, 1967).

two-hour sessions a week was offered to from seventy-five to ninety aides currently employed in the Washington area. Students were selected on the basis of their motivation to attend, able job performance, and the commitment of the employing agency to foster their career advancement. The curriculum includes growth and development, group fundamentals, and understanding the urban setting, as well as remediation techniques. The project hopes to demonstrate that residents of poor neighborhoods with little formal education can benefit from a college-level course which attempts to broaden their intellectual understanding and improve their job performance, and that such a course will also encourage social agencies to develop a permanent career ladder for aides.

Another promising scheme for upgrading, developed by the Newark Board of Education, Newark and Montclair State Colleges, and Scientific Resources, Inc., seems to incorporate most of the recommendations of the new careers proposal.[43] In contrast to the Georgetown Institute, it combines education with an explicit promise of job mobility. It proposes differential levels of subprofessional teachers, each with instructional responsibilities. A combination of employment, in-service training, and university courses permits them eventually to acquire professional status. An aide can be employed without a high school diploma but must acquire one during the first two years of employment. There has been considerable involvement of teaching staff in the planning phase, and institutional changes, including modifications of the instructional program for the socially disadvantaged, are integral to the plan.

Professionals and Nonprofessionals

Professional reactions to the employment of nonprofessionals are not limited solely to an objective evaluation of their ability to perform the required tasks. There are, in addition, what may be termed professional *qua* professional resistances which lead some professionals to conclude that the use of untrained workers in positions of responsibility would adversely affect the quality of services. Furthermore, there is justifiable anxiety about the effect of new

---

[43] Newark Board of Education, *A Proposal from the Newark Board of Education to the Ford Foundation.*

careerists, not so much on clients, but on professional status and role. Finally, professionals face genuine difficulties in working with nonprofessionals which may stem from factors other than their capability.[44]

Many professionals, unwilling to be driven by manpower exigencies, take the position that most human service tasks demand a full understanding of the client's situation—the ability, as it were, to recognize both symptoms and underlying problems. Thus a professional social worker with long experience in public welfare commented that even in the simple delivery of a special grant check there is "so much dynamics": the implication being that the trained worker is likely to understand the meaning of the client's reaction to his receipt of a check and would be able to make diagnostic or therapeutic use of such knowledge in subsequent contacts. That such professional knowledge can seldom be utilized because of the size of caseloads, not to speak of the client's possible disinterest in interpersonal assistance, seemed not to alter the worker's position. On the other hand, Human Rights Commissioner Mitchell Ginsberg, commenting on the job of the caseworker in the New York City Department of Welfare, which he formerly headed, flatly states that "eighty per cent [of the job] is often clerical in nature and doesn't require an iota of professional skill."[45] Ginsberg's subsequent remark that much of this work might well be done by machines leads one to wonder whether the portion of professional tasks to be allocated to nonprofessionals would be so resistant to automation as new careers proponents assume. But it is clear that Ginsberg, in proposing a subprofessional level in a city department of welfare, would also assign some human service tasks to the new workers, for he alludes to the need of many clients for "someone who will take some interest in them, who will talk to them, who will take them from their home to the clinic or to the hospital. . . ." Where nonprofessionals are used to perform tasks which overlap those of the professionals—as opposed to currently neglected tasks

[44] This section and the subsequent discussion of organizational issues are reworkings of Gordon and Goldberg, *op. cit.*, Chapter Four, "The Job Development and Training Program," pp. 105–136.

[45] "Forum: Credentials, Careers, and Conflicts," *American Child*, 49 (Winter 1967), pp. 25–26.

or the more routine professional tasks—there would seem to be more reason for professionals to resist new nonprofessionals.

Inasmuch as a considerable portion of many nonprofessional roles is more demanding than clerical work, escort services, and friendly visiting, it is often difficult to distinguish between professional and nonprofessional activities. A scheme proposed by Willard Richan, which categorizes workers on the basis of levels of "client vulnerability" and "worker autonomy," appears to clarify assignments until it is applied to the current use of nonprofessionals.[46] For some feel that the most innovative and valuable work performed by nonprofessionals has been with vulnerable clients and has required considerable initiative and independence of both the agency and professional supervision, Grosser asserts, it should be remembered, that direct services exploited nonprofessional assets most effectively; and the bridge function, which many regard as the nonprofessionals' most efficacious role, by definition spans the agency and client worlds. Although it may be that work requiring professional skill is offered by a professional after the bridge has been crossed, it is significant that during the fifties it was thought that a great amount of professional skill was involved in the process of reaching out to and engaging low-income problem families— much of which work seems to be implied in the bridge function.

It is clear that there is genuine disagreement between those who maintain that the professional is, if not the only, the preferable person for most service tasks and those who insist either that the technician can perform simpler tasks adequately or that the nonprofessional brings a special understanding which is in some instances more helpful to the low-income clientele than the assistance of a professional. The extreme generic position would perhaps be that even if community persons have more information about the environment of the client, it is the trained person who has the dynamic understanding to utilize this knowledge in the helping process. Sherman Barr, moreover, has argued that neither the knowledge nor the know-how of the indigenous worker is so special that

[46] Willard C. Richan, "A Theoretical Scheme for Determining Roles of Professional and Nonprofessional Personnel," *Social Work,* 6 (October 1961), pp. 22–28.

it cannot be learned by good professionals[47] (although in practice professional training has not stressed such understanding). This argument deals with that rationale for using indigenous staff which is related to their proximity to the clientele, but it overlooks that aspect of the manpower issue which concerns not whether over-worked professionals can acquire more skills but whether they can be relieved of some of their tasks by skilled nonprofessionals. Clearly there are a variety of questions raised by this problem, the resolution of which is dependent partly on philosophical commitments and partly on unavailable data.

Proponents of the new careers proposal argue that professionals will be upgraded by the employment of nonprofessionals because they will no longer be required to perform the more menial aspects of their assignments, will become supervisors and trainers of nonprofessionals, or will by implication be enhanced with the addition of lower-rung personnel. Once again, much depends on what parts of the former tasks are assigned to nonprofessionals. If direct service, itself encompassing many levels of competence, is offered by nonprofessionals, then it is understandable that professionals would be resentful of untrained persons who perform a role for which they were prepared by years of education. A major strength of the new careers proposal, that it offers an alternative route to professional status than the present one of acquiring credentials prior to employment, may at the same time be a source of friction unless it is clearly understood that nonprofessionals will also have to earn credentials—the difference being that they can do so subsequent to employment. Further, in fields such as teaching, where status is based largely on education and experience rather than on standards of performance, the employment of persons whose sole qualifications are service-defined is not only revolutionary but threatening to professional staff.[48] Finally, many professionals chose their life's work because they most wanted to be directly engaged in helping those in need, and such persons may find supervision and training of nonprofessionals or administration less rewarding than work with clients. If there is so much satisfaction for the nonpro-

---

[47] Barr, *op. cit.*, p. 6.
[48] I am indebted to Edith Lynton for help in developing this point.

fessional in the helping role, are some professionals going to be content to give it up? On the other hand, continuing to perform tasks which have been assumed by nonprofessionals—perhaps even former clients—may be inconsistent with the professional's career aspirations. Once again, a strength of the new careers plan—its blurring of the line between donor and donee—may threaten both the satisfactions and the privileged standing of professionals. If only a portion of the new careerists—for example, one-fourth, or 250,000 —were to enter the social-welfare field, they not only would outnumber the professional social workers but would exceed the total number of social welfare personnel currently employed in the United States. Regardless of the division of assignments, their employment would cause massive dislocations, the effects of which must be anticipated as clearly as possible.

The supervision and training of nonprofessionals tax even those professionals who are most convinced of their capabilities and least concerned about the status problems which their employment poses. (That there are many such professionals is suggested by the Yankelovich study, which concluded that friction between professionals and nonprofessionals is confined to a small minority and that "the majority of social workers in these programs are committed to the nonprofessional concept and are trying to make it work.")[49] Since nonprofessionals do not belong to the professional culture, they are often likely to question its basic assumptions and, in a setting which encourages their independence, to openly express resentment of professionals. Such hostility often arises from differences of social class and racial or ethnic identity, and while much of it may be a projection of past bitter experiences, the indigenous worker may also be reacting to the current prejudices of many professionals toward lower-class groups and to the status structures of many organizations which institutionalize these prejudices.

The professional who can learn to face these various assaults and to deal differentially with biases according to whether they are his own, the nonprofessional's, or the institution's is likely to become a much more competent worker, particularly with clientele resembling the nonprofessional. It is also likely, however, to be unusually

[49] Yankelovich, *op. cit.*, p. 74.

confident and competent. If such competence is to become commonplace, it will need to be deliberately developed in the course of professional study and in-service training.

Organizational Issues

The organizational issues raised by implementation of the new careers programs are naturally related to the characteristics of the institutions in which the nonprofessionals will be employed. Many, though not all, observers agree that the vast majority of new careerists should work in the large public health, educational, or welfare agencies.[50] These agencies are not only the largest dispensers of human services and hence the largest employers of human service workers; they are also chronically understaffed. Moreover, they serve the poor—that is, the clientele with whom new careerists are thought to have special rapport. However, for those who feel that nonprofessionals may diminish the quality of services, the fact that the poor will be their clients is a drawback. Some have warned that the nonprofessional movement may simply perpetuate the tradition of offering poor services to the poor. Another reason for choosing the public welfare institutions is that these agencies are poorly attuned to lower-income clientele; indigenous nonprofessionals would seem to offer a special advantage. Specht and Pruger, however, point out that there are special obstacles to their employment where they are most needed—that is, where the institution lacks rapport with the community;[51] teacher aides might be employed in Harlem but probably not in Scarsdale. Frequently too, they note, institutions seek to know how they are perceived by a community, but reject such information and the informers when it is candidly given.[52] On the other hand, two of the attributes that these authors suggest are conducive to the employment of new careerists are characteristic of large welfare agencies: a prior differentiation

[50] The Yankelovich report suggests using the Community Action Agency programs for nonprofessionals as a stepping stone to outside jobs in industry as well as in voluntary and government agencies. See pp. 85–88.

[51] Robert Pruger and Harry Specht, *Working with Organizations to Develop New Careers Programs*, Monograph No. 110 (Walnut Creek, Calif.: Contra Costa Council for Community Services, 1966), p. 31.

[52] *Ibid.*, pp. 20–21.

and specialization of staff in terms of both occupation and level of authority, and a tradition of employing subprofessionals.[53] The stability of employment which these institutions provide and their policy of offering training incentives, at least to high-status employees, also make them compatible with the new careers concept.

Although they are the appropriate sources of employment for nonprofessionals, these institutions present a number of legal, civil service, and funding problems which must be identified and dealt with by planners. There may be both legal and quasi-legal problems in restructuring, the former resulting from enabling legislation, and the latter from civil service, licensing, or departmental regulations. Federal, state, or local laws may stipulate that only certain kinds of tasks can be performed by certain kinds of people. For example, the laws may require that initial or continuing eligibility for public assistance be established by persons with a college education. Thus the inclusion of persons without a high school diploma in certain aspects of the eligibility process may well pose legal problems. The second type of difficulty pertains to the inviolability of job descriptions. For example, even though there may be no law stating that a probation officer is the employee charged with visiting the probationer in order to assess his home situation, this task may nevertheless be included in civil service or departmental classifications or descriptions of the job. Consequently, it may be difficult, although not legally impossible, to assign it to other members of the staff, particularly those with less education. Such factors have in some instances seemed amenable to compromise. Ginsberg, for example, reports that civil service authorities in New York have been quite cooperative in his efforts to institute subprofessional welfare workers, and he reports no legal barriers. And the city council of Richmond, California, voted to change the statutes which apparently made it illegal to reserve public service positions for poor people.[54] Temporarily waiving civil service regulations is a means of gaining a foothold for nonprofessional jobs in public agencies, although legislative change may be necessary for establishing permanent positions.

[53] *Ibid.*, p. 30.
[54] *Ibid.*, pp. 45–46.

The fact that many public service agencies are unionized may pose an obstacle to restructuring. Thus far experiences with unions have been mixed. In New York City, Commissioner Ginsberg reports that the union to which welfare workers belong opposes reassignment of investigators' tasks to new subprofessional staff and will assent to the creation of a new job only if it consists of activities not currently performed by professionals. In the same city, however, District Council 37 of the American Federation of State, County, and Municipal Employees is jointly administering, with the city Department of Hospitals, a program through which nurse's aides may be trained and promoted to practical nurses.[55]

Another serious obstacle to restructuring jobs to permit new entry levels may grow out of the status concerns typical of bureaucratic employees,[56] which are sometimes reinforced by union membership. The supervisors of present line staff and the line staff themselves are likely to be most influenced by restructuring, but the entire staff may well be affected, including the administrators. The supervisors of present entry staff may fear that their status and salary scale will be lowered, since in large bureaucracies these tend to be related to the level of staff supervised. Thus a supervisor of investigator aides might have less prestige and lower wages than a supervisor of investigators. Even workers who are not professionally trained for their jobs, as many line staff of public agencies are not, may share the fears of professionals concerning the lowering of their status if persons with less education perform some tasks formerly assigned to them. Related to these points is the objection, often raised by administrators, that the introduction of persons with a special status is likely to lower the morale of existing staff.

Perhaps because a stable marriage is impossible without a sound financial base, the question of funding has received increasing attention, although it remains a confusing issue. The wide-scale employment of nonprofessionals would be costly. J. Douglas

[55] Lynton, *op. cit.*, p. 13.

[56] Professional and bureaucratic responses to restructuring are by no means discrete. For a general discussion of contrasts and similarities between bureaucratic and professional orientations, see Peter M. Blau and W. Richard Scott, *Formal Organizations: A Comparative Approach* (San Francisco: Chandler, 1962), pp. 60–74.

Grant has proposed three strategies for financing new careers: through utilization of existing human service budgets; through diversion of funds from the budget of the welfare or other sectors of the economy—for example, from national defense; or through increased spending on human services, irrespective of reductions in other areas.[57]

The third strategy, increased welfare spending, will be necessary to finance new careers at this time. It may be feasible to hire a certain number of nonprofessionals by means of the first strategy, as Grant himself has done in California. (He has initiated a policy whereby the state allocates a percentage of annual budgetary increases in certain departments for subprofessional employment.)' But in view of the expenses of training and supervising the new workers, and the kinds of financial incentive which may be necessary to win the compliance of higher status workers and their unions, the creation of a million new jobs will require budgetary increases considerably beyond projected annual increments. Many professional salaries are so low that the wages of subprofessionals, which must necessarily be lower, will fall below the poverty level unless the professionals win sizable raises.[58] Furthermore, even though an agency might not be able to attract the number of professionals for whom funds are allocated, a proposal to utilize these monies to hire nonprofessionals might be rejected because this realistic response to manpower shortages would formally substitute nonprofessionals for professionals. In the past, the characteristic response to such shortages has been to do nothing, usually at the client's expense.[59] Besides, it is not clear whether such monies are indeed available, since some agency budgets may be predicated on the use of previously unused funds.

[57] J. Douglas Grant, "A Strategy for New Careers," in Pearl and Riessman, eds., *op. cit.*, pp. 209–214.

[58] Many present nonprofessional wages are near the poverty level. Edith Lynton, commenting on the findings of the Yankelovich and NCEY studies in fourteen cities, concludes, "In the vast majority only one job level was provided—an entry level at a wage just over the poverty line of $3,000." (Lynton, *op. cit.*, p. 11.) The Yankelovich survey reports that 39 per cent of the aides received between $4,000 and $5,000 per annum, but over 33 per cent are paid below $4,000. (Yankelovich, *op. cit.*, p. 13.)

[59] National Committee on Employment of Youth, *op. cit.*

Riessman estimates that hiring a million nonprofessionals would cost $5 billion; this is not much compared with military expenditures, but rather unlikely in view of them. Conversion of military budgets is out of the question at present. The public agencies at local and state levels are both short-staffed and shortchanged. It is clear, therefore, that implementation of the new careers program requires federal support considerably beyond the current financial commitments of the grant-in-aid programs. It is not at all certain that such increased federal support for welfare will be forthcoming.

Professionals and Implementation

This overview may be unduly overcast, possibly because of the seriousness of the situation. It is, after all, one thing to be enthusiastic about casual dating—or, in this case, scattered demonstration programs—but another to contemplate a serious courtship which may culminate in a permanent alliance. If the poor have most to gain from this engagement, they may also have much to lose. There is the chance that if the new careers are not properly designed, service will fail to improve and employment will prove temporary after all. There is also the question of priorities, particularly in view of the apparent retreat from the war on poverty. Employment in the human services may be more permanent than, for example, jobs in mass public works programs to build hospitals, housing, and schools. But the latter programs may offer more substantial aid and employment to more of the hard-core poor than programs to hire the less unemployable as nonprofessionals.

The question of the public and political support for the legislation, funds, and institutional adjustments necessary for implementation of the new careers concept may lie beyond the scope of most professionals, although Riessman has been pressing for a movement in which professionals join the present nonprofessional, civil rights, and antipoverty groups to develop mass support for new careers. Our primary responsibility as professionals, however, is to encourage and design research and demonstration which will permit more definitive evaluation of the new careers concept than this overview could possibly report.

CHAPTER II

Sociological Comments

Henry J. Meyer

Professionalization has been defined as the process through which an occupation, or cluster of related occupations, achieves a distinctive form.[1] Social work has emerged as an identifiable specialization engaging a considerable number of persons in full-time remunerative employment; these persons have acquired a set of distinctive skills based on an accumulated body of presumed fundamental knowledge. They identify with one another and share the conviction that a necessary social function can be best executed through their occupational group.

[1] This conception has been presented in Henry J. Meyer, "The Effect of Social Work Professionalization on Manpower," in Edward E. Schwartz, ed., *Manpower in Social Welfare: Research Perspectives* (New York: National Association of Social Workers, 1966), pp. 68–70.

40

The trappings of professional identity—symbols of membership, associations, regularized channels of entrance and legitimacy, norms of appropriate behavior in relation to clientele and fellow professionals, codified as well as informally inculcated values, and an apparatus of boundary defenses—all are evident in social work. Like other professions, it is subject to external and internal forces that generate new professional segments as the tasks of the profession become differentiated, as new demands and new knowledge press on it, and as new roles become defined in the changing systems where social work is practiced.

What can be said about the state of professionalization in social work today? First, social work is an uneasy profession. Still in the process of professionalizing, it lays uncertain claim to competent performance of tasks unclearly specified in a domain with vaguely defined boundaries. The profession is not sure what its skills are or what the criteria of skillful performance should be. It struggles to distinguish the central components of professional skill and responsibility from those which are shared with other professions. It is not universally recognized, and it is scarcely protected by law or custom.

Social work is a profession under pressure. It is subject to impossible demands for performance, and it is defensive about its inability to meet them. The burgeoning demands for manpower in sheer quantity alone threaten its sense of standards and its capacity to fill the positions it feels a responsibility to fill. It is also pressed by new knowledge inputs from the social and behavioral sciences, often imported by rising elements within the profession that strive to achieve status by espousing dramatic new approaches to supersede unfruitful older ways. New inputs—whether supported knowledge, plausible theories, or fads and fashions—assail the established store of professional knowledge and the wisdom of practitioners. The threat of obsolescence is often made to seem more imminent by the attempts of institutes and professional conferences to bring practitioners up to date.

Social work is a profession locked into bureaucracies. Its practitioners cannot escape the strains that beset the professional in the complex organization, even where the agency itself is staffed almost entirely by social workers and the bureaucracy is composed of professionals. More commonly, professional social workers are subject to organizational demands, determinations, and evaluations from laymen and other professions. In a very real sense, it is the agency that can in many instances be said to perform the professional services. We may properly think of the agency as the user of both professional and nonprofessional workers.

Social work is a changing profession. Like other social forms, social work is adaptive, unevenly and often reluctantly and not necessarily in ways that reduce the pressures on it. And finally, it is an indispensable profession. By *indispensable* I mean only to recognize that the responsibilities placed on social work must be performed, and that, in the present social system, it is expected that social work will perform them.

After making these sweeping generalizations about the social welfare profession today, I must caution the reader that the statement is incomplete, that the variation within social work is great, and that the concept of "profession" itself probably implies both more unity and more stability than detailed analysis would reveal. What I mean to convey is: (1) that social work has characteristics of uncertainty, tension under pressure, and dependence on bureaucratic structures, as well as indications of change and inescapable responsibility; (2) that social work as a profession has sufficient organic unity through its associational structure, its responsiveness to leadership, and its sense of identity to respond in some way to changes that affect the occupational structure of social welfare; (3) that the socialization of professionals into social work —largely through the schools and especially the apprenticeship features of field instruction—tends to confer on the practitioner the characteristics I have attributed to the profession; and (4) that a consequence of the current stage of professionalization in social work is ambivalence—both rigidity and fluidity, defensiveness and receptivity to change. As one example, note that the demand for professional social workers generates at the same time a sense of urgency to respond in some way and a feeling that there is no need to change, a willingness to experiment and a conviction that the old ways are good enough.

Professional and Not-professional

Arthur Pearl and Frank Riessman,[2] among others, have given a special meaning to the term *nonprofessional,* and they themselves recognize that this is but one of the not-professional categories that have significance to the social work profession.[3] They mean the indigenous worker, selected from the population class from which clients are drawn, and used with professional supervision in the execution of agency or program purposes. The concept carries the double meaning of an addition to service personnel, performing some of the functions otherwise done by professionals and a complex method of intervention; thus the nonprofessional is both a means of increasing manpower and an embodiment of the "helper" therapy principle[4] of "new careers for the poor." The *non*professional is distinguished from the *sub*professional in that he performs different but not lower functions than the professional. He is distinguished from the untrained worker who performs professional functions without professional training. The nonprofessional is assumed to be lower class, since his employment is intended as a first step in social mobility. He is assumed to be uneducated, not differently educated. The nonprofessional is conceived as both a target and an agent of intervention.

Whatever other purposes there may be in the employment of the nonprofessional, he has been deliberately introduced into the service enterprise as an addition to the manpower resource. As such he takes his place beside other not-professionals and, like them, forces attention to the definition of the role, tasks, and relative position of the professional social worker. If the nonprofessional

---

[2] Arthur Pearl and Frank Riessman, eds., *New Careers for the Poor* (New York: Free Press, 1965). See also Frank Riessman, "The Revolution in Social Work: The New Nonprofessional," *Trans-Action,* 2 (November–December 1964), pp. 12–17; and George Brager, "The Indigenous Worker: A New Approach to the Social Work Technician," *Social Work,* 10 (April 1965), pp. 33–40.

[3] See Jack Otis, "Problems and Promise in the Use of Indigenous Personnel," *Welfare in Review,* 3 (June 1965), pp. 12–19.

[4] See Frank Riessman, "The 'Helper' Therapy Principle," *Social Work,* 10 (April 1965), pp. 27–32.

takes on professional orientations without professional legitimacy,[5] if he does what professionals presumably should do but have not been or cannot be trained to do, if he develops a possessive identification with his functional role in the service complex—he adds to the problem of delineating the distinctive qualifications of the professional social worker and thereby the distinctive claims of the profession to a special status.

It seems to me that there is no other way to view the nonprofessional worker from the standpoint of the profession than as another not-professional who has to be placed and held within some definition of competitor or auxiliary participant in an enterprise where the professional must lay claim to dominance.

The Agency

Another aspect of the use of nonprofessionals is related to the fact that the agency as an organization constitutes the operating system to which professional and nonprofessional alike are bound. There has been considerable analysis of the consequences for organizations and for professionals when these alternative approaches to the achievement of complex goals are combined. One approach—through the complex organization—depends on specialization of activities as components of a division of labor, coordinated by externally specified rules whose determination, application, and performance are necessarily supervised by some organizational means of authority. The other approach—that of the profession—depends on the acceptance of goals and the definition of task activities and norms and standards of performance as internalized in prior training and socialization.[6] Social agencies are typically structures in which these forms are combined in varying proportions, and agencies

[5] This has been reported to be the case by Charles F. Grosser, *Perceptions of Professional, Indigenous Workers, and Lower Class Clients*, unpublished doctoral dissertation, Columbia University School of Social Work, 1965, as cited by Sherman Barr, "Some Observations on the Practice of Indigenous Nonprofessional Workers," paper presented to the Fourteenth Annual Program Meeting, Council on Social Work Education, New York, January 1966.

[6] See W. Richard Scott, "Professionals in Bureaucracies—Areas of Conflict," in Howard M. Vollmer and Donald L. Mills, eds., *Professionalization* (Englewood Cliffs, N. J.: Prentice-Hall, 1966), pp. 265–275.

are thus subject to the types of conflict reported as characteristic within such structures: the professional's resistance to organizational rules, his rejection of organizational standards, his restiveness under bureaucratic supervision, and his conditional loyalty to the organization.[7] Attention has been given to modes of adaptation to such conflicts, mechanisms to minimize them, and organizational forms that maximize the advantages of both approaches. Consequences of bureaucratic location for the profession as such—as distinguished from the professional worker—have been less thoroughly explored although often noted with respect to social work, education, and other "captive," "nonindependent" professions.

The social agency as a company of professionals stands as one polar model of organization, and the agency as an administered division of labor represents an opposite model. The distinction serves to suggest some issues if we examine what the use of nonprofessionals may mean to the professionals in the agency. In the former case (the company of professionals), the employment of nonprofessionals introduces into the organization persons whose presence necessitates explicit task specification and supervision on a hierarchical rather than collegial basis, and whose performance must therefore be organizationally evaluated. In terms of the autonomy of the professional in his work, it is of great importance whether the nonprofessional is the professional's helper or the agency's employee, especially if the nonprofessional is assigned responsibilities defined as within the professional's competence whether or not they are typically executed by him. We may expect competition for control over the nonprofessional to persist as a distracting problem, an additional source of intra-agency conflict between profession and bureaucracy. If the professional controls as well as supervises the nonprofessional, we may expect the nonprofessional to be socialized toward professional orientations and norms, to be rewarded in terms of his adaptation to them, and in this manner to become "professionalized" at the expense of the very qualities that are supposed to represent his major source of effectiveness. In this sense, one of the agency's purposes in using nonprofessionals may be subverted. Since the nonprofessional worker cannot by this means be-

[7] *Ibid.*, p. 269.

come a legitimated professional, he must either become a subprofessional, attaining at best the status in the agency of "untrained worker," or an unprofessional employee whose direction is organizationally determined. Thus, the role of the nonprofessional can be expected to be persistently unstable, and his presence can be expected to introduce a new element of instability in the role of the professional. From a broader perspective, these results may not be undesirable, but they should be recognized.

If the agency tends to be an administered division of labor —the second polar model—the nonprofessional worker constitutes merely another functionally defined performer, and the professional is affected in the same manner, and to the same extent, as when the organization introduces any new functional specialization. The professional's central concern in such circumstances is to protect his domain of responsibilities and his autonomy to make decisions in terms of his professional reference group. His attention will, I think, be turned toward means of insulating his professional role from a possible organizational intrusion.

We may turn now to possible consequences of the use of nonprofessionals for the agency as an organization. We regard the agency as goal-directed (often with multiple and complex goals, some explicit and others implicit) and as using personnel, structure, technology, and resources as means toward its goals. A primary reason that organizations use professionals is that professionals are presumed to have needed expertise. Therefore, organizational structure is adapted so as to attract, hold, and utilize that expertise. The structure, as previously implied, must tolerate sufficient freedom of performance and unconditional loyalty to call forth effective professional work. When tasks of the professional can become rationalized, they become available in varying degrees (depending on their relation to still unrationalizable tasks and to training, supervision, and other conditions) for incorporation into a not-professional component of the structure. If tasks are unstandardized, if the technology required to perform them is uncertain, and if exercising judgment, rather than merely following rules, is required, some degree of autonomy must obtain, and achievement of the organization's goals must depend on internalization of those objectives as well as on the skills and norms of responsibility which training into a profession is intended to provide. This is an organizational reason why the indigenous nonprofessional worker, whose tasks have been imaginatively conceived on the assumption that he has professional-like competencies in working with the special populations he comes from, needs to be tied closely to the trained professional, and why, if this bond does exist, the agency may find that its purposes are not being advanced.

The assets of the indigenous nonprofessional are usually said to include his special capacity to communicate with the agency's target population, particularly to reach across the social class barrier that hampers the middle-class professional in his dealings with clients. If the nonprofessional becomes a front-line worker, some of the features and problems of what Dorothy Smith calls the "front-line organization" may arise.[8] Smith based her analysis on observations of the structure of communication and the power to affect policy in a state mental hospital. In this essentially custodial and closed organization she found a tendency for power to be distributed to the periphery, where ward attendants made *de facto* decisions for the organization by virtue of their crucial location at the point where communications with respect to patients and often actions toward them took place. Of course, the community agency dealing with the poor, the delinquent, the welfare recipient, or the released patient differs from the state mental hospital, but it may be instructive to adapt some of Smith's observations to the community agency which is proposing to make extensive use of nonprofessional workers.

One feature of organizational significance is the fact that the front-line nonprofessional has a potential monopoly of, and almost certain influence on, input information to the agency. He can become, as March and Simon put it, "an important source of informational premises for organizational action. . . . By the very nature and limits of the communication system, a great deal of discretion and influence is exercised by those persons who are in direct contact with some part of the 'reality' that is of concern to the organiza-

---

[8] Dorothy E. Smith, "Front-line Organization of the State Mental Hospital," *Administrative Science Quarterly,* 10 (December 1965), pp. 380–399. I am indebted to Rosemary C. Sarri for suggesting the applicability of this article to consideration of the nonprofessional in the agency.

tion."[9] I do not argue that this is necessarily bad, but only that it creates special needs for intra-organizational communication procedures and that central decisions are thereby limited and agency direction affected.

Furthermore, obstacles to supervision arise from the need to allow the front-line nonprofessional sufficient autonomy to use his own ways of bridging to the client population. This may make it possible for actions to be taken on behalf of the agency that commit it to some significant degree without involving other segments of the organization in the decision-making process. And this situation may require a continuous series of bail-out, back-up, or back-down maneuvers by the agency in order to square organization policy with the various commitments that have been made. The implication is, of course, that nonprofessionals must be professionalized (so as to act independently but in accord with internalized standards and understandings of agency purpose), or very intensively supervised from the center, or made subject to a control structure that represents decentralization of decision-making and policy formulation by the collegium of professionals.

Smith observes that front-line organizations "will be likely to develop mechanisms of control adapted to regulating and restricting the autonomy of front-line units." The consequence "if such mechanisms fail to develop or are ineffective" is that the "operative policies of the organization will be decided at the front line rather than at the center."[10] She notes that charismatic leadership at the center may for a time generate unity of purpose, but that this is a doubtful mechanism over the long run; its limits are apparent in the perceptible waning, over time, of the enthusiasm and inspiration with which agencies begin ventures. A professional control structure, Smith concludes, seems particularly relevant to control problems of the front-line organization, especially where center and front line are filled with persons of common professional membership. This suggests that the professional type of social agency may more effectively manage front-line organization problems than other types of agency and, hence, may be more likely to use nonpro-

[9] James G. March and Herbert A. Simon, *Organizations* (New York: Wiley, 1958), p. 165, as cited in Smith, *op. cit.*
[10] Smith, *op. cit.*, p. 397.

fessionals successfully. It also suggests that the nonprofessional needs to be closely tied to professionals, at least for the sake of organizational effectiveness.

The foregoing analysis does not imply a restrictive concept of either the agency or the professional within it. Indeed, the introduction of nonprofessionals on the initiative of agency management may serve to shake loose rigid concepts of professional social-work functions and responsibilities and to generate new modes of professional practice, particularly those calling for supervision, coordination, organizational manipulation, and community linkages. The clinical skills of the professional social worker in these circumstances are likely to be placed in a broader context in the agency that uses nonprofessional workers. Thus, a result of the use of nonprofessionals may be to stimulate new professional organizations as well as new modes of professional practice and new kinds of professional practitioners. The use of nonprofessionals may quite properly, I think, be seen as itself a strategy of agency change.

Before leaving the topic of the nonprofessional in the agency, I want to comment briefly on the concept of career as applied to the nonprofessional and its relation to the profession. However dependent or independent he is as regards the professional, it is evident that the nonprofessional can rise only in the *organizational* structure; he cannot enter the profession. Conceivably, the necessary series of achieved statuses—high school and college graduation and professional school—could be accomplished by some persons, but they must go outside the agency to do so. Apprenticeship to the social work profession is limited to professional-school students who are professionals in training. With present definitions, prior work experience is irrelevant to the legitimation system. The openings for career advancement would seem to be especially limited in the professional agency. There might be more opportunity in the less professionalized agency, but such an agency is less likely to use nonprofessionals in the first place, and if they are used, is quite likely to see them in positions that are functionally fixed rather than the first steps in a career. A substitute for career advancement in a dead-end job is improvement of the conditions of the job. In the circumstances faced by the nonprofessional worker, he may be expected as a structural consequence to develop an individual and probably a collective interest in strengthening wages and job security. This adds another basis for strain within the organization and between the nonprofessional and the professional.

Nonprofessional as Bridge

The "bridging" function of the nonprofessional[11] is often stressed as a major advantage to the agency in the use of such workers. It is said to rest on the nonprofessional's interclass communication and mediation skills, which can increase the access of the professional and thus of the agency to the target population. The nonprofessional is a two-way communication channel. It may be useful to consider briefly some of the characteristics of the nonprofessional within a broader view of linkages between the agency and its potential clientele.

Attention has been given recently to the complementary functions of the formal organization and community social groups (families, neighborhoods, voluntary associations, and the like) in the achievement of social objectives such as education, control of delinquency, and adjustment of new or returning persons and families in the community.[12] Theoretical analysis and observation lead to the conclusion that organizations must and do find means of linkage with the social world of their clientele, and that mechanisms of coordination can be deliberately utilized to enhance the achievement of agency goals. These linking mechanisms range from those that are limited in intensity, control or initiative by the agency, and provision of professional expertise but have wide coverage (for example, mass media) to those that provide more focused expertise, intensity, and initiative, but somewhat less scope (for example, the detached professional worker). If we regard the nonprofessional worker as a bridge, a communication channel, what sort of linking mechanism does he provide?

The strength of the nonprofessional as a link stems from his double position as a member of the community and its groups, on

[11] Pearl and Riessman, *op. cit.,* p. 86.

[12] Eugene Litwak and Henry J. Meyer, "A Balance Theory of Coordination Between Bureaucratic Organizations and Community Primary Groups," *Administrative Science Quarterly,* 11 (June 1966), pp. 31–58.

the one hand, and a member of the agency, on the other hand. Having access to both, he can serve as a common messenger in their interaction, much as the school child can serve as a liaison between school and family. The nonprofessional's identification with both agency and community is essential; if he loses identification with either, his function as a linking mechanism is greatly diminished. The most obvious threat to this double identification arises from the previously discussed processes that move the nonprofessional toward a professionalized or an agency-defined orientation; however, it is also possible that he will become a representative of, rather than a participant in, the community from which he comes.

If we broaden the meaning of nonprofessional worker to include any persons drawn from the potential client population, paid or voluntary, who participate in agency-determined activities, we broaden our recognition of the communication function they can serve as common messengers. It would be well to recognize that the use of clients in as many organizational roles as possible will strengthen the bridge between agency and its community. Therefore, positions which seem remote from the service functions that are often identified as the special province of the nonprofessional can be deliberately developed and clients deliberately selected and placed in these positions so that they can serve as common messengers in the linking process.

In the public schools, we have seen the development of the school-community agent as the professional person who attempts to exploit the wide range of linking mechanisms that may be available. The counterpart might be developed in any agency, and he would use the nonprofessional worker as but one of the several potential linkages available to the agency. I am sure that this possibility has already been recognized and that it is a deliberate part of the effort of some agencies. I think it might be given more emphasis as programs to use nonprofessionals are instituted.

If this is done, the nonprofessional in the agency will need to be supervised with as much attention to his linking function to the wider community as to his bridging function to the particular clients or client groups with which he works. This suggests that the *agency* function of the nonprofessional as well as his program function should be clearly recognized by the professional staff. As a means of linking the agency and its community, the nonprofessional might be given different tasks and his role more broadly defined.

Role Strains

The foregoing discussion has noted some of the implications of using nonprofessionals in the organizational setting. I now turn briefly to some of the strains introduced in the role of the professional person placed in the position of using nonprofessionals.

The most obvious strain arises from the ambiguity of dealing with the nonprofessional both as a client to be helped and as an agent in the helping process. This is a structured strain built into the concept of the nonprofessional worker. In the face of role ambiguity, the professional worker is likely to fluctuate but finally to resolve the ambiguity by acting in terms of one or the other expectation. This resolution does not remove the strain, however, since the double definition will persist and will affect the role relations of professional and nonprofessional.

Decisions by the professional can often be made in such a way as to satisfy both expectations placed on his role, but it cannot be assumed that the decision required of the nonprofessional on behalf of another client or client group will always be the one most helpful to the nonprofessional himself. We do not have enough information to specify when the helper-therapy principle is operative, when it succeeds or fails in helping the nonprofessional or another client or both. In any event, the professional is put in a position of uncertainty with respect to his responsibility in the situation.

The professional who uses the nonprofessional is also likely to experience strain with respect to his norm of accountability as a result of role ambiguity. How can he fulfill his responsibility for a client once removed? The nonprofessional cannot be assumed to have professional standards of accountability in his dealings with clients, and it is not surprising that some of the reports of experience in using nonprofessionals indicate that more attention has to be given to training the nonprofessional in this kind of responsibility. Furthermore, whatever other qualifications he may have that make him more effective with clients, the nonprofessional cannot be expected to have the special expertise of the professional. Relinquishing the responsibility to use what he believes—rightly or wrongly—to be his professional expertise is likely to be another source of strain for the professional.

The ambiguity noted also puts the professional in a position where another of his professional norms may be threatened. The nonprofessional as helper acquires, at least to some degree, the status of colleague of the professional. They are co-helpers and in some respects on equal footing. What norms are available to define such a relationship?

Finally, in more than a semantic sense, the idea of "using" the client as a worker may give some pause to the professional worker socialized in the norm of service. To be sure, such use may also be service; but then again it may not be. In any event, the professional will have to reconcile potential conflicts with what he has had firmly built into his definition of the proper role behavior of the professional.

The role of the nonprofessional is itself an unstable one, as Levinson and Schiller indicate in their analysis.[13] The strain in the professional role is its counterpart.

I do not mean to imply that there are no compensations for the professional in the use of nonprofessionals. Not the least of these may be a sense of extending the reach of potential benefit by bringing otherwise unavailable forms of influence and help to bear, both on the client-nonprofessional himself and on other clients through the nonprofessional. But the role redefinition required will be accompanied by uncertainty and strain. Advocates of the use of nonprofessionals generally believe, as I do, that such a redefinition of the professional role is desirable, even overdue, and that the concomitant strain is small price to pay for the potential benefits both to the professional and to the profession. Nevertheless, we would underestimate the problem of effectively using the nonprofessional if we did not take seriously the professional's role strain.

Problem for the Profession

I want to conclude by returning to consideration of the profession in its broadest sense, at the level of abstraction on which

[13] Perry Levinson and Jeffry Schiller, "Role Anaylsis of the Indigenous Nonprofessional," *Social Work*, 11 (July 1966), pp. 95–101.

we may speak of the "behavior of the profession." It is hard to operationalize with any sense of validity the concepts and observations we can make at this level, but we can predict some of the reactions of the profession to the idea of using nonprofessionals. The underlying assumption is that a profession seeks to guard or extend its boundaries, to increase its relative status, and to minimize internal conflict while adapting to external pressures. I assume, too, that my earlier characterization of the social work profession is a plausible sketch of what the profession faces today.

The manpower problem is a central fact for the profession. It is a primary source of pressure to grow, to expand the definition of what constitutes legitimate status as a professional, to differentiate professional from not-professional responsibilities and tasks and skills, and to justify the profession's claim to superior knowledge and competence. As members of the profession well know, the vast majority of social workers—approximately three out of four—are untrained and hence outside the legitimated profession, although many of them perform work that differs little, if at all, from that performed by trained professionals. I mentioned earlier that the profession will have to classify the nonprofessional with all the other not-professionals who contribute to the manpower pool within which social work seeks special professional status.

However, the nonprofessional worker, as a lower-class person drawn from the client population, represents a lesser threat to the profession in terms of direct competition than most other not-professionals. Lack of education and lower-class disqualifications, as well as client-potential status, keep the nonprofessional worker from knocking at the profession's door or usurping all its jobs. Indeed, if the nonprofessional may be conceived as an extension of the professional's scope and as subject to his control, the use of nonprofessionals may well be viewed as a manageable and desirable addition to social welfare manpower.

The claim that the nonprofessional should be used because he is especially effective where the professional social worker is not represents a different order of concern to the profession. So as not to admit shortcomings of professional competence, the work of the nonprofessional must be defined as beneath professional level or as effective only when performed under professional supervision and control. This seems an acceptable interpretation to some proponents of the use of nonprofessionals as well as to the profession. Any claim that the skills of the nonprofessional are not "natural," that is, a by-product of class, ethnic, or cultural life experience, but are produced by training will raise the issue of why other nonprofessionals cannot be trained in these skills; hence such a claim may be viewed as a challenge to professional training.

The theory of the nonprofessional movement—if I may call it that—assumes the nonprofessional's effectiveness and the profession's ineffectiveness in working with lower-class clients. This places a demand on the profession for special knowledge content in place of content presumed to have universal applicability. The significance of social class differences in behavior and their implications for intervention have been increasingly thrust on the helping professions, most vividly with the work of Hollingshead and Redlich, Oscar Lewis, and the literature of the antipoverty program. The curricular content of the schools of social work already reflects the pressures from these sources.

The use of nonprofessionals also puts emphasis on structural features more than on clinical aspects of behavior. The clinical tradition in social work has been dominant and is still strong. It cannot be expected to acknowledge gracefully the equivalent values of intervention methods at structural levels. Nevertheless, such methods are emerging and finding their place.

The social work profession has struggled to free itself from dependence on the agency, to distinguish the professional from the employee. The use of nonprofessionals in direct service functions, even if under professional supervision, reemphasizes the agency as crucial because it is the agency rather than the professional practitioner that can provide the varied forms of intervention that apparently are needed to deal with the complex social problems forced on the profession as its responsibility. The development of agency management, supervision, coordination, and other organizational and interorganizational functions as dominant professional roles will require new conceptions of professional practice in social work. It is not merely the shift in the relative importance of these new roles and their associated methods of practice that will be hard for the profession. The profession will find itself competing with sets of other incipient professions as it attempts to distinguish its special claim to competence and its claim to a special part of the job market. A new round of specializations will open for the profession a period of uncertainty about what is and what is not social work.

These problems for the profession have been presented in ideological language, but they could be translated into structural terms and viewed as pressures on the recruitment, training, associational, and other components of the profession. The pressures for change are not, of course, generated exclusively by the movement to use nonprofessionals; they are exerted by wider forces to which the idea of using nonprofessional workers is itself one response. The social work profession cannot ignore these forces, and we may expect both resistances and innovations.

CHAPTER **III**

Dilemmas of Professionalism

Robert Reiff

It is because professionals see them-
selves independently of social forces that they are able to assume
that their practices are based exclusively on "objective scientific
principles." They are made uncomfortable by the thought that
factors beyond their control play a determining role in their professional behavior.

In the last few years, numerous studies, beginning with the
Hollingshead and Redlich report,[1] have amply demonstrated that

---

[1] August B. Hollingshead and F. Redlich, *Social Class and Mental
Illness* (New York: Wiley, 1958).

57

professional practices in the mental health field have in large part been determined by social factors. The issues raised by the Hollingshead and Redlich report were timely. Awareness of poverty as a social problem was growing. There were many signs that we were entering a period of social reform, particularly in the area of social services. In the Community Mental Health Services Act of 1965, the substantive nature of a mental health program was written into legislation for the first time. The act provided for the participation of consumer groups in the planning of mental health services. The Economic Opportunity Act followed in 1964, with its proclamation that "maximum feasible participation" by the poor in the planning and the program of its large community action component was to be a fundamental guiding principle. Soon thereafter there began the development of what has since become the nonprofessional and new careers movement. One theme runs through all these reform programs: the poor must have a voice in the planning and an active part in the delivery of social services to the poor; in short, they must play a role in determining what happens to them.

This central theme of the social reform movement during the past ten years did not spring full-blown from the brow of social reformers. It developed partly in response to the civil rights movement, the struggle of a disenfranchised people to have a voice in our democratic society. But it is not only the Negro who is disenfranchised. The aged poor, the mentally ill poor, the immigrant poor, the migrant poor, all have suffered from a sense of powerlessness and rejection by our affluent society. And the social service professions—medicine, mental health, welfare, social work, and even education—have contributed to the disenfranchisement of the poor and reinforced their feelings of powerlessness and rejection, as agencies which once effectively delivered services to the poor have been transformed to a great extent into agencies for the distribution of services to the advantaged.[2] This has occurred, not out of

[2] Cf. August B. Hollingshead, *Elmtown's Youth* (New York: Wiley, 1949), Chapter 12; William F. Whyte, *Street Corner Society,* second edition (Chicago: University of Chicago Press, 1955); H. C. Bredemeir, "The Socially Handicapped and the Agencies," in Riessman, Cohen, and Pearl, eds., *Mental Health of the Poor* (New York: Free Press, 1964); Richard

malice or stupidity of choice, but as a consequence of the brand of professionalism that has developed over the last twenty years, itself as a result of certain social and cultural forces.

A major effect of the rapid and significant advances in the natural sciences during the past two decades has been the increasing thrust toward specialization and division of labor in the health services. This division of labor affects the established patterns of relationships within the profession, among professionals, and between professionals and the recipient of service. It creates a prestige caste system within the professions. The tendency toward greater and greater specialization and a hierarchical organization of these special- ties with status implications is one of the fundamental characteris- tics of professionalism today and has important social consequences for the distribution of services as well as the substantive nature of the services provided. The wish to protect the status hierarchy of a profession has led to the development of an advancement system based on titles, diplomas, certificates, and the like rather than on competence. If one possesses the proper credentials one is considered to be competent and effective; one who lacks these credentials is not regarded competent and effective. And this unfortunate tendency is becoming more widespread and entrenched. Thus, when Mar- garet Rioch trained a group of middle-class, mature housewives to be psychotherapists, there was great resistance by the professional agencies to using their skills, even though the trainees were highly competent. On the other side of the coin, the emphasis on cre- dentials not only deprives the public of the services of many effective practitioners but also forces the consumer of social services to "buy a pig in a poke."

Recently I chaired a committee for the New York State Psychological Association which was charged with answering a re- quest from Medicaid administrators to issue specialty certifications so that they would have a basis for judging the competence of psychologists who applied to be reimbursed under Medicaid. We maintained that we could not certify the competence of any psy-

Cloward and Irwin Epstein, "Private Social Welfare's Disengagement from the Poor," in Mayer Zald, ed., *Social Welfare Institutions* (New York: Wiley, 1965).

chologist; all we could do was provide a list of those in the state who had met certain standards of training and experience. We took this position fully cognizant of our failure as professionals to provide the public with the protection it was entitled to and failed to develop a meaningful mechanism of public accountability.

The professional takes the view that his colleagues in the professional organization are the only ones qualified to judge his competence. But, as Levine points out:

> Our colleagues have become so concerned with form at the expense of substance, they have become so concerned with respectability and with the trappings of professional credentials, that they no longer look upon what anyone actually does. What is important is not demonstrable competence or ideas or empirical verification but degrees, number of courses, amount of supervised experience, and legal and para-legal certification, without any evidence that any of these in any quantity or combination produce better practitioners.[3]

Professional organizations which justify their existence on the ground that they provide "protection of the public" are more accurately seen as vehicles for the perpetuation of professional privilege, status, and self-interest. This professional "autonomism" places professional needs above social needs and the advancement of professionalism above social advancement.

Professional autonomism has affected the relationship between the professional and the consumer of his services. The professional designates the consumer as a client and thereby strips him of many of his consumer rights. The ordinary rules of supply and demand which govern the relationship between the consumer and the producer in our free economy are suspended for clients. A client cannot choose the service he feels is best suited to his needs. His dissatisfaction with a service has no effect on the service, nor do his expectations differ from what the service actually provides, or if he is dissatisfied with the service for any other reason, he is likely to be considered unsuited for the service and denied further access to it. A client who attempts to do comparison shopping is likely to

---

[3] Murray Levine, "Training Community Psychologists," paper presented at an informal symposium, University of Texas, Austin, April 1967.

be labeled a multiproblem case and demoted to the status of patient. The social consequences of this unique relationship can be seen in the lack of utilization of these services by the poor and the absence of any *effective* demand for services in spite of the great existing need.

Another factor with important consequences for the relationship between the professional and his client is the method of payment. We are accustomed to think of the method of payment as a simple economic mechanism for the exchange of services, but in reality it is a social process, a dynamic force, which in part determines the nature of services and the patterns of distribution.

Professional services in America are organized on a fee-for-service basis in a society which has developed a middle class large enough to purchase all the available professional services. Under these conditions, the fee-for-service method of payment has resulted in the professional's private practice becoming a measure of his success. More specifically, the status measure of the professional practitioner today is the income level of his patients. I am certain that if one studied the career development of a psychiatrist today one would find that his status advancement is marked by constant increases in the level of his patients' income. Most psychologists profess to abhor this situation with regard to psychiatrists, but they privately seek to emulate it. It is interesting that in most European countries status is associated with professional practice in hospitals and public institutions, not in private practice. The men of highest standing are based in hospitals and public institutions, and the brightest young students compete for the opportunity to work with them. In America, private practice is the mark of status, and the bright young men can hardly wait to finish their training before opening an office. Hospitals and public institutions have notoriously been regarded as places for the mediocrities, the professionals who "can't make it" in the rich Elysian fields of private fees.

This has created another status dichotomy, between the salaried professional and the fee-for-service professional. The glamor and status associated with working for a fee result in a constant drain on the public services which depend on salaried professionals. It has become commonplace for salaried professionals to conduct a part-time private practice so as to more nearly match the income of their private-practice colleagues and thus avoid being considered of lower status.

The poor can no longer compete for the services of the professionals. They are almost entirely dependent on publicly organized professional services. But, as we have implied, the public institutions and agencies have traditionally employed professionals with less training and skill. The poor are aware that the professional services they get are often second or third rate, a fact which reinforces their feelings of powerlessness and rejection.

Possible Solution

It seems utopian to expect that the professions will of themselves respond to this challenge and make efforts to change. They can still sell all their services to the middle class while paying lip service to the programs which they agree ought to be started but which cannot get under way for lack of manpower. Some strategy must be developed which will move the professions away from these undesirable consequences of their professionalism and which can at the same time begin to meet the needs of the poor. Such a strategy is the use of the nonprofessional, whose attributes and competencies make it possible for him to serve the poor, not in the same way that the professional does, but in a way which is still helpful and which brings the poor and the professional in closer touch with each other.

The effectiveness and competence of the nonprofessional are based on natural skills, acquired not through education but through life experience. Through the natural unfolding of his life as part of a lower socioeconomic group he has learned the necessary relationship skills that make him effective. His effectiveness does not depend on acquiring credentials or becoming expert in any organized body of knowledge or prescribed skills which he learns to practice. In fact, he does not "practice"; that is to say, he is not a "practitioner." There is no organized body of knowledge today that forms the basis for a nonprofessional practice. If such a body of knowledge were ever to be evolved it is very likely that we would see the development of a profession of nonprofessionals, which would soon develop some of the least desirable characteristics of professionalism.

I see the larger social purpose of the nonprofessional movement as restoring the disenfranchised poor to active participation in society. This cannot be achieved without building career lines and a career advancement system. The problem is, can we provide for this reentry of the poor without developing a career advancement system that has all the undesirable social characteristics of professionalism? Let me state here that even if the answer is negative, I would still be unequivocally for the nonprofessional movement. It would be infinitely better than what exists today. But need we be satisfied with half a loaf? There has been some discussion about whether or not the development of new careers is simply a way of making middle-class professionals out of nonprofessionals. To which the reply is often made, "What's wrong with that?" The answer is as naive as the question is superficial. The problem is that the poor are disenfranchised. They have no viable place or role in society. The middle class cannot absorb the poor and make a place for them. Building a bridge to the middle class may help some individuals escape but it cannot solve the social problem. Many of the immigrant poor took this route successfully. In fact, a good part of the middle class today is comprised of the sons and daughters of the immigrant poor. But they were not disenfranchised. The status-advancement systems, such as education and employment opportunities, were open to them, and they used them well. Today's poor are different, and yesterday's solution is not available to them. The education system is an alien and irrelevant structure, and the old employment opportunities no longer exist in a society with decreasing needs for the unskilled. The first step is to find or create a place for the poor where they can play a role that seems relevant to them, where they are needed and effective. The next step is to create a status-advancement system leading to new employment opportunities that are realistic, realizable, and relevant because they grow out of their effectiveness in their new place and role in society. That is how I understand the nonprofessional–new careers movement.

If, as I have argued, one of the social consequences of professionalism is that it has created a vacuum in the distribution of human services to the poor, what could be more relevant than to have the poor themselves fill the vacuum? That is the role of the nonprofessional. That is the first step in the creation of a viable place and role in society. We have had enough of a demonstration to know that it works. The next step is the development of new careers and a career-advancement system that works.

It is in this phase of the program that we will face some important problems. Because a new careers movement for nonprofessionals cannot succeed without the participation of professionals, their understanding, acceptance, and cooperation must be sought and encouraged. Until now most nonprofessionals have been employed in the poverty programs. The professionals in these programs have been dedicated and cooperative. But when the nonprofessional moves outside the poverty programs into community agencies and public institutions, he may meet with resistance and even open resentment. A recent evaluation of CAP nonprofessional programs[4] found that even the most cooperative professionals tended to resent demands on their time for training and supervising nonprofessionals. Can we solve these problems by helping the nonprofessionals to develop into trainees and supervisors themselves? This is certainly an important way to develop career advancement. But it still leaves us with the problem of dealing with professionalism. The more career-advancement system of nonprofessionals resembles the status-advancement system of professionals, the more resistant we can expect the professionals to become. The more the work of the nonprofessional resembles what professionals do, the more threatened they will be. By this token, we may expect that social workers will be the most threatened, with psychologists following close behind.

For these reasons it seems to me essential that the role of the nonprofessional in providing real and needed services that the professional cannot and should not provide needs to be stressed over and over again. In structuring the functions and training of the nonprofessional, his uniquely nonprofessional assets should be emphasized. Training exercises which are traditionally professional, such as T-groups and seminars in psychodynamics, should be avoided. The ambiguities in role relationships between the professional and the nonprofessional should be clarified as early as possible. Structure will be important in minimizing conflict. But some conflict is inevitable.

[4] Daniel Yankelovich, Inc., *A Study of the Nonprofessional in the CAP* (New York, September 1966).

Many a professional individual who, as a citizen, supports civil rights, the antipoverty program, and community mental health would, as a professional, resist with every ounce of his strength the proposal to give the disenfranchised a voice in the planning and an active role in the distribution of social services. Yet this is the central theme and the major strategy of the social reform movement of our time. The potential for conflict rests in the dilemma of modern professionalism, which is self-perpetuating and accountable only to itself, but which today faces great pressure to give the poor a voice and a place in social service. This is a dilemma which all of us have to face, for without a change in the nature of professionalism the nonprofessional–new careers movement is in danger of being aborted. Without such a change the best that can be hoped for is the creation of a new caste of persons who, although employed, are still powerless, still rejected, still disenfranchised, and still resentful recipients of professional service. Always a client but never a consumer.

These comments about professionals and professionalism are generalizations, of course, referring to social trends and institutional practices rather than to individuals. Needless to say, there are professionals who abhor these developments and are struggling against them. Included among them are leaders of the professional organizations. Through the efforts of such professionals, responsive to social needs, professionalism can become a vital force in effecting desirable social change.

CHAPTER **IV**

Nonprofessional Social Work Personnel

Bertram M. Beck

The severe shortage of manpower in the helping professions has been extensively documented.[1] One proposed remedy for the shortage, to which the social work profession has given much attention, is to make more effective use of persons who lack the master's degree.

Even before the advent of the antipoverty program, only about 20 per cent of those employed in social welfare occupations in America held the master's degree. Nevertheless, the general as-

[1] See *Closing the Gap in Social Work Manpower* (Washington, D. C.: U.S. Department of Health, Education, and Welfare, 1965).

sumption was that one day all social workers would have the degree. Since 1955, compelling statistical analysis has forced social work to forsake this goal.[2] Beginning in the early sixties, Frank Riessman and others began to talk about the "nonprofessional" in social work, not in terms of a necessary or tolerated adjunct to the professional, but as a person who could make a unique and extremely valuable contribution to the helping process.

This creative approach was picked up by the antipoverty programs, and, like most good ideas given popular currency, was vulgarized. An infatuation developed with the notion that we can now solve the manpower problem in social welfare as well as the unemployment problem created by automation by employing huge numbers of so-called indigenous workers. It was held that such workers not only could find gainful employment in social work but that because of certain personal qualities, they could be even more successful than their professional colleagues in dealing with the problems of the poor. These romantic notions are being vigorously fostered by the Office of Economic Opportunity as well as a variety of individuals and organizations which fancy themselves as "anti-establishment." In general, organized social work has taken no steps in response to this unrealistic infatuation with the nonprofessional, possibly because it fears being thought reactionary or self-seeking, or possibly because it has no better answer. Instead, the profession has devoted itself to the attempt to define the tasks or the clients that can be assigned to the social-work associate.

While social work is pondering what the possessor of a master's degree might relinquish to some ancillary occupation, tens of thousands of individuals with no formal qualifications are being placed in social work jobs. There is abroad a new brand of know-nothingism which forsakes education as a route to competence and promotes the notion that social and economic deprivation are the best preparation for certain helping tasks. As a consequence of this sort of thinking, individuals who have long been locked into the ghetto are now being employed in the name of curing poverty, at minimum wages. They are now being locked into social work oc-

[2] See, for example, John Folger, "Manpower Demand and Supply in the Social Work Professions," unpublished paper delivered at National Conference on Social Welfare, 1966 (mimeo.), 12 pp.

cupations bearing the label *nonprofessional* or *indigenous,* cheated
of their right to receive education, which remains our major means
of transmitting knowledge from one generation to another, and of
their right of access to occupational ladders that will lead them to
the skills and salaries of the middle-class professional. Worst of all,
the poor, who heretofore have received little first-class social work
service, are henceforth to receive second-class service. This may be
better than nothing, but it is not good enough. Obviously, the use
of the nonprofessional in social work requires creative rethinking.

Barker and Briggs, reviewing the literature concerned with
trends in the utilization of social welfare personnel,[3] report that this
literature is universally concerned with the effort to differentiate
between the tasks, services, problems, and clients that can best be
handled by persons with the master's degree and those within the
capacity of personnel with less formal education. The approach
that awards the more complex tasks or problems to the possessor of
the master's degree may protect the client, but it also protects and,
in fact, enhances the status and dignity of the profession by con-
juring up the entrancing vision of the certified social worker at the
head of a team of technicians, subtechnicians, auxiliaries, and aides
who relieve their chief of the scut work while he is free to—guess
what—"conceptualize."

Despite all the effort that has gone into the task of defining
the job of the certified social worker's handmaidens, there is still
no agreement; the Board of Directors of the NASW has suggested
that that organization must wait another four years before it can
decide whether there should be any class of membership for the
members of the yet-to-be-defined auxiliary profession.[4] We suggest
that it is inherently impossible at present to classify problems or
tasks in a fashion that would be acceptable to possessors of the
graduate social work degree, for two major reasons. The first is
apparent in all efforts to establish personnel classification schemes
for social work jobs. Even when we are dealing only with indi-

[3] Robert L. Barker and Thomas L. Briggs, *Trends in Utilization of
Social Work Personnel: An Evaluative Research of the Literature,* Research
Report No. 2, Utilization of Social Work Personnel in Mental Hospitals
Project (New York: National Association of Social Workers, 1964).
[4] NASW *News,* January 1967.

viduals who possess the master's degree, we find that each level of social worker is doing the same thing; the hope is that those with more experience do it better. In other words, virtually all persons engaged in social work, whether they are merely high-school graduates or have the doctorate degree, do interviewing, for example. The task does not vary; the difference is in the skill with which it is performed.

Because of the difficulty of distinguishing tasks suitable for the possessor of the master's degree and those appropriate for the less favored, efforts have been made to distinguish among clients or problems that do and do not require the attention of an M.S.W. But these attempts are of limited value; problems are constantly being redefined, and the needs of various clients shift. One cannot, therefore, anticipate the degree of knowledge and skill required on the basis of the nature of the client or the nature of the presenting problem.

Social work is not alone in this dilemma. Studies of nursing practice have not been outstandingly successful in differentiating the tasks of the registered nurse, the practical nurse, and the nurse's aide. Because of the acute shortage, the tendency has been for the registered nurse to become the supervisor; this has led to the lamentation that the most knowledgeable and skilled nurses are not directly engaged in service to patients. There are similar developments in social work, and we may anticipate similar lamentations. Medicine has been more successful in differentiating tasks, at least partly because of the authority and prestige of the profession. The acts prohibited to those who do not possess the doctor of medicine degree are not necessarily acts they *cannot* perform. They are acts they *must not* perform according to state statutes which the medical profession has been reasonably successful in promoting.

The second, and more significant, obstacle in the way of the effort to differentiate the tasks of the social work professional and the nonprofessional arises out of social work's failure to define its own practice. Obviously, it is difficult to talk sensibly about what the so-called nonprofessionals should do in social work without a definition of what it is that the so-called professionals do.

In 1956, shortly after the National Association of Social Workers was formed, the first meeting of a national membership group called the Commission on Practice was convened. Persons from all fields of social work practice came together to consider a variety of issues, all of which led to one question: What are the common elements of social work practice, and how are they refracted through the glass of particular fields of social work practice? This effort, under the guidance of Harriett Bartlett, produced the current working definition of social work practice.[5]

The working definition holds that social work's uniqueness lies in its configuration of values, sanctions, purposes, knowledges, and skills, rather than in any one element. Out of the work of the first NASW Commission on Practice came the notion of fields of practice as distinct from settings, and the idea of generic social work, not as something that is practiced, but as an abstraction brought to life in interaction with a particular field.[6] By focusing on the knowledge and skills required of all persons who perform a social work job, regardless of whether those persons are classified as professional or nonprofessional, the working definition moves social work away from the dead end of trying to factor out the tasks, services, or problems that can be handled by persons without a master's degree and toward the attempt to discover how we can develop the optimal command of the required knowledge and skills.

The various bodies of knowledge enumerated in the working definition as necessary to the practice of social work include the following: (1) human development and behavior, characterized by emphasis on the wholeness of the individual and the reciprocal influences of man and his total environment—human, social, economic, and cultural; (2) the psychology of giving help to and taking it from another person; (3) ways in which people communicate with one another and express inner feelings, in words, gestures, and activities; (4) group process—the reciprocal effects of the group upon the individual and the individual upon the group; (5) the meaning and effect on individuals, groups, and the community

[5] Harriett M. Bartlett, "Toward the Clarification and Improvement of Social Work Practice," *Social Work,* 3 (1958), pp. 3–9.

[6] Miss Bartlett and William Gordon eleborated these ideas in a series of writings, constantly reminding us that fundamental studies of practice should precede studies of educational, not vice versa. Unfortunately, funds with which to launch studies of pratice of the nature and scope demanded by the commission formulations never materialized.

of cultural heritage, including religious beliefs, spiritual values, law, and other social institutions; (6) the interactional process between individuals, between the individual and the group, and between groups; (7) the community, its internal processes, modes of development and change, social services and resources; (8) the social services, their structure, organization, and methods; and (9) the individual practitioner himself.

According to the working definition of social work practice, skill is technical expertness, or the ability to use knowledge effectively and readily in performance. Competence in social work practice is defined as the possession of skill in the use of the following techniques: (1) support, (2) classification, (3) information-giving, (4) interpretation, (5) development of insight, (6) differentiation of the social worker from the individual or group, (7) identification with agency function, (8) creation and use of structure, (9) use of activities and projects, (10) provision of positive experiences, (11) teaching, (12) stimulation of group interaction, (13) limit-setting, (14) utilization of available social resources, (15) effecting changes in immediate environmental forces operating upon the individual or groups, and (16) synthesis.

Using the working definition as a frame of reference, five graduate schools of social work in New York have joined with Mobilization for Youth in an attempt to develop a statement of expectations concerning the social work knowledge and techniques which should be manifest in the practice of social workers at five different levels.[7] The statement concerning Level I, the point of entrance, will set forth what is expected of a socially and economically disadvantaged person with no less than a grammar school education who is employed to work with clients in carrying out the objectives of a social welfare agency. Level II will set forth our expectations in respect to a person who has entered at Level I and spent a year as a trainee. Level III will set forth the command of social work knowledge and techniques that might be expected of someone with a bachelor's degree in social work. Level IV is the statement of expectations of the master's degree graduate, and

[7] The schools are Adelphi, Fordham, Hunter, New York University, and Yeshiva. Hunter will serve in an advisory capacity. The others will be co-sponsors.

Level V, at the other end of the spectrum, will define the social work knowledges and skills to be expected of a member of the Academy of Certified Social Workers. In developing the statement, particularly in relation to Level V, we will draw upon the work done by the NASW Committee on Definition of Social Work Competence.[8]

In our attempt to develop a statement along the lines indicated here, we will view knowledge as relative. Most people know at least something about, for example, the extent and nature of social services. We will attempt to state the extent to which command over the nine areas of knowledge listed in the working definition should be developed at each of the five levels. For example, "knowledge of the social services, their structure, organization, and method" may be broken down as follows: (1) has knowledge of certain social services and their central purpose; (2) has knowledge of the major social services in the neighborhood and their central purpose; (3) has knowledge of the major social services in the city, their structure and purposes; (4) has knowledge of the social services, their structure, organization, and method; and (5) has knowledge of the social services, their structure and their informal and formal organization, as well as their actual methods of operation.

We will take a somewhat different approach to the development of technique. By Level II we would expect all workers to have *some* command of all of the knowledges listed. Deliberate use of technique comes more slowly; it is not until Level IV that the social worker is expected to be in command of all techniques.

As a consequence of the development and deepening of knowledge over time and the acquisition and growing mastery of skills, we would expect the individual to be capable of assuming responsibility for ever more complex social work tasks. We therefore have listed five sets of tasks which we would expect of workers at each of the five levels. These are not dissimilar to the conventional listing of tasks in standard personnel classifications for social work jobs. The difference is that we will try to relate the tasks to the time span for professional development.

We further propose to determine what combination of class-

---

[8] *Personnel Information,* 8 (March 1965), p. 1.

room instruction and on-the-job training will enable a worker who starts at Level I to develop his maximum capacity for competence in the practice of social work. We hope to develop a research design that will examine, on the one hand, the variables in the trainee's background that influence this basic capacity and, on the other, the variables in the educational program that have to do with its development. We begin with no set ideas concerning learning potential. As a consequence of our experiment we hope to develop some notions about the extent to which a person without a master's degree in social work can approach the level of knowledge and techniques we can rightfully expect from a person who has the degree. It may be that we will find that the M.S.W. is but one road to competence. Alternatively, we may find that people without a college degree tend to go no further than Level II or III.

In this endeavor we are for the most part abandoning the conventional personnel classification approach, in which each job grade is in its own little box with a job title, a job description, and a salary range; instead, we are plotting an anticipated rate of professional development, knowing that some will follow the normal curve, some will be above it, and some below. Progressive personnel authorities have long advocated the abandonment of a rigidly defined classification for professional personnel.[9] We are merely applying this idea to social work, examining the varieties of life experiences that will promote growth on the curve.

It may be that a profile will be developed based on the expectation that workers will develop unevenly.[10] Numerical weights could be attached to various knowledges and techniques and other numerical weights would reflect mastery of the various tasks. Thus each worker would receive a composite numerical score at the end of each year. These scores would be supplemented by objective measuring devices developed around the content of the training program and a combination of sociological and social-psychological instruments and techniques. We might use interview data gathered systematically, objective tests administered as part of the academic

[9] Robert L. Sibson, *Wages, Salaries and Management* (New York: American Management Association, 1967).

[10] I am indebted to Dr. Helen Strauss of Scientific Resources, Inc., for her assistance in preparing this section of the paper.

program, evaluations and judgments by supervisors and teaching staff, and video-taped interviews to evaluate skills as they develop. These devices would provide the basis for comparative judgments of the trainees and master's candidates.

Once the measuring devices are developed, it would be possible to apply them equally to the workers we are trying to educate and to those with a master's degree. We will want to know: (1) How do students at various periods of their training compare with B.A.'s in social service, first-year graduate students, M.A.'s, and social workers in agencies where similar client needs are present? (2) How long does it take to reach these various levels of competence?

The role of research is to document systematically the steps taken to achieve the program's goals, to provide some of the measures to be used in the assessment of competence, and to obtain other measures which have to do with the effects of the program.

The attainment of some objective measures for assessing social work competence would constitute a major advance for the profession. Without such assessment we cannot have a hierarchy of the superbly competent, the competent, and the less competent. We can only have hierarchies based on longevity, gamesmanship, credentials, luck, and, to some small extent, competence.

The original intent in the creation of the ACSW was not that this be a reward for two years' survival under supervision, but that it would provide the funds whereby social work could establish objective measures of competence. Although fully reliable and objective measures of competence have not been established for any profession, it would certainly seem possible, even at our present stage, to have a national board of social work examiners which might, after observation and case reading, with an examination and references, grant a certificate based on an individual's proficiency without regard to his formal education. With this safeguard, we might stop thinking about what a person with a master's degree can do, as opposed to what a person with minimal formal education can do, and instead try to spell out how we expect a person to grow in his command of social work knowledge, skills, and abilities.

I have described the proposed experiment at some length because, whatever its scientific failings, it does illustrate, in my estimation, a *professional* approach to the use of the so-called nonprofessional. It is professional because it is focused on knowledge, which is the key attribute of any profession, and not on educational credentials, which have meaning only insofar as they imply the possession of knowledge useful for competent practice.[11] It is an approach consistent with social work values because it postulates an open society in which an individual is assisted to develop his potential to the maximum, free of the artificial barriers of academic credentials. It is professional because it does not denigrate knowledge as the major vehicle through which man gains control over his environment or formal education as the major means of transmitting a body of knowledge. It seeks only to test the relative efficacy of different learning experiences made available to different populations. It seeks a route alternative to, but not in substitution for, the M.S.W., because of an awareness of the high correlation between middle- or upper-class status and the possession of the college or graduate school degree. It seeks an alternative, not with any certainty that there is one, but in the conviction that social work and all other professions and occupations whose gates have been closed to the poor must now seek to provide new routes of access.

But however professional this or any other approach to the use of the nonprofessional, they are "unnatural" in that they seek to determine whether persons without a high school education can approach the competence level of the holder of the master's degree. This is quite different from whether the social work aide can or cannot relieve the certified social worker of certain paperwork. It would be a quite natural line of inquiry if professions were concerned with knowledge, skill, and service only. But professions are also guilds engaged in polite but fierce warfare to protect their boundaries and crush insurgent forces that would displace them. Professions by nature seek a monopoly of certain acts of practice, and requirements for admission to the profession are a major means of enforcement. Thus it would be most unnatural for any profession to forsake arduous initiation rites.

This would be particularly unnatural for social work since

[11] Ernest Greenwood, "Attributes of a Profession," *Social Work*, 2 (July 1957), pp. 51–53.

it has uncertain rank within the hierarchy of professions.[12] Social workers with the master's degree tend to be quite sensitive to any suggestion that their profession is not equal in rank, dignity, and difficulty to the most honored. In one of the most frequently mulled-over papers in the professional literature, Abraham Flexner, in 1914, questioned the professional status of social work.[13] Obviously, a profession that lacks high status among its sisters, struggling for its place in the sun, is not likely to follow an innovative course.

The approach I am proposing does not put social work in the position of saying, "You can't come in unless you have a master's degree"; nor does it glorify deprivation as the ideal preparation for social work practice. Rather, it says that there is room in social work for all who have the capacity to grow, and that they all are social workers. It puts the responsibility on the social work profession for helping those who come in at the entry position without formal education to gain maximum command of social work knowledge and skill. It does not argue that everyone can get to the top of the curve, but it does uphold everyone's right to develop his potential and our responsibility to enhance competence and to reward it above the possession of educational credentials.

The solution I have presented requires that social work desert the traditional pattern of growth of a profession. This pattern is to define the knowledge base of the profession and then to achieve a professional monopoly over the acts that spring from this knowledge base. Although this can be properly defended as serving the public interest, it also serves the personal interests of the professional practitioner. Social work's pursuit of the unorthodox, dangerous, and unnatural idea that the currently prescribed formal education may not be the only road to a command of professional competence is, of course, supported by the profession's value commitment and the fact that it has always combined the characteristics of a social movement with those of a profession. From these roots may come the notion that a hierarchy of competence might be a better way of

[12] Alfred Kadushin, "Prestige of Social Work—Facts and Factors," *Social Work*, 4 (April 1958), pp. 37–43.

[13] Abraham Flexner, "Is Social Work a Profession?" *Proceedings of the National Conference on Charities and Corrections* (Chicago: Hindmann, 1914), pp. 576–590.

relieving the manpower shortage than a hierarchy of academic credentials—always with the proviso that the growth of professional education must be protected. There are millions of people in modern society who have been exiled through discrimination and who now want entry. If the master's degree is the proper ticket for entry, then it must be demanded. If, however, we can welcome new recruits into the social work fellowship and help them gain maximum competence through a variety of life experiences, then we may not only ease our manpower problem but also make an enormously valuable contribution to an open and free society.

CHAPTER V

Nonprofessionals
in Mental Health

Lonnie E. Mitchell

The possibility of social change
and the many problems any change system is likely to involve are
no longer academic issues. No longer can psychologists afford the
luxury of relative noninvolvement in the affairs of the community
in which they and others live. Planned programs of social change
in the areas of racial attitudes, civil rights, poverty and the disadvantaged, and job opportunities for the poor are being instituted
in our country at such an unprecedented rate that our whole system
of beliefs, values, perspectives—indeed, our very lives—are being
reshaped, whether or not we participate actively in the change
process. One might expect that social and clinical psychologists

would be deeply absorbed in these issues and one might hope, therefore, to find our journals full of research reports, discussions, and arguments on matters pertaining to the psychological aspects of these social change issues, particularly as they relate to the deprived and the role the nonprofessional will play in reshaping the social structure.

But when we psychologists are questioned about our involvement in these issues, we are likely to say that "reliable" data cannot be easily obtained, that the methodological problems of model building are too many and difficult. This answer may well be a self-fulfilling prophecy; believing that appropriate data are not available, we make no effort to find them. The hardships of data collection and research design, although real enough, are perhaps only half of the story. We must look for deeper reasons for the general diffidence which characterizes our involvement with the psychological effects of change on the poor and our pursuit of work with the nonprofessional in the larger context of social change. It would be more honest if we were to say that good work in the area demands not only a grasp of psychological and sociological processes in all their many and tangled interactions, but also a sense of the historical, a capacity to deal with human and social phenomena as they happen in time. This would mean an involvement with the nonprofessional, the poor, and the deprived. Although we can certainly drag our feet, adhering to obsolete models of research, treatment, and training in mental health, we cannot help but be influenced by events in fields of interest outside our own. Psychologists are behavioral scientists, concerned with the problems of bringing about change in individuals and groups; therefore, they should form the vanguard of those concerned with effecting social change in a responsible fashion.

It is no secret that fewer and fewer people are needed for material production jobs and more and more are needed in the professional fields. One may legitimately raise the question as to whether or not we have at our disposal a model sufficiently well developed to handle the problem.

Recent national projections of requirements for health manpower suggest that between now and 1975 at least one million new positions will have to be filled in order to provide minimal health services to an ever-increasing population. This estimate is probably conservative in view of the multiplication of health services in a variety of federal, state, and community programs, such as Medicare, OEO neighborhood services, community mental health centers, and regional centers. In addition, many new roles in the field of health have yet to be identified or defined. It is obvious that our current manpower training policies are totally inadequate to cope with the rapidly increasing shortage of trained health personnel.

In the area of delinquency and crime alone there are serious shortages of personnel to work with offenders. Antisocial behavior is a major problem in American society. The social structure of the society is changing, and there is a need for psychology to shift attention from the study and treatment of mental illness and deviance to creative ways of fostering human development.

Implications for Mental Health

With the increased need for mental health resources, one must logically raise the question of for whom service is to be supplied, and how. We must then define the concept of community mental health. In my view, it is not the treatment and prevention of mental illness. It is a positive condition requiring active strategies for its achievement and maintenance. One of the major tasks for the professions concerned with mental health is to provide more adequate and more meaningful services for the poor. The availability of funds from the Mental Health Act of 1965 creates many opportunities for the establishment of new kinds of clinical facility, but the danger exists that the new mental health centers will tend to follow conventional patterns of treatment rather than develop more flexible approaches to meet the needs of the deprived and disadvantaged.

Psychologists have a particular stake in community mental health because of their central concern with the development and functioning of the normal human being. From a very general base, they have developed a wide variety of specializations which have relevance for community mental health. Psychologists who have specialized in speech, child development, perception, learning, motor coordination, and other areas can be of assistance as consultants or staff in schools and child care centers. Many social psychologists have had specialized interests in the relationship between mental health and living conditions, in family interaction and structure; others have had long experience as human relations consultants. Clinical psychologists have specialized in the study and treatment of the abnormal, and counselors in the resolution of normal problems of adjustment. Many psychologists have experience and competence in program development and direction as well as a basic research orientation. The implication of the role of the nonprofessional is therefore significant and meaningful in view of the increased needs for mental health services.

When we consider the use of the nonprofessional in mental health work, we need to be aware of some of the implications of the employment of indigenous workers for the mental health of the workers themselves, for the relationship between the poor and the rest of the society, for the organization of the institutions directly concerned with the mental health of the community, particularly on the philosophy, approach, amount, and nature of their services, and for the evaluation of the society which the changes themselves create.

It would seem desirable to use the nonprofessional in many of the human services areas. Screening may be accomplished through a redefinition of those aspects of professional roles which do not require formal training. New roles may also be created. It has already been demonstrated that the nonprofessional can perform tasks which a professional is not so well equipped to meet. It is well documented in the field of corrections that the main influences on our institutionalized offenders are other offenders.

The evidence now available from studies and programs utilizing nonprofessionals and other self-help movements suggests that the involvement of the poor in new nonprofessional roles does not necessarily reduce the quality of services offered. Programs have been mounted to demonstrate the use of the nonprofessional as teacher, homemaker, and mental health, child care, and police relations aide. Evidence from some of these efforts suggests that when the uneducated nonprofessional is used to provide service for the poor, service is generally improved. My own experiences in the Baker's Dozen Community Mental Health Center for Adolescents suggest that the utilization of the poor as mental health aides is rehabilitative in its own right. This project will be discussed later in this paper. It is important to note at this point that the nonprofessional who participates in the helping services himself gains a sense of value, worth, and dignity.

It goes without saying that when we consider the role of the nonprofessional in a mental health discipline, whether psychology, social work, or any other, we must think about the kind of training he will need to develop competence in his role as well as particular training strategies.

Growing awareness of the problems of nonprofessionals and of disadvantaged groups generally has led to the establishment of many creative new training programs designed to free them from the descending spiral of poverty and defeat which engulfs them. New insights into the motivations of human behavior have made it clear that the cycle will never be broken unless the poor are helped to help themselves. This means, first of all, that they must have hope. They must have reason to believe that life does not have to be an endless and futile struggle for survival in a hostile environment. It means that they must have confidence in their own ability to bring about change in their lives. It means that they must have the assurance of decent jobs; and this, in turn, means that they must have training to equip them to hold their own in an increasingly competitive labor market. It means, finally, that they must learn to see their personal problems in the larger perspective of the community and society, and to understand that the solution to their problems is intimately related to the solution of the problems of others.

Howard University Model

As the goals and life standards of society have risen, programs of human services have proliferated, and growing personnel shortages have resulted. With the increasing size and administrative complexity of these programs, hard-pressed professional staffs have had to spend too high a proportion of their time in duties which could be performed by staff with special skills and abilities but less training. Recognizing this situation, the Howard University Institute for Youth Studies undertook to develop a program to train members of the disadvantaged population to meet the acute personnel needs in the human services area. One of the strengths of this concept of new careers is the unique quality that poverty-level workers can bring to human services programs: their firsthand knowledge of the problems and the way of life of the poor.

The potential success of such a program, the Institute recognized, rested on several factors:

1. the willingness of the community and its social institutions to accept and make use of such workers;
2. the willingness of community agencies to provide actual job opportunities, ranging from on-the-job training through permanent career status;
3. the ability of the program to select trainees with the necessary persistence and drive to complete their training and become effective workers in permanent jobs;
4. the development of special training techniques which can reach and hold trainees who do not respond to standard academic techniques;
5. the ability of the agencies and the training program to define the jobs to be done and the kinds of training that are needed;
6. the development of curriculum content which will provide the basic knowledge needed in all human services and the special skills needed for particular duties;
7. the development of training sufficiently flexible to enable the workers to move easily from one job to another as new needs and opportunities arise;
8. the ability of professional workers to readjust their thinking to encompass comfortable working relationships with new nonprofessional colleagues;
9. the constant feedback into the program of what is learned from each new step and technique, so that the quality of training can be constantly improved;
10. the outflow of this experience to other communities and other programs facing similar challenges.[1]

In considering aspects of training the nonprofessional, it became clear that both training phases and training content had

[1] *Training Nonprofessional Workers for Human Services, A Manual of Organization and Process*, Institute for Youth Studies, Howard University, May 1966.

to be taken into account. There was a need to look at orientation versus in-service training, as well as training for upgrading. Training had to be regarded from the skill-information-content as well as interpersonal-content point of view.

The goals of the training programs for the nonprofessional went far beyond the teaching of specific skills, reaching into the underlying areas of human relationships which are equally crucial to job success. Training therefore encompassed the following elements:

(1) teaching trainees to understand the nature and meanings of various types of behavior in different situations; (2) providing an understanding of the complexities of interpersonal, group, and community relationships; (3) helping trainees to develop a sense of personal and occupational identity; (4) helping trainees to develop goals, values, and attitudes that will enable them to function effectively within the organizational systems of society; (5) teaching the basic general skills and viewpoints needed for all nonprofessional jobs in human services; (6)' developing the personal and social coping skills needed for successful job performance; (7) helping trainees to develop sufficient knowledge and flexibility so that they will not be confined to one job but can transfer from one to another as opportunities for advancement arise; and (8) helping trainees learn to accept and make use of supervision, and training professionals to supervise and work effectively with nonprofessionals.

Training Methods. For several reasons, these training goals could not be achieved through a traditional academic approach. First, many of the nonprofessional trainees had been unhappy and unsuccessful in school and would not have been able to respond to training which seemed like more of the same old thing. Second, the hypothesis of the need for positive interpersonal relationships as an element of job success called for training situations in which various types of personal and social relationships could be acted out and experienced rather than "taught." Third, the trainees, many of whom felt isolated from society in general, could gain a sense of identity and support and could learn more easily as members of small, informal groups of their peers. Fourth, if the interest of the nonprofessional trainees was to be retained, they needed to experience some immediate rewards for their efforts.

In terms of this last element, training professionals to work with the nonprofessionals always presented special concern.[2] It was found that attention tends to be focused on professional resistance rather than on the type of training to be done. Professional resistance is often manifested in condescending attitudes toward the nonprofessionals. Often there is lack of sympathy for the nonprofessional movement and a feeling that nonprofessionals know nothing and cannot be effective workers. The possibility of lowering standards is another area about which the professional expresses concern. Professionals may be threatened by having their hard-won status or career shared by someone with less training and experience. (Perhaps the professional organizations may tend to be more upset about this than anyone else.) Reluctance to give up parts of the professional job is seen as another form of resistance.

> One problem is that functions often considered most appropriate to turn over to nonprofessionals are those aspects of the job that are most psychologically rewarding to professionals, namely, contact with clients. Few professionals or nonprofessionals are much interested in the noninterpersonal (housekeeping, record-keeping) aspects of the job, yet the concern of those developing jobs for the nonprofessionals is that this group does not get relegated to just these functions.[3]

Reluctance to assume a supervisory role is another way in which the professional may resist involvement with the nonprofessional. In our experience, the older professional displayed a greater need to resist than the younger professional. The younger professionals seemed better able to handle the concept of cultural difference and more likely to be concerned about how they might work effectively with nonprofessionals. In one situation it appeared that the smaller the social distance between professional and nonprofessional, the greater the threat to the professional's job.

For existing professionals, approaches to the issue of pro-

[2] Joan Grant discusses many of the problems and issues in this area in *A Strategy for California's Use of Training Resources in the Development of New Careers for the Poor* (Sacramento: Institute for the Study of Crime and Delinquency, New Careers Development Project, 1966).
[3] *Ibid.*

fessional resistance may include specific training in techniques of supervision of more general orientation to the problem of "cultural differences." Probably more important is the involvement of the professional in helping define both his own and the nonprofessional's role and actual participation in training with the nonprofessional.

For future professionals, concern centers more on the adequacy of college and university training. The concern comes from students and faculty as well as from outside critics of academic institutions. Suggestions for change include modification of the curriculum (courses that are more relevant to social problems) ; integration of course with field work; and the development of problem-oriented institutes or schools that cut across academic disciplines.[4]

Demonstration Project. The Baker's Dozen Community Mental Health Center for Adolescents, sponsored by NIMH, illustates a new approach in community mental health utilizing the nonprofessional. The program trains and employs youth, themselves suffering from a variety of psychosocial problems, as mental health aides in a group treatment program for neighborhood children. The project serves a high-poverty, high-crime and delinquency neighborhood and is operated by the Institute for Youth Studies and the Center for Mental Health and Behavioral Sciences of Howard University College of Medicine.

This program is part of an ongoing exploration at Howard which we call training for new careers. The larger program involves the recruitment, training, counseling, and employment of problem youth and young adults from the urban ghetto in a variety of jobs as nonprofessional aides in human services, including not only mental health but also education, child care, recreation, community health, neighborhood organization, institutional work with children, and social service. The program is an attempt to combine prevention, therapy, education, meaningful job training, and a career perspective. The concept of human services is utilized as a generic approach to training in all fields involving person-to-person helping services. This approach has been found to be an effective combination of therapy, training, and rehabilitation for these young people in that it involves meaningful preparation for jobs with a future perspective in fields concerned with helping others.

[4] *Ibid.*

Our experience suggests that the traditional approach of the psychiatrist to the problems of lower-class clients, particularly adolescents, is generally inadequate, lacks attracting and holding power, and is irrelevant to the daily needs of these youth. The fifty-minute hour seldom makes any difference in the life of the youth. If the youth is fortunate or unfortunate enough to wind up in a residential center, he spends his time in activities and therapy unrelated to his major needs and interests—education, employment, group identity, and realistic social skills for negotiating the system to which he will return. During the past six years, despite the investment of large amounts of federal funds, delinquency in Washington, D. C., has doubled, and 65 per cent of the delinquents last year were repeaters or school dropouts with a variety of social and personal problems.

The following points are relevant in this regard:

First, resolution of the normal problems of adolescents—development of a personal identity, commitment to meaningful life goals, and absorption into the mainstream of the community—is difficult for teenagers in general, but particularly so for youth in the urban ghetto. Meaningful, dignified employment with a future is not adequately available, and the usual public educational channels lack holding or motivating powers. They also frequently lead nowhere—as youth are quick to perceive.

Second, the incidence of mental health problems is dramatically higher among lower-class children and youth than in other parts of the community.

Third, most professionals in mental health fields have difficulty understanding or communicating with lower-class patients. They are not familiar with the values, attitudes, cognitive styles, or identification of these youth. The adolescent becomes particularly unwelcome when he shows so-called acting-out behavior as opposed to clean-cut neurotic symptoms.

Fourth, in the lower-class community much stigma is attached to attendance at psychiatric facilities.

Fifth, treatment process generally has not been integrated with the important needs and relevant institutions affecting the lives of youth. These include schools, employment resources, social agencies, and the like.

The present project involves the training of youth in the

new careers model as mental health aides, acting as Group I leaders
in a uniquely developed activity therapy for children and youth in
the neighborhood.

Youth Leaders. Eight youths, four boys and four girls, were
selected for training and ultimate employment as aides in the project. A matched cohort was selected to serve as a control group,
not to be involved in the program. Trainees and members of the
control group ranged from seventeen to twenty-one in age; the
educational level ranged from seventh-grade dropout to high school
graduate (one only). The reading level ranged from the fifth to the
eleventh grade. The eight trainees were divided into high- and low-
risk groups of four each. High-risk youth are defined as deprived
youth who have had a series of police, delinquency, and crime in-
volvements and who may or may not have spent time in an institution for such an offense. They read at a minimal fifth-grade level,
dropped out of school early, worked only at odd jobs, and never
worked longer than three months at any given job. The low-risk
youth are defined as deprived youth with no police record, who
continued in school until family or poverty circumstances forced
them out, and who worked at menial jobs but for longer periods
than the high-risk group. Maximum employment time was about
one year. The average number of siblings in the family was five. All
had multiple social problems.

Training Program. The training program lasted three months,
after which youth were employed as aides at the GS-2 level ($3,680
per year) under professional supervision in the Baker's Dozen program.

Major training goals were: (1) to develop in these youth
the necessary motivation, identity, values, and capabilities for maxi-
mally utilizing the offered training; (2) to help them learn the
basic personal, social, and interpersonal skills, attitudes, and knowledge needed to cope with and solve group, client, and personal
problems; (3) to provide specialized skills for their role in mental
health; and (4) to help them develop flexibility of attitude, role,
and viewpoint.

A further task involved the orientation of training of professional staff to work effectively with the aides. Training was pro-

vided in three concurrent phases—core group, specialty workshop, and on-the-job training.

The nonprofessional was trained to carry out a set of specific roles, including: (1) acting as group leader, helper, and planner for ten children in each of two groups; (2) participating with the psychologist, psychiatrist, or social worker in developing a structured therapeutic program for the group; (3) observing and recording individual and group behavior; (4) conducting interviews with group members and providing information to professional staff for feedback and quality control purposes; (5) escorting groups on trips and tours; (6) participating in individual and group supervision; (7) attending staff conferences; and (8) writing progress reports and keeping records of daily observations on the children.

Training activities were held five days each week, eight hours each day. The mornings were devoted to discussion of specific issues and information in the following areas: the world of work, human growth and development, conceptions and misconceptions of mental health, mental mechanisms, group intervention, remedial reading and skills training, social history and interview recording, and observing. The afternoons were spent in visiting the major youth caretaking agencies in the community, such as receiving home, juvenile court, training schools for youth, psychiatric facilities for children, and residential treatment establishments; role playing; interviewing children for group participation; supervision; and reviewing mental health films.

Treatment Program. The core of the treatment program is a series of activity groups led by the trained aide. Activities are structured to provide ego-strengthening and therapeutic benefits and include recreational, cultural, social, and community activities. The program for the group is designed to create a common desire to raise the group standards as means of attaining goals. The strategy is to use group leadership as a vehicle for establishing beneficial controls over individual youth, with strong emphasis on the relationship of the leader to the group members. The changes sought include symptom reduction, fewer police contacts, better social functioning, attitudinal change, acceptance of the larger society's values and norms of behavior, and development of more acceptable ways of handling situations. The emphasis on structured, goal-directed activity is intended to help the youth increase his self-esteem and self-confidence, to behave less impulsively, to develop meaningful relationships with peers and adults, and to become concerned for others. Youth are expected to take responsibility for themselves, to plan programs and solve problems and make decisions in a socially realistic and democratic fashion. The group emphasis reduces anxiety and uncertainty and thus helps the youth to cope successfully with a wide variety of social and personal problems and frustrations.

Employment and Institutional Consequences

The employment of the nonprofessional involves the creation of a new hierarchy—the service team. The professional must now concentrate on planning and directing programs, supervising less highly trained personnel, and performing the most highly skilled tasks. Direct service must be broken down into simpler tasks which can be undertaken by the nonprofessional; graduated steps of increasing work difficulty and responsibility must be created so that the nonprofessional can advance and, if he has the motivation and the capacity, eventually become a professional. Continuing training and education must be devised and provisions made so that workers can make use of these opportunities. This could mean that employment would include a combination of work and education to be undertaken over a period of years. Such employment involves not only the structural reorganization of institutions but a change in the concept of work and a consequent reorganization of work and education programs.

Thought also needs to be given to those who do not wish to participate in the battle for more status and goods. Can new satisfactions, material rewards, respect, and interest be built into possibly less significant positions? In fact, the lowest paid jobs, requiring less education and training, are often crucial to society and should be so regarded. Nonprofessionals must be able to feel proud of their jobs. Advancement should be not only from aide to technician to professional, but also within the aide hierarchy itself, to supervisor and administrator. However, in order to provide for the maximum of retraining, the aide should be able to move horizontally from specialty to specialty. The problem, however, still remains that low-level jobs are not well respected.

The employment of the nonprofessional creates an urgent need to reconsider the organization of professional roles in community mental health. Is it current work division between school counselor, family social worker, probation officer, employment counselor, remedial expert, public health nurse, and child guidance personnel really functional? Do we wish to preserve this distribution by creating nonprofessional hierarchies along these lines, or should we consider whether some other organization would prove more effective?

Institutional Functioning. In the meantime, however, the fact that these roles are being created and occupied by people—youth and adults—who have felt alienated from society and who have had difficulty in benefiting from educational opportunities and in holding jobs means that with short-term intensive training, the entry job in the institution must itself be conceived as a mental health and training intervention, and that the employment of the nonprofessional must be regarded as a human service as important as any other human services the institution provides. Initially, this raises the problem of ensuring that the quality of service does not suffer unduly in the process. In our experience, however, the gains in improved communication, more relevant service, and greater concern and respect for the population being served have offset the occasional awkwardness, impulsivity, or irresponsibility of the nonprofessional.

Through the employment of indigenous personnel, it is expected that the services of the institutions can become more related to the needs of the segments of society which are now so inadequately served. A teacher's aide who is himself an Appalachian youth will presumably treat small children from the "hollow" with knowledge and respect and, through his association with the teacher, will help her to better understand the lives and struggles of the people who live in the backwoods. Similarly, a mental health or counseling aide can help a professional psychologist or social worker to assess the local meaning of specific behaviors and to provide a familiar climate in a strange environment for the patient or client.

The Neighborhood. When local people are employed in community mental health agencies the impersonality of the institution is reduced. Neighborhood people can take pride in institutions when they can help to mold them to satisfy their needs. The employment of local people changes the relationship between human service personnel and the local population in two ways. Now the poor are both servers and served, and to the extent that they can plan for themselves the human services become their servants rather than the bringers of charity.

Further, a member of the same population who has moved up in the world, provided that he is still accepting and respectful of his origins, can often be more readily accepted as a model and a source of inspiration and hope than a person from another social group. As the one who is most closely concerned with direct services, particularly to the young, the nonprofessional becomes the primary transmitter of the culture, the one who conveys attitudes to authority and teaches what is and is not acceptable behavior.

The employment of local people as community workers and as members of local planning and agency boards is designed to create a new sense of neighborhood and to give the individual a say in the planning and operation of his world—thus combatting the feeling that he is a pawn in the game and has no obligation to act responsibly because no responsibility or power is accorded him. He has less need to protest in deviant ways because he can now make his opinions felt more directly.

Such engagement of indigenous nonprofessionals has profound mental health implications in that it engenders a different view of themselves as worthwhile persons and serves to combat the feelings of powerlessness and alienation from which many of the poor suffer. As the sense of self-respect and power increases, people frequently desire to create a changed society with which they can feel more identified rather than to find themselves incorporated into a higher level of the old society. Thus, there is a pressure to review old ways and values and evolve something new. To the extent that these citizens can remain identified with the oppressed and can use their new power to achieve a wider distribution of community resources, there can be a lessening of dissension between different segments of society. As they gain power and importance, they are also in a position to insist on increased communication between classes with the ultimate hope of better understanding.

In summary, we have been concerned in this paper with the implications of the employment of indigenous nonprofessionals for the creation of communities which are mentally healthy in a positive and not a reactive sense. Rapid change is an intrinsic aspect of modern living, and communities must be capable of accommodating to change without severe dislocation. Institutions have to develop flexible structures, readily adapted to new conditions, and individuals must have sufficient personal security to be able to change roles and functions without loss of identity. The civil rights movement and the war on poverty have launched a social revolution which forces reexamination of our values and institutions, a basic mental health operation.

The employment of the indigenous nonprofessional, both as a mental health specialist and as a contributor to mental health through human service and community action, has implications for the individual, the organization of institutions, the social organization, and the future of society.

Such employment is designed to: reengage the individual and reduce his feelings of alienation, powerlessness, and depression; increase his competence and his capacity to take responsibility; encourage the poor to function as their own models and as transmitters of their culture; narrow the distance between the server and the served and change relationships so that the served can command the service; facilitate the spread of knowledge and communication between the poor and the rest of society; reduce the gap between classes and engage them jointly in making a new society; change the structure of institutions so that there are service teams and the possibility of both upward and horizontal mobility; create new opportunities for both education and careers; and stimulate a reexamination of the fundamental values and institutions of American society in which the nonprofessional can raise questions from a different perspective, particularly regarding the role of the family within the American culture and the dilemma created by the value placed on the present work and career position.

It is difficult to estimate the lasting impact of any program while it is in the early stages of evolution. There is, however, already clear evidence that the use of indigenous nonprofessional workers in the human services (including mental health) has become an established trend in this country. Approximately 40,000 or more of them have been employed in the United States since the passage of the Economic Opportunity Act of 1965. How permanent and how successful the use of such workers will be depends, I believe, on the quality of training they receive, the adequacy with which professional personnel are prepared to welcome the workers as contributing members of agency staffs, and the possibility for upward mobility in the system.

Much more research and many additional innovative demonstrations are needed. We are, however, glad to be able to share what we feel to be significant preliminary findings for the development of other programs. They reflect the institution's conviction that the training process itself can be utilized as an important agent of social change.

CHAPTER **VI**

Editorial: Social Work

Alvin L. Schorr

The steady rise in professional standards of social work—more trained social workers, the development of a cadre of Ph.D.'s, more carefully rationalized curricula—has been some cause for satisfaction. Public appreciation of social workers has increased and salaries and status have shifted for the better. However, the change also gives cause for anxiety, because of the evidence that the membership of NASW is not all or even most of social work. Preoccupation with standards among professionals may be widening rather than narrowing the gap between NASW and the others who are practicing social work.

In 1960, a third of all practicing social workers were employed in public assistance; a negligible proportion of them were trained. The disdainful attitude toward them of many fully trained workers is probably reciprocated by those in public assistance. Their

consequent attitudes toward the task of social work are painfully
apparent in high turnover rates and callous treatment of recipients.
Another large and growing group of social workers are in antipoverty programs—programs that deliberately employ the untrained,
in our terms and in anyone's terms. In the last issue of *Social Work*[1]
(July 1966), Bertram Beck put the lesson of the antipoverty program with some vigor. He said:

> Our country cries out for people with technical knowledge of the
> order here described—plus deep commitment. We have the ability
> if we have the will to meet this need. To do so, we must welcome
> into the ranks those who have not been anointed with the . . .
> benefits of any important formal education . . . we must find
> ways so that they too may become officers.

Public assistance and antipoverty programs account for half
the nation's corps of social workers, not to mention other fields in
which untrained workers are common.

In a choice between the unqualified and improving the
qualified, self-interest and the needs of the clients of social work
divide. We should recognize this. We should not pretend that our
interests coincide with those of our clients. In one direction lie more
Ph.D. sequences, higher standards of practice, and more technical
papers and conferences. (Are esoteric conferences the LSD parties
of the middle aged?) The result of taking this route will be better
practice for comparatively few people. Other results will be higher
salaries and more respect from other professions and public groups
—and a wider gulf between an elite professional group and the bulk
of social workers. It is just possible that quite a lot of clients will
suffer at the hands of social workers—by whatever name—who
feel themselves excluded and denigrated.

In the other direction lies a movement toward a single profession, with everyone who practices social work accorded full title.
Professional knowledge will increase, but possibly not as rapidly in
certain directions. Salaries and status may rise less rapidly. The profession may find itself invigorated by new ideas and a new dedica-
tion. And all the clients of social workers will receive a higher

[1] This chapter is reprinted by permission of the National Association
of Social Workers from *Social Work*, 11 (October 1966).

standard of practice. All will benefit from the field's knowledge. All will benefit from the single most important contribution of professional social work: the invaluable code of ethics and sense of responsibility of professional social work. This contribution can be enforced without reliance upon advanced training.

The choice is not so simple as this comparison may imply because, unless standards are enforced in some manner, there will be little incentive to general improvement. On the other hand, standards are not absolute qualities; rather, they represent a judgment that a specified level of knowledge and skill have become attainable. The level that is specified represents a balance point between ideal professional preparation, whatever that may be, and the resources available (schools, salary levels, and so forth) to tempt and prepare the bulk of the people who must practice. Thus, standards should probably always be moving up, with the *rate* of improvement determined by weighing conflicting demands. A cool appraisal of our situation must lead to the conclusion that, in terms of the profession's objective, we are moving too quickly and, in particular, *have* moved too quickly. If we leave half the social workers behind, it may be the other half rather than we who will be doing the real job of social work, however poorly.

There might be no single moment at which the profession makes an irrevocable choice. Almost two years ago, the NASW Delegate Assembly rejected (by 174 to 111 votes) a proposal to include individuals without professional training and doubtless a similar opportunity will be offered at the next assembly. We could temporize or compromise for years. Caught between self-interest and the high purposes in which we believe, will temporizing appeal to us or can we choose?

CHAPTER VII

Social Policy Formulation

Harry Specht, J. Douglas Grant

$$\text{ʊʊʊʊʊʊʊʊʊʊʊʊʊʊʊʊʊ}$$

U ntil recently, the professional's role in human service organizations has been limited primarily to tactics— that is, providing expertise in specific operations, such as testing, diagnosing, treating, teaching, and researching. These limited functions no longer constitute a viable model for professional activity. What is needed now from the professional, and what will be needed increasingly in the future, are contributions to agency policy formulated as social agencies attempt to meet the demands of a rapidly increasing rate of institutional and organizational change. It is time, in short, for professionals to move from tactics to strategies.[1] Such

[1] See Arthur Pearl, conference on "The Utilization and Training of Counselor Aides in Vocational Rehabilitation," sponsored by the Division of Education, Sacramento State College, San Diego, California, March 15–17, 1967.

strategies will complement concurrent efforts to bring institutions into step with the times through the use of vast nonprofessional resources.

Our argument for a shift from tactics to strategy is based upon three premises: (1) our current higher education systems cannot produce enough professionals to perform even the present level of tactical services; (2) the society's demands for human services will continue to expand with the increasing affluence of the economy; and (3) the self-help and client-participation demonstrations demand a change in social agency programs from those in which clients are the passive recipients to programs in which clients participate actively and meaningfully.

It follows from these assumptions that organizations and institutions will be under increasing pressure to change. There will be frantic searches for both staff and procedures for program development. The emphasis in organizations will change from writing manuals describing standard procedures to writing proposals for program innovations. How will we keep some semblance of order in an accelerating change process? How will we develop systems to change systems?

Studies producing data in support of a given program innovation will not be enough. There will be increasing concern with systematic study of policy decisions themselves. We will turn not only to measuring the effectiveness of decisions[2] but to the social psychology of the decision-making process.[3] Organizations will require staff to help them to obtain and apply relevant information in changing their policies. Research utilization will become an extensive science in its own right.

Participation will be another crucial issue. To what extent should staff and clients participate in changing policy decisions? How can procedures be developed to bring about the optimal participation of service users? How can the ideas, reactions, and innovations of staff and clients be fed effectively into the organiza-

[2] See J. D. Grant, "It's Time to Start Counting," *Crime and Delinquency* (1962), pp. 259–264.

[3] See R. A. Bauer, "Social Psychology and the Study of Policy Formation," *American Psychologist,* 10 (1966), pp. 933–942.

tion-change process?[4] The question of whether or not professions *should* be concerned about social change will no longer be relevant. Rather, the change process itself will be seen as the central content of professional studies and practice.[5]

Roles for Professionals

The growing use of nonprofessionals in service organizations can be regarded as an indication of professional concern with change and with the process by which policy decisions are made in organizations. In *New Careers for the Poor*,[6] Riessman and Pearl brought together information concerning the potentials of nonprofessionals, the implications of self-help movements, and the social and economic forces in American life which are generating change. They then outlined new roles for professionals as supervisors, trainers, and innovators rather than as direct providers of service.

But the professional role is not limited to these functions. Frank Riessman himself has worked with Congressman James Scheuer of New York to implement new careers ideas. A loose network of professionals and legislators are jointly developing a strategy for building the implementation of new careers into legislation (for example, the "Safe Streets" bill, the Delinquency Prevention Act, the Elementary and Secondary Education Act, the Law Enforcement Assistance Act, and the Model Cities program). Bills currently being considered by Congress propose to provide technical staff and guidelines for revising federal and state civil service procedures to make them consistent with a new careers manpower strategy. These bills are based upon similar actions previously taken by the California and New Jersey Personnel Boards.

These "organization-change" roles for professionals have

---

[4] For a highly relevant discussion of this problem see N. Foote and L. Cottrell, *Identity and Interpersonal Competence* (Chicago: University of Chicago Press, 1955).

[5] See Seymour B. Sarason, "Toward a Psychology of Change and Innovation," *American Psychologist*, 22 (1967), pp. 227–233; and J. D. Grant, *Progress in Clinical Psychology* (New York: Grune and Stratton, 1966), pp. 29–46, "The Psychologist as an Agent for Scientific Approaches to Social Change."

[6] Arthur Pearl and Frank Riessman, *New Careers for the Poor* (New York: Free Press, 1965).

been formalized in two large contracts to New York University and Howard University for technical assistance in developing new careers programs in nineteen cities under the present Nelson-Scheuer Addendum to the Economic Opportunity Act.[7] This technical assistance helps cities to prepare proposals, develop and conduct programs, train trainers, prepare curricular material, and work with specific organizations in redefining as well as expanding job functions so as to establish career ladders for nonprofessionals who are working in entry positions.

The conference for which the present paper was prepared, organized by the American Psychological Association and National Association of Social Workers, is an example of the professions engaging in policy decisions and program change. National study groups like the Joint Commission on Correctional Manpower and Training, as well as the President's Commission on Law Enforcement and Administration of Justice, are using professionals to implement change and development. Increasing numbers of professionals are serving on review panels, making decisions regarding program development and the changing of institutions.

In addition to directly implementing changes, we are beginning to study and conceptualize ways of improving the change process. It has been suggested that many agency staff members who are now resistant to organizational change could be transformed into champions of innovation if priority were given to new program budgets over workload increase budgets.[8] Survival needs dictate that much of the administrative talent of agencies is concerned with budget procurement; changing the requirements for budget approval might, therefore, bring about more basic change in the point of view of the staff concerned with agency policy and development than sensitivity training or any other method directed at staff personality change. We are only starting to think of systems for changing systems, but the need for such study and conceptualization is fast becoming apparent.

[7] Nelson-Scheuer Addendum, U.S. Department of Labor, *Standards and Procedures for Work-Training Experience Program Under the Economic Opportunity Act of 1964*, as amended, Washington, D. C., February 1967.

[8] New Careers Development Project, "Job and Career Development for the Poor," a paper presented to the California Office of Economic Opportunity, October 1, 1965.

Along with studies of policy decision-making and program evaluation, there needs to be methodological development in ways of systematizing emerging trends. How can we use empiricism in developing theories and hypotheses, as well as in hypothesis testing? Efforts are being made to expand the subject-researcher role in studying areas of innovation in which the programs and their processes are only vaguely understood. One example is a study of the perfoming arts in delinquency prevention and youth development.[9] In this effort social scientists and program staff are brought together to clarify the rationale and objectives of specific uses of the performing arts. From these explorations the social scientists are preparing statements on the nature of the trends suggested by the programs, and testable hypotheses from such frames of reference as communication theory, the study of social movements, community organization, new careers development, organization change, and human development.

Another example is a study of how nonprofessionals are being integrated into social agencies.[10] Ex-offenders employed as new careerists in social agencies participate in the study of the change process, whereby the organization, its existing staff, and the nonprofessionals take on new roles. The ex-offenders, as well as significant others in their lives such as wives, peer workers, and supervisors, are used as subject-researchers in trying to understand the nature of this innovation and to formulate hypotheses for testing.

Change Implementation

The case has been made that the major role of the professional in service agencies will and should shift from practicing techniques to developing and implementing strategies to cope with the forces for and against change, both inside and outside the agency.

This shift calls for a reorientational current professional practice and modification of our training of graduate students. A recent NIMH demonstration project attempted to train program

[9] Joan H. Grant, "Use of the Performing Arts in Delinquency and Youth Development," Office of Juvenile Delinquency and Youth Development, Department of Health, Education and Welfare, February 28, 1967.

[10] J. D. Grant, "Beyond the Opportunity Structure," February 1967 (mimeo.).

development teams composed of a part-time professional, a half-time graduate student, and two nonprofessionals (ex-offenders).[11] The project subjects are now working throughout the country in program development roles. The nonprofessionals have assumed the formal title of Program Development Assistants.

This project gives us some experience for creating program development institutes which could offer training in organizational change strategies to professionals and graduate students from several disciplines, as well as to nonprofessionals. Public health has been offering such special training to established professionals in several disciplines through its fellowship and master's degree programs.

Policy Change Model

The problems which will be encountered in introducing nonprofessional personnel into institutional systems must be estimated in light of the forces for change in the larger society, some of which are described above. Essentially, these are the forces which necessitate changes in the policies of our institutions.[12] In order to discuss how professional associations can participate in the formulation of these policies, we shall have to consider the process by which policy is shaped.

In the past decade increasing concern has been expressed about the need for mental health professionals to play a more direct role in the formulation of the social policies which guide our social

[11] J. D. Grant, "The Offender as a Correctional Manpower Resource," paper presented at the First National Symposium on Law Enforcement Science and Technology, Illinois Institute of Technology, Chicago, March 9, 1967.

[12] *Social policy* refers to the goals of social transactions in private and public institutions which serve human needs. Kenneth E. Boulding, in distinguishing social policy from economic policy, says that the former refers to "those aspects of social life that are characterized not so much by exchange in which a quid is got for a quo as by unilateral transfers that are justified by some kind of appeal to a status or legitimacy, identity, or community." Later he adds, "Social policy is that which is centered in those institutions that create integration and discourage alienation" ("The Boundaries of Social Policy," *Social Work,* 12 [January 1967]). The utility of using *goal* to define policy is that it suggests that concepts related to organization, structure, economics, and administration should be viewed as the independent variables which affect policy but are not themselves policy, since goals remain constant whether or not they are actualized.

service institutions. This concern is reflected in cliches asking the professionals to "get into the political arena,"[13] or to learn to deal more effectively with the "community power structure"; in general, the call is for more social action and for a more aggressive professional stance in policy formulation. However, such demands can be demoralizing to professionals in certain roles, particularly to practitioners, such as the therapist in the psychological clinic or the social worker in the family counseling agency. At best, a general call to arms without more specific instructions about which arms to use or how to use them is only temporarily inspiring; at worst it is likely to produce feelings of inadequacy. This occurs because of the tendency to conceive of social policy formulation in . . . exclusively substantive terms,[14] and thus to see participation in policy formulation as requiring expertise—comprehensive and extensive knowledge of a field—in a major area of service. If policy formulation is recognized as a process that can be taught to all in a profession, if it is seen as a process that entails many different tasks and roles, then all professionals can learn to contribute to it in the ways most appropriate for them.

Part of the reason for a sense of inadequacy, then, is that the process of actually dealing with policy is not so well defined as are other professional tasks.

In casework, for example, what one actually does (counseling) and the units with which one deals (cases) are relatively clear. Most of the methods we use in direct practice allow professionals to work within a series of fairly well-defined roles which usually have a high degree of consonance and each of which can generally be filled by a single person. However, the process by which policy is formulated involves a wide range of roles which often strain against one another and which must be filled by several people.

The model we shall present describes the process by which social policy is formulated. We shall identify the various stages of

[13] Alan D. Wade, "The Social Worker in the Political Process," *Social Welfare Forum 1966* (New York: Columbia University Press, 1966).

[14] See Don Howard, "Social Policy Formulation as Process," unpublished paper prepared for the School of Social Welfare, University of California at Los Angeles, February 1965 (mimeo.).

the process, the tasks involved at each stage, the institutional resources needed to carry out these tasks, and, finally, the professional roles required at each stage of the process. We shall then consider the points at which the professional association can play a strategic role in policy formulation. Utilizing the model, we shall indicate the gaps in the role sets of the professional groups participating in this process.

Many authors have developed models of policy formulation along similar processual lines.[15] We believe that the particular utility of the following discussion lies in its identification of the different professional tasks and roles which are relevant at the several stages of the process.

The table below identifies all of the elements mentioned. The process may be summarized as one of uncovering both developing needs and existing unmet needs, and evolving new methods of meeting those needs. This process might take place in a variety of settings—within one small agency, in one department of a large agency, or in a nationwide bureaucracy. The process might involve the various resources and subsystems of only one institution, or a wide variety of institutional resources and organizations.

In referring to professional roles, we mean those roles that must be filled in the process of policy formulation, whether or not those who fill them are actually members of the mental health professions.

Let us discuss the stages briefly, mentioning the ways in which each of the elements fits into the model.

Identification of Problem. The basis for institutional policy change is the identification of a developing or unmet need in the community, a need which the originator of the policy goal believes that the institution is responsible for meeting. Perception of the problem and of the institution's responsibility is, of course, related to the political, economic, and social forces which bear upon the perceiver, and to his institutional position. Thus, for example, a con-

[15] For example: Elizabeth Wickenden, *How to Influence Public Policy* (New York: American Association of Social Workers, 1954); and Robert E. Agger, Daniel Goldrich, and Bert E. Swanson, *The Rulers and the Ruled* (New York: Wiley, 1964).

Stages of Policy Formulation

Stage	Tasks	Institutional Resources	Professional Roles
1. Identification of problem	Casefinding; recording; discovery of gaps in service	Agency	Practitioner
2. Analysis; fact gathering	Counting; analysis; conceptualization	Research organization (e.g., a university)	Researcher
3. Bringing problem to attention of public(s)	Dramatizing; public relations; communications (writing, speaking)	Public relations unit; communications channels; voluntary associations	Muckraker; community organizer; public relations man
4. Developing policy goals	Creating a strategy; program analysis	Planning bodies; voluntary associations	Planner; community organizer; administrator
5. Building public support	Developing leadership; achieving consensus	Voluntary associations; political parties; legislative and agency committees	Lobbyist; community organizer; public relations man
6. Legislating (formulating program in statutory terms)	Drafting legislation; program design	Legislative bodies; agency boards	Legislative analyst; planner
7. Implementing, administering	Program organizing; administration	Courts; agencies	Administrator; practitioner; lawyer
8. Evaluating, assessing	Casefinding; recording; discovery of gaps in service; counting	Agency; research organization	Practitioner; researcher

106

cern for institutional maintenance might be more likely to guide the perceptions of professionals in certain positions than a concern for providing better service for clients.

Professionals who are alert to the forces dictating institutional change will be more likely to perceive certain gaps in services. And if they are aware of the process by which policy is formulated, they will be in a better position to make use of their findings.

Tasks that must be completed during this stage are casefinding, recording instances of unmet needs, and generally discovering gaps in services. The institution itself is the resource to be utilized at this point in the process, and the practitioner role is the most important.

Practitioners, then, can play an important role in the policy formulation process if they are alert to the potential for change in certain aspects of their practice. There are many problems which practitioners regularly confront in their work to which the concept of new careers is relevant, such as too-large caseloads, "hard-to-reach" clients, long waiting lists, high turnover staff and personnel shortages, and apathy and alienation in the community to be served. Practitioners must have the knowledge and skill to utilize their practice experiences in the formulation of policy to deal with these problems.

Analysis. Once a problem has been identified, it is necessary to develop some factual data about the numbers of people who are affected and a clear-cut statement about how the problem is actually being measured. For example, what kinds of information do members of the community lack about mental health services? What is meant by mental health services? Specifically, what members of the community are being referred to, and what kinds of information are considered essential?

A good example of the use of research to deal with problems suggested in stage one is the series of studies conducted by the Veterans' Administration on the use of social work assistants.[16] From a processual point of view, the knowledge required is how to move from an expression of concern about an unmet need to an

[16] Veterans' Administration, Department of Medicine and Surgery, *A Study of the Use of the Social Work Assistant in the Veterans' Administration,* June 1965.

organized program of information gathering. The institutional resource involved is a research operation, whether it is a single consultant, an agency research department, or a university research center. The professional role is that of researcher.

Bringing the Problem to the Attention of the Public. The public, or publics, are those subsystems in the institution or the general community that must become informed about the problem. This might be as widely defined as the community at large or as limited as the administration of the institution, depending upon the nature of the problem and the stage of the process. The tasks involved are to present the problem in a form that will capture the interest and attention of these publics by use of appropriate media. The institutional resources involved are these media, but these could be limited to channels within the institution, such as the public relations department or the staff meeting, or extended to outside institutional resources, such as the press. Although the form of action may vary, this is the stage at which counterdemands will essentially determine the extent to which activities in the following stages are consensual or conflictful.

The professional roles required differ from those previously mentioned. The muckraker, the community organizer, the public relations man (all of which themselves differ) are the roles which put the public in touch with the institutional problem.

Developing Policy Goals. Once the problem has been identified, analyzed, and brought to public attention, many suggestions will be offered for dealing with it, all of which must be sifted and examined, to arrive at a strategy. Essentially, a "strategy" is a set of program goals which is based on a theory about how the problem originates. Various voluntary associations and planning bodies within and outside the organization become involved at this point. This is the point at which the professional association, as a voluntary organization, can become most actively engaged in policy formulation. The professional roles involved are those of planner, community organizer, and administrator.

It would be well to bear in mind that strategies must change as goals change. For example, policy issues relevant to new careers might move from: (a)' the viability of using the poor to serve the poor in selected, specialized communicating roles; to (b)' using the poor in all aspects of service to relieve professionals of some of the responsibility they currently carry; to (c) approaching the staffing patterns in social services as mechanisms for broadening community participation in the design and implementation of programs. These policy goals are vastly different from one another and will require the involvement of different people in their formulation. In the next stage, "building public support," different kinds of leadership will be needed for each kind of goal, and a consensus for each would be based on a different set of relationships.

Building Public Support. Many different subsystems of the institution and of the community will have a stake in the formulation of policy. The originator of the policy will have to find those groups in the system that can lend support to the goals enunciated in the previous stage and translate them into instruments for action. That is, a consensus must be achieved among those groups which can support the policy. Compromises may be made at this stage, and the processes of bargaining, exchanging, and persuading will be used.

The culmination of this stage is the development of a platform by the group supporting the goals, or a general statement of direction by the administration of the agency.

Major tasks involved at this point are the development of leadership for the coalition and the negotiation of consensus among the supporting groups. Voluntary associations, political parties, legislative committees, and committees of the board of directors are the institutional resources most likely to be involved, and the professional will be called upon to fill the roles of lobbyist, community organizer, and public relations man.

Legislating. The program must be formulated in statutory terms, whether it is written as a law for consideration by some legislative body or as a statement of program to be considered by the agency board of directors. Legislation must be drafted that will describe the allocation of responsibility for the program and deal with organizational structure, financing, and program operation. Legislative analyst and social planner are the professional roles required.[17]

[17] Wilbur J. Cohen, "What Every Social Worker Should Know About Political Action," *Social Work,* 11 (July 1966).

Implementing, Administering. Depending upon how detailed the legislation is, a large part of the process of policy formulation may be left for this stage, when the concrete policies of program may be established by practice, precedent, and experimentation. A good example of this is the Economic Opportunity Act, in which the policy specifying the "maximum feasible participation" of the poor left the practical details of involving the clients to the administrators of the program. Policy formulation may take place informally within the structure of government, without fanfare or public proclamation, when what is required is not formal changes in the law, but rather an altered pattern of action within the law. The chief tasks involved here are administrative and programmatic, that is, getting the program organized and the policy clarified. The institution itself and the courts are the chief institutional resources that will be involved in determination of policy at this stage.

The courts become a significant institution for determination of policy at this stage because it is by establishing a system of rights and guarantees through judicial procedures that a body of accepted administrative practice develops for any social program. Thus, social service personnel must be able to utilize the skills of lawyers in determining how the goals of policy can be affected through legal mechanisms.

Evaluating, Assessing. In a sense, the goals of social policy are ever receding before us. New programs create new expectations and new needs, and uncover additional unmet needs. Programs themselves become a major element in the "demand environment" of policy. This stage requires an assessment of the impact of policy and an evaluation of how effectively the policy meets the problem. Actually this stage is the first stage all over again, for the process of policy formulation is an ongoing one that has neither a discrete beginning nor an end.

This model suggests many questions about the process of policy formulation:

It has been traditional, in social planning and community action, to conceive of the process of policy formation as an orderly one, based on rational appraisal of the best alternatives available for the community. The model described above, however, is better understood as a bargaining or negotiation process, akin to what

political scientists describe as political behavior.[18] And although it
has been customary to think of the analysis of social policy as taking
place in the mind of one man or a small group of men, the kind of
"fragmentation" of analysis that is presented here, to use Lindblom's term for it, may actually be an asset in developing a correct
weighting of values in policy formulation. Lindblom's view of how
the participation of many individuals and groups affects policy
formulation is different from the view of community organization
people:

> Policies are set as a resultant of such conflict, not because some
> one policy-making individual or group achieves an integration but
> because the pulling and hauling of various views accomplishes
> finally some kind of decision, probably different from what any
> one advocate of the final solution intended and probably different
> from what any one advocate could comfortably defend by reference
> to his own limited values. The weighing or aggregation is a politi-
> cal process, not an intellectual process.[19]

Although the process can originate in many different sources
and can start or stop at any point, and although different stages
may overlap or occur simultaneously, there is the question of
whether or not each of these elements is essential in the process.
Assume, for example, that a professional association were to initiate
the process at stage three through a series of public meetings at
which the association begins to sensitize its publics to the need for
subprofessionals in mental health services. Even if this were done
successfully, we believe that at some point the tasks that are nor-
mally carried out in stages one and two—casefinding and research
—will have to be undertaken, and that the initiators of policy must
remain aware of this requirement of the process. Similarly, the professional who undertakes policy formulation through research can
benefit from understanding the other tasks that must be performed
in order to translate knowledge into policy.

We describe policy formulation as a process that goes on

[18] Edward C. Banfield, *Political Influence* (New York: Free Press,
1961); and Agger et al., *op. cit.*
[19] Charles E. Lindblom, "The Handling of Policy Norms in Analysis," in Moses Abramowitz, ed., *The Allocation of Economic Resources*
(Stanford, Calif.: Stanford University Press, 1959).

between the institution and its environment, of which the professional is only one part—and a small one at that. The question to be considered by the professional association is at what points they can exert the greatest influence on the institutional environment, and what resources are required for them to do this? At what points do professional associations generally come in?

The part the professional association plays in moving the goals of policy forward is most important at the third, fourth, and fifth steps of the process. This suggests that from the association's view, channels must be opened to agency practitioners and researchers who play a large role in the initiation of policy formulation and to the legislative bodies, lobbyists, boards of directors, and planners who play an important role in the later stages of the process.

How much knowledge of other roles and institutional resources is required for successful performance in any one professional role? What are the combinations of professional roles required in policy formulation that produce the greatest strain, and which combinations have the greatest consonance? For example, there is a high degree of consonance between the role of community organizer and that of lobbyist, and it is very likely that one individual could fill both roles. Conversely, there is a great deal of dissonance between the researcher and practitioner roles, and strain is likely to occur between the two. What mechanisms are available to deal with such strain?

To what extent can the professional staff of a given agency undertake these tasks and fill these roles? The larger the institution, the greater the probability that there will be a variety of professionals available with the different skills required to fill a wide range of roles. In a small agency the limited staff will make it necessary to find other ways to carry out the tasks and fill the roles needed in policy making.

Related to these questions is the question of the kinds of links and transitions that are required to move the process of policy formulation forward between the various institutions that are involved and the different professional roles—between the practitioner and researcher, between the service department and the research department, between the agency and the legislature.

Here, essentially, is what might be regarded as the substantive knowledge to build a practice of policy formulation. For example, what methods and techniques are available to move the knowledge acquired by the practitioner in the first stage to later stages? How are organizational mechanisms such as staff meetings, supervision, and reporting used for this? What other ways are available to the practitioner to link his knowledge with the researcher and with other institutional personnel?

Although the role of the administrator is relevant to carrying out specific tasks at certain stages of the process, there also exist administrative functions which are important and required for the overall process. By definition, it is the administrator's function to coordinate the other functions and roles played by professionals at different stages. It is the administrator who links together the various professionals and institutions that must work together throughout this process because it is his job to assign tasks and to allocate resources. Thus, the administrative function is a strategic one in the process of policy formulation, and the administrator's orientation toward policy formulation is of crucial importance.

As we look at the various resources and role responsibilities involved in the process, it is interesting to note that, by and large, these are institutionally defined; that is, the resources and roles which play a part in moving the process forward are not usually independent bodies. It is true that the force for change can spring from many sources, but that force will inevitably encounter the many gatekeepers and facilitators in various institutional positions who control access to other institutional resources.

Implications of Policy Formulation

The professional association is only one element in the process by which policy is formulated. As a voluntary association, it might be expected that the association would ordinarily become involved rather late in the process, and also that it would not ordinarily play a major role in the final stages of the process. Thus, when the association identifies an area in which it would like to play a role in policy determination, conscious planning is required to link its efforts with the earlier and later stages of the process. One chapter of the National Association of Social Workers, for example, having determined that it wished to be actively involved in the development of policy in regard to the use of nonprofessionals in social agencies, organized a committee of professionals who had some familiarity with the issues. The committee met for several weeks to identify the problems about which they would focus their concern. A subcommittee was organized to gather data from local agencies on the extent to which they were using subprofessionals and the various conditions under which they were working. Future plans of the committee are stated in a charge developed out of the first series of meetings: "to work with existing groups on the development of new careers in the human services . . . to provide technical assistance to agencies interested in the development of such programs . . . to develop a position statement for the chapter's consideration, and to encourage chapter members to examine these new career concepts as they apply to their own practice." This last goal is to be implemented by means of an all-day workshop on new careers which the committee is planning to conduct. It is apparent that the committee made an effort to link their efforts to what was taking place in agencies. Once some of these tasks are completed—for example, developing a position statement—the association will be able to play a part in the later stages of the process. It does appear, though, that the committee did not consider what it would do later on in thinking through its charge.

Finally, the model we have described should draw the attention of the professional association to the various gaps in the series of roles which professional members must be able to fill if the profession is to play a meaningful part in the formulation of policy. If there are not professionally trained workers within institutions who are prepared to undertake these tasks, the assignment will fall to other professionals who may not be fully able to represent the interests of the profession. Therefore, the association must be attentive to the extent to which the educational preparation of professionals helps to build both basic knowledge about the process of social policy formulation for all professionals and specialized training for roles which are not currently being filled—for example, the legal tasks in the seventh stage. In the absence of professionals who can fill such roles, the association must consider ways of helping professionals to develop the knowledge required to work productively with other professionals, who can fill the required roles. The inability of many social workers and lawyers to communicate with one another is a good example of this kind of knowledge gap.[20]

Secondly, although there may be some members of the profession who are able to fill all roles, the professional association has to determine the extent to which professionals in different roles can represent the interests of the profession, as against, say, the interests of the institution. For example, the interests of the professional who is an administrator are more likely to be influenced by his organizational commitments and concerns than are those of the practitioner. If that is the case, then the professional association must develop strategies by which to enlist the support of professionals who are administrators because of their strategic role in policy formulation.

---

[20] See Homer W. Sloane, "The Relationship of Law and Social Work," *Social Work*, 12 (January 1967); and Paul E. Weinberger and Peggy J. Smith, "The Disposition of Child Neglect Cases Referred by Caseworkers to a Juvenile Court," *Child and Welfare* (October 1966).

CHAPTER **VIII**

Manpower Development Programs

Charles Grosser

The Manpower Development and Training Act–sponsored youth training programs have frequently been part of comprehensive projects which encompass many services, centrally administered. These projects have utilized nonprofessionals in various program divisions. Although this report is concerned primarily with youth employment programs, we will refer to the use of nonprofessionals in other divisions as well, in the belief that the experience of the nonprofessional in the project as a whole is relevant to the manpower program in particular.

This paper is based on a comprehensive review of documents prepared by various MDTA-sponsored youth training programs and numerous other materials collected by the Office of Manpower Policy, Evaluation, and Research (OMPER). From among the many projects, five were chosen for site visits, not because they represent the typical experience of Office of Manpower Automation and Training (OMAT) youth projects but, rather, because their written material suggested that they were using nonprofessional staff in innovative or significant ways. The five programs are geographically disparate. Although all are located in large cities, no city represents a "typical" urban setting.

Interviews on project sites were conducted with agency administrators and practitioners as well as with the relevant community residents.[1] The conclusions reported here are those of the author; they do not necessarily represent project or community consensus or the position of the Department of Labor. Estimates of the frequency of phenomena described in this report are based on impressions gleaned from the site visits and from written reports, not on systematic enumeration.

Objectives in Using Nonprofessionals

Filling Manpower Needs. Since the historic social legislation enacted in the thirties, the number of agencies providing health, education, and welfare services has greatly increased. The past three decades have seen the creation of what is virtually a new industry, designed to meet the service demand of an increasingly urban, industrial, highly organized, technical nation. The complexity and specialization of our contemporary society have required public programs to provide for such contingencies as retirement, unemployment, illness, and disability, as well as for the recreational, educational, and vocational needs of the populace. The personnel requirements of this industry comprise a major portion of the nation's job market.

[1] The author is grateful to the staff of the five projects visited for their gracious assistance and to Joseph Seiler of OMPER for providing written materials, arranging project contacts, facilitating administrative matters, and being otherwise helpful. The projects visited are Mobilization for Youth, New York, New York; Mayor's Committee on Human Resources, Pittsburgh, Pennsylvania; Neighborhood House, Richmond, California; Youth Opportunities Board, Los Angeles, California; and PAL Joey, New York, New York.

The development of the highly industrial American economic system has tended to direct available manpower to manufacturing and commercial enterprises rather than to service. As a result, throughout the history of the welfare service complex, its manpower needs have never been adequately filled. Even as new sources of personnel are developed, constantly increasing demand has maintained a state of continuous shortage.

In the last five or six years, this crisis in personnel has been intensified by the expansion of existing programs, such as services provided under the Social Security Act, as well as by new programs such as community mental health and urban renewal. In addition, the early demonstration projects funded under the Manpower Development and Training Act and the Juvenile Delinquency and Youth Offenses Control Act[2] have evolved into an all-out war on poverty, based essentially on the provision of additional services to the millions of poor. The manpower needs of this vast mandate impose impossible demands on the service professions and thus have stimulated much of the current activity regarding the use of nonprofessionals.

Bridging the Gap. Accompanying the increase in welfare and service institutions over the last several decades has been an expansion in the range of the persons served by these institutions. This reflects a public policy objective, to provide service to a full spectrum of the nation's population. Services originally limited to those who were most amenable to treatment and whose prognosis was most positive have been extended to those whose problems are numerous, acute, and unlikely to be solved rapidly.[3] Thus ethnic minorities, the unemployed, the undereducated, migrant workers, and matriarchal families, among other groups, have become the concern of employment bureaus, vocational rehabilitation and guidance agencies, social security and welfare bureaus, and voluntary agencies as well as poverty programs. This interest in serving the total community reflects both the developing welfare-state phi-

[2] These laws were administered through the Office of Manpower Automation and Training and the Office of Juvenile Delinquency and Youth Development, respectively.

[3] Cf. E. Burns, "Social Security in Evolution Toward What?" *Social Service Review,* 29 (January 1965).

losophy and a growing sensitivity to practical politics. The trend to urbanization (three-fourths of the nation's population is located in urban centers) has awarded the city enormous influence in national politics. The elective process, in the reapportionment and one-man, one-vote issues, acknowledges this new power.

In an earlier day, welfare agencies denied service to persons whom they judged to be unemployable, uneducable, unmotivated, immoral, or incorrigible. But the same factors which have led welfare agencies to serve new deprived groups today keep them from abandoning these clients when it appears that the programs they offer are unsuited to the clients' needs.

Agency programs have generally been offered in a style very different from that of the target population and have been staffed by professionals who tend to differ from the clients in ethnicity, education, and other social class indices. Agency programs and policies have usually been created by central decision-making bodies far removed from the service neighborhood. These factors have produced a gap between the service institution and the target population. The nonprofessional worker, indigenous to the population served, is seen as a bridge between the institution and the lower-class community. The expansion of staff to include some members of this class as dispensers of service does not require the service agency to alter its program, replace its present staff, or revise the legislative or corporate mandate under which it operates. The use of local persons is perhaps the least threatening way of developing rapport with the new client.

The indigenous nonprofessional is seen as having mutual interests and common cause with program participants, as being able to communicate freely with them because, like them, he is poor, resides in the neighborhood, and shares minority-group status, common background, and language. It is assumed that nonprofessional staff, being of the community, will not render judgments, either clinical or moral, about client behavior.

Local nonprofessionals are often hired because they have succeeded in mastering the intricacies of urban slum life and can teach program participants how to do likewise. The service they offer, unlike that provided by the more clinically oriented professional, is direct, immediate, and pragmatic. For example, the nonprofessional may help a work trainee to succeed in a job culture by teaching him not to be a rate-buster, how to show proper deference to a foreman, and the like. He may provide a welfare client with knowledge, inadvertently or deliberately withheld by the department, which enables her to obtain larger benefits. In both instances, techniques will be both informal and unofficial. The nonprofessional may suggest stretching or bending rules and regulations on behalf of the client. This should cause no alarm, for it is apparent that professionals and administrators similarly stretch rules on behalf of agency, or for expedience or economy.

In all these ways, local nonprofessionals provide the institution with sufficient flexibility to remain in contact with program participants who otherwise would be excluded from service. Yet there is considerable opposition to the use of such personnel. Even in agencies which operate under directives that indigenous nonprofessionals be employed, compliance is often reluctant, and every effort is made to ensure that the service program remains intact.

Providing Jobs. The fact that, in the midst of great national prosperity, chronic unemployment and widespread poverty persist among certain segments of the population was forcibly brought to public attention by Michael Harrington[4] and others in the early sixties. Many proposals have been offered to remedy this situation. As a solution to poverty in plenty, for example, Robert Theobold[5] has proposed that a minimum income level be established below which no family would be permitted to drop. Pearl and Riessman[6] seek the solution in the creation of a million welfare service jobs for the poor. They claim that the bulk of professional time is spent in activity which could be handled no less effectively by the nonprofessional and suggest that their approach will not only provide jobs for the technologically unemployed but reduce estrangement between service agency and disadvantaged client and fill a chronic manpower need.

Fulfilling Democratic Ideology. The democratic, egalitarian

[4] Michael Harrington, *The Other America* (New York: Macmillan, 1963).

[5] Robert Theobold, *Free Men and Free Markets* (New York: Potter, 1963).

[6] Arthur Pearl and Frank Riessman, *New Careers for the Poor* (New York: Free Press, 1965).

traditions of our nation are based on the idea that all citizens must participate actively in governmental and decision-making processes. Numerous studies indicate, however, that by such indices as membership in voluntary associations and voting behavior, the lower classes are significantly less active than the middle and upper classes. In fact, by any absolute measure of activism they do not exercise their franchise or participate in the affairs of community life. They are therefore without voice, power, and influence, and thus belie our democratic image.

Among the many sociopolitical strategies put forward to rectify this situation are programs designed for the "maximum feasible participation" of the poor, such as the community action projects established under Title II of the Economic Opportunity Act.[7] The involvement of the poor in the development and the administration of these programs, as called for in the act, has aroused considerable controversy. Participation of the poor on a policy-making level has been opposed by such diverse critics as the Bureau of the Budget, a southern governor's office, and various councils of social agencies. It is for this reason that the majority of antipoverty programs meet their mandate to involve the poor by employing local residents in the "conducting" function, or in the dispensation of largesse. Some service programs thus employ nonprofessionals without regard for how they might best be used, but simply as a means of bringing into existence a program for which the employment of local persons is a requirement.

The "Helper Therapy" Principle. Observers have been struck by the fact that programs which use people in trouble to help others with similar difficulties are often as successful in helping the provider of service as the recipient.[8]

Such programs as Synanon and Parents Without Partners appear to have regularized this phenomenon to the point where the roles of patient and therapist become indistinguishable; the course

---

[7] Public Law 88–452, August 20, 1964, Title II, Section 202, a3. "The term *community action program* means a program which is developed, conducted and administered with the maximum feasible participation of residents of the areas and members of the groups served. . . ."

[8] Cf. Frank Riessman, "The 'Helper Therapy' Principle," *Social Work*, 10 (April 1965).

of treatment is for the patient to devote his energies to the rehabilitation of others. One of the projects reviewed illustrates this phenomenon most dramatically. The project assigned local high school students to tutor fourth- and fifth-grade pupils who were severely retarded in reading development. Many of the tutors themselves were below grade in their school work, and their educational and employment future was bleak. Over a study period of several months, the youngsters who were tutored as much as four hours a week showed significant improvement when compared to a control group. Even more striking—and unexpected—was the improvement made by the tutors, which exceeded the gains made by pupils.[9]

The ultimate objective of many nonprofessional approaches is to channel some of the forces within the deprived community itself into rehabilitative and restorative efforts so that the client becomes able to help himself. Complementing the service component in such efforts are attempts to break the cycle of pessimism and defeat which plagues low-income persons. In a society which places the highest value on success in the world of work, there is no more potent device for enhancing self-esteem than meaningful, productive employment. The employment of nonprofessionals may therefore produce therapeutic results simply by awarding these workers status, regardless of the benefits derived in the helping process.

Nonprofessionals and Assignments

Background of Workers. Nonprofessionals associated with the various youth projects have been drawn from diverse backgrounds. They include indigenous local residents and clients, middle-class volunteers, graduate and undergraduate college students (both as volunteers and on field training assignments), VISTA volunteers, and Peace Corps trainees. Both youth and adults have been utilized as nonprofessional program personnel. In one single large-scale project, virtually all these categories of nonprofessionals have been used concurrently, as follows:

1. Student Project Assistants: Graduates of the youth employment counseling program were given general ancillary respon-

[9] Robert Cloward, *Studies in Tutoring*, Research Center, Columbia University School of Social Work, 1966 (mimeo.).

sibilities, such as driver, assistant receptionist, interpreters of the youth training program to the community.

2. Interns: Part-time (thirty hours per week) college students were assigned tutoring, counseling, job development, and other professional responsibilities.

3. VISTA Volunteers: Full-time volunteers were assigned to tutoring and community work.

4. Neighborhood Youth Corps Trainees: Youngsters enrolled in the Neighborhood Youth Corps and placed in project programs were assigned such ancillary responsibilities as clerical, research, and custodial assistants.

5. Neighborhood Adult-Participation Project Aides: Full-time employees in the project's community development program. NAPPs carried many responsibilities among which were assignments to the youth training program as work-crew foremen.

6. Volunteers (students, professionals, and housewives): Middle-class residents offered a variety of services, both professional (psychotherapy, tattoo removal, legal services) and nonprofessional (tutoring assistant).

7. Work-Study Students: College students from low-income families being assisted under Title IC of the Economic Opportunity Act were assigned to assist in job development, counseling, tutoring, and so on.

8. Vocational-Rehabilitation and Social Work Trainees: These trainees were assigned to programs which would facilitate their professional training.

Nonprofessionals may be categorized as indigenous to the target community or separate from it. Indigenous workers reside in the target area, engage in social, economic, and political processes similar to those of the program participants, and are matched with them in such characteristics as social class, ethnicity, race, religion, language, culture, and mores. Many projects have recruited such nonprofessional staff from the broader community beyond the target area, but we shall continue to call these workers indigenous if they are matched with clients on general face-sheet characteristics. In attempting to fill crew chief positions, for example, projects have frequently had difficulty in finding local residents with the necessary work skills. The search for such persons in the broader community was often futile as well, since for many crafts the candidate's racial and ethnic characteristics, which provide the indigenous match, preclude the acquisition of work-skill qualifications. In projects which attempted to prepare youth for work through training in carpentry, masonry, plumbing, and other building trades, the crew chief often matched the client only on certain working-class attributes but not on residential, racial, or cultural characteristics. Other divisions in the same project which did not require the work-related skills were able to employ nonprofessionals who were native to the target area and representative of its population. In general, the projects appear to have been most successful in hiring indigenous nonprofessionals for assignments which did not require a high degree of formal technical skill.

Nonprofessional staff that was separate from the target population and community sometimes became associated with the program almost accidentally. This was particularly true of volunteers. The experiences of the projects with volunteers are so disparate as to defy classification. Some of these nonprofessionals were typical social agency volunteers, members of the middle and upper classes offering their services in their leisure as a gesture of noblesse oblige. At the opposite end of the scale were young radicals who settled in ghettos as a matter of personal choice, virtually as missionaries or colonizers, who offered their services as part of their political ideological commitment. In a number of instances, volunteers were arbitrarily thrust upon the projects and were accepted with resentment and misgivings. In these cases relationships with the project tended to become pro forma and were usually short-lived.

In their early attempts to reach unemployed youth, training projects located in Spanish-speaking ghettos were faced with language barriers. In order to provide counseling as well as other services, it was necessary to find Spanish-speaking professionals. The search soon revealed that Spanish-speaking minority-group members had been systematically excluded from the professions.

Because of the need to establish a relationship as a functional therapeutic device, there is an inordinate dependence on the spoken word in counseling, tutoring, social work, and other such rehabilitation services. For this reason the use of translators with

English-speaking professionals is impractical. Projects therefore recruited Spanish-speaking persons with some college or a college degree to provide such services. These workers were sometimes called aides or intake workers to distinguish them from their fully trained counterparts, but these distinctions tended to fade rather quickly. Recruitment of nonindigenous Negro staff took place for similar reasons, in the belief that Negro clients would communicate more fully with Negro workers than with white personnel.[10] Many projects also recruited Negro and Spanish personnel in an attempt to meet political pressure for integration exerted by civil rights and other activist and community groups.

Often such nonprofessional personnel were selected instead of indigenous lower-class persons. One project describes an extensive screening process which eliminated thirty or forty indigenous applicants because they were deficient in communication skills and lacked preprofessional experience. The positions in question were ultimately filled by Negro and Puerto Rican workers, all of whom had had at least three years of college. These applicants had work backgrounds in teaching in the rural South, recreation work in a large city, and work as research assistants.

Most projects employed nonprofessionals on a full-time, paid basis, most of whom were adults. With few exceptions youth used in service positions have been assigned to various projects for work experience. In these instances, of course, the project is not the employer of the nonprofessional youth, nor does it assume direct responsibility for supervising him.

Types of Assignments. The wide variety of tasks to which nonprofessionals have been assigned may be subsumed under four categories: direct service responsibilities, responsibilities ancillary to the professional service, responsibilities establishing bridges or ties to the target community, and assignments totally apart from the professional services of the project. This last category, which simply needs to be acknowledged rather than discussed, consists in the main of clerical and custodial assignments often given to N.Y.C. or Peace Corps trainees and others, particularly volunteers, whom the project is forced to accept. Although this pattern is not uncommon,

[10] Cf. John Martin, "Social-Cultural Differences: Barriers in Casework with Delinquents," *Social Work,* 2 (July 1957).

it does not characterize every assignment made to such nonprofessionals.

Direct service responsibilities—the least common of the four categories—refers to services usually transmitted to the client through the professional worker, for example, counseling, remediation, job development, tutoring, and teaching. In the projects reviewed, there were examples of nonprofessionals providing each of these services directly to the client. Such assignments make best use of the skills peculiar to the nonprofessional, for example, his enthusiasm and spontaneity.

Direct assignment also tends to utilize such nonprofessional qualities as the ability to communicate with clients, through common language or style; empathy with the client through shared life experience; and the ability to help clients negotiate the complexities of the ghetto.

Assignment to responsibilities ancillary to the provision of professional service is the most common way of using nonprofessionals. Some of these assignments are rather remote from the professional services being offered. In contrast to the wholly unrelated assignment, however, they are located within the program and are related to the client group. Ancillary responsibilities may consist of clerical, administrative, transport, and other such duties which help to bring the client and the service into productive contact. Further along the continuum toward direct assignment are tasks which are instrumental in preparing the client for the professional service—for example, reception, intake, and vestibule services—which are frequently assigned to nonprofessional personnel.

Such assignments as recruitment and follow-up involve a large measure of independent service. Nonprofessionals on these assignments generally operate directly in the neighborhood, away from the supports and structure of the project agency. They are called upon to exercise considerable imagination and ingenuity, particularly when they deal with youth whom the agency has failed to induct or for whom service has been ineffective. Although successful recruitment or follow-up ultimately entails turning the client over to a professional for service, the nonprofessional task is perhaps more accurately viewed as contiguous than as ancillary. Within the ancillary assignment, as one moves from the remote to the contiguous, the opportunities for exploiting indigenous qualities appear to increase.

Recruitment and follow-up to some degree serve a bridge function. However, the assignments which we classify as bridge have more to do with project community relations on an institutional basis. In speaking engagements, door-to-door canvassing, leaflet distribution, and visiting youth groups and P.T.A.s, the non-professional acts as agency spokesman to the target community and the community at large. The use of nonprofessionals in these capacities is often a viable device for persuading the target community that services are being offered by a congenial institution. (It can, however, become a public relations gimmick, an attempt to represent the agency as ethnically or culturally indigenous when in fact it is not. It is something of an anomaly that the employment of nonprofessionals can be offered as tokenism to avoid the actual reordering of a public institution along congenial indigenous lines.)

Work-training projects tend to discriminate between indigenous and middle-class, more formally trained nonprofessionals. The former group gets more irrelevant and fewer direct assignments. The ancillary tasks assigned them tend to be remote rather than contiguous. Middle-class nonprofessionals are utilized more frequently in direct assignment, often in ways indistinguishable from the professional. Agency representatives indicated that they would be willing to promote such nonprofessionals into professional positions, although few actually did. Where youth employment projects were part of comprehensive programs, this tendency was not so pronounced in other program divisions. Although indigenous nonprofessionals in employment projects were not assigned to provide counseling or remediation, they did provide social work services (casework, group work, and especially community organization) and educational services (tutoring, citizenship, and consumer) in other divisions of the same project. The failure to use indigenous nonprofessionals in employment was more pronounced in counseling than in work-readiness programs. Crew chiefs and on-the-job training personnel did include numbers of indigenous persons.

Substantive Issues

Nonprofessional and Agency. The use of nonprofessionals in MDTA youth programs was in large part the result of influence exerted by the federal funding agencies. Federal agencies not only provided the service agencies with funds for the employment of nonprofessionals but threatened to set up parallel organizations if these moneys were not used for that purpose. A number of respondents were convinced that without this threat the agencies and projects would not have hired nonprofessionals, and that should federal supports be removed, they would stop using nonprofessionals. It is significant that this opinion appears to apply primarily to nonprofessional employees who are indigenous to the service community.

In part this reluctance reflects the resentment that many project administrators and agency executives feel at being compelled to employ large numbers of minority-group indigenous persons. According to one respondent, the project was "paying the price for a hundred years of discrimination by the entire community." Although others expressed their conviction that nonprofessionals were vital to successful project programs, they frequently felt inhibited in reassigning or dismissing indigenous personnel because of fear of community reprisals. When the administrative head of one project dismissed the director of a neighborhood program which employed many indigenous nonprofessionals, these workers picketed project headquarters and eventually involved the local congressman and the regional Office of Economic Opportunity. As a result, in large measure, of the public turmoil the workers were able to raise, the professional director was rehired, with considerable loss of face for the project administration. This incident resulted in widespread enmity among professionals associated with the project regarding this program in particular and indigenous workers in general. The potential for a reenactment of this situation exists in all projects, programs, and agencies which employ local residents.

The attitude of various state employment service offices illustrates that they perceive a threat in the use of local personnel because the employment of such persons forces the agency to a degree of accountability to the client community. This is contrary to the traditional pattern in all service agencies of professional self-regulation and accountability to the total community[11] and to the employment service's views of its responsibility to the employer.

The district manager of a state employment service office which itself employs nonprofessional staff complained that the nonprofessional does not play by the rules. The persistence with which such workers undertake job development, he claimed, often alienates employers: they tend to demand rather than ask for job placements. In addition, these workers are not content to stay within the parameters of their assigned tasks; they want to "take over the entire agency."

A demonstration project staff member observed that turnover among nonprofessional provisional workers in the Bureau of Employment Security was inordinately high. "The best provisions end up being the ones who fail the tests and get fired." According to this respondent, this phenomenon cannot be explained in terms of the workers' failure to meet state job standards, since the employment service could train provisionals to take tests just as the project prepares trainees to take tests. The phenomenon illustrates the reluctance of the employment service to hire and to retain local nonprofessionals. Once hired, these staff are generally abrasive to the operation of the office as conceived by its executive, and a high turnover rate ensues. According to project informants, further evidence would be found in the high turnover rate of project counselors in the employment service.

A nonprofessional who served as a neighborhood extension worker for the employment service office voiced a number of grievances regarding lack of employment service cooperation. She charged that supportive counseling services were not provided, that only certain kinds of jobs were made available to her people, and, most particularly, that the employment service did not take her word for anything. What was the use, she asked, of a neighborhood extension program if all the information gathered through that program was verified independently by the downtown office? The employment service office felt that nonprofessionals were useful in preemployment and intake functions but lacked the skill and train-

[11] *Total community* generally means the formal organizations and representative groups of the community. It apparently never includes the unaffiliated poor.

ing to operate effectively beyond this point; professional counselors therefore had to take over. This view in part reflected an ideological disparity between the professional and the nonprofessional. The nonprofessional apparently feels that the most important thing to be done for the client is to get him a job while the professional feels that "one has to correct the root of the unemployment problem through programs of counseling, training, and education which will make the person employable." The professional also tends to select the most amenable candidates, excluding "drifters, gamblers, and hustlers," while the nonprofessional believes that the service should be available to all on a first-come, first-served basis. It is clear that there are both merits and problems in each point of view. Despite the strains, the employment service has managed to contain both elements. Its administration describes the nonprofessional in program as a "must."

The use of nonprofessionals in the projects and in the public welfare service agencies in particular must be seen in terms of institutional change, as well as service objectives. The introduction of a program device as innovative as this one, even if the original intention is only to improve service, must soon produce strains leading to alterations in patterns of agency function. A somewhat anomalous circumstance surrounds this social change objective in that it is articulated by the staff of the CAP agency which administers the federal funds but not by the public agencies which are the targets of the change. Thus the antipoverty administrators conceive of the nonprofessionals as change agents while the welfare agency sees them as facilitating existing services. It would appear that the stress inherent in this situation is exacerbated by this dual perception.[12]

The experience of a nonprofessional in a neighborhood employment office illustrates the way in which alterations in service impinge on general agency function. Because of this worker's roots in the community, she is contacted on matters pertaining to all programs offered by the local CAP. While being interviewed for this

[12] It may very well be that this disparity is essential if the nonprofessional is to be accepted by the service agency at all. If this is the case, there is little that can be done about this complication beyond recognizing its genesis and some of its consequences.

review, the worker received a call from a local resident, greatly agitated because her welfare worker was investigating a report that the client was receiving income for baby-sitting. The information had been given to the welfare worker by the Head Start coordinator, who was working with the family for which the baby-sitting was said to have taken place. After hearing from the client, the employment aide called the Head Start worker, the welfare worker, and the neighborhood family to ascertain the facts. She then explained to the welfare worker that no payment had been made for sitting, that funds were not being diverted from the regular family food budget for this purpose, and that this was, after all, the kind of neighborliness to be encouraged in building community pride and spirit.

The indigenous worker then explained to the Head Start worker, politely but firmly, that the baby-sitting arrangements of the client family were none of the worker's business. If she inadvertently became privy to such information she should keep it to herself. Later, describing her own work, she said that if she succeeds in helping a person on public assistance to get a job, she does not share this fact with the welfare department. She points out to the client that he is required to inform the department and that she hopes he will do so. However, she can understand that need may drive the client to withhold information, and she will not interfere with his decision.

In this instance, the worker remained loyal to indigenous rather than professional values and behavior patterns. The community's acceptance of this worker as interpreter, confidante, and advocate is undoubtedly a response to this loyalty. Her professional associates in the CAP agency regard her with some fear and suspicion. The employment service people look upon her as a troublemaker, and top agency administrators tend to see her as a model of what the indigenous nonprofessional ought to be. The question of whether the indigenous worker is loyal to the neighborhood from which he is drawn or to the agency is not always resolved in so clear-cut a manner.

In another project, another nonprofessional indigenous worker faced with the same dilemma indicated that she would share information with her agency, but not with the welfare department, if the client refused to do so. This worker expressed a sense of alienation from her own community. Regarding her relationships with her neighbors after being employed by the youth project, she indicated that "the people do stand off, they feel that you are not the same." It appears that nonprofessionals who feel this alienation tend to seek acceptance from the agency staff group, where they are likely to take on additional values, attitudes, and norms of behavior alien to the neighborhood.

Another factor which appears to have a bearing on where the indigenous nonprofessional will build continuing loyalties is the nature of the job assignment. In the first instance described above the worker was employed in a direct service capacity; the responsibilities of the second worker were ancillary. Primary identification with the community seems to be enhanced if the nonprofessional is engaged in activity that can stand on its own. Where the nonprofessional's successful performance was tied to a client's amenability to service to be provided by a professional colleague, high professional identification and orientation ensued. Where performance was independent and community participation by heretofore unserved persons was esteemed, identification with community was primary. In the project in which the professionally oriented ancillary worker is located, there is a division in which nonprofessionals are used in direct service capacities. These workers, drawn from the same community, of identical class and racial background and employed under the same project executive, are militantly identified with community.

Recruitment and Selection. Although professional and non-program staff are systematically and regularly recruited through conventional channels (that is, employment services, ads, and so on), nonprofessionals are apparently recruited on an ad hoc basis. Community informants, particularly such influentials as local welfare agency executives, clergymen, political leaders, and school officials, are often asked to refer local persons for employment. Sometimes "outstanding" residents are specified. Even when this is not explicitly done, the persons referred tend to be those who have assumed some leadership in the organization with which the referrer is affiliated. As will be noted later, there is reason to believe that relying on local institutional leaders as a source of candidates screens the applicants in light of the qualities which the recruiter deems desirable. In addition, unrelated factors may influence selection; for example, positions may be seen by those who make the referrals as rewards for service, political patronage, or largesse for the deserving poor.

In most cases, neither the local institutions which do the recruiting nor the projects have formally specified the qualities they seek in nonprofessional staff. One informant indicated, however, that his project sought "quickness of mind and a capacity for growth," along with "a public capability to lead and organize." Nonprofessionals in this project appear to have a good measure of the qualities sought. In a project in another city, staff have indicated that they seek nonprofessionals with white-collar experience. High priority has been placed on the ability to prepare written reports and to participate easily in staff meetings and conferences. This project expressly attempts to avoid nonprofessionals who are "too overidentified with the client." It is interesting to note that the white-collar experience which this project seeks apparently successfully screens out those who tend to be "overidentified." In still another city, the project staff sought persons with a strong personality and a strong positive commitment to the agency; "do-gooders" were not welcome in staff positions.

Still another agency at its inception developed differential recruitment practices and standards for its various categories of nonprofessional staff, depending on the function they were intended to fill. One group, which helped local residents with household management, was selected from a list of women recommended by local settlements and churches. The qualities sought were home-making skills, demonstrated mastery of the intricacies of urban slum living, and good feeling toward people. Members of another group, hired to teach a craft or work skills to young people, were recruited directly from industry. They were not local residents or affiliated with local welfare or religious institutions. Community workers were recruited from among the local unaffiliated residents. The quality sought was leadership, which was measured in terms of following; thus, influential community persons who were not involved in community institutions were selected. As is apparent, very different kinds of nonprofessionals were hired in each of these job categories.

One project developed written specifications which described job qualifications and requirements (as well as responsibilities and benefits).[13] Requirements included local residence, prior work experience, and participation in the P.T.A., the Scouts, a union, a fraternal group, or a similar organization. Personal characteristics sought were maturity, ability to work with people, agency loyalty, participation in some form of personal upgrading, and willingness to undertake training, if necessary. Educational requirements are listed as high school, General Education Diploma (G.E.D.), or strong potential for G.E.D. The specifications noted that the position for which the nonprofessional was to be hired was regarded, not as an end in itself, but as a means of helping him find a permanent place in the labor force or encouraging him to seek additional training. Although many of the requirements and conditions listed in these documents are the same as those of other projects, the fact that they are available to candidates and recruiters makes for a consistency in the selection of nonprofessionals that is too often lacking in practice.

Two of the projects surveyed in connection with this report indicated that they had interviewed candidates for nonprofessional employment who had been trained under an OMAT grant to the National Committee for the Employment of Youth. One project found none of these candidates suitable for employment as counseling and job development aides. The other project employed seven of these trainees in such direct assignments as recruiters, work-readiness evaluators, and assistant crew chiefs. Apparently a project's ability to make effective use of nonprofessionals depends more on its willingness to surrender areas of professional discretion to them than on issues of training or the availability of trained applicants. Competence is judged differently by different projects, and it is likely that each sees the nonprofessional as serving a different organizational purpose.

Nonprofessional staff have also been drawn from among local people who were active in the project as volunteers. Recruits

[13] It is of interest, with regard to possible replication of MDTA experience, that this community subsequently developed a highly sophisticated CAP program which included specifications for each distinctive nonprofessional position.

of this kind pose problems for local residents who continue to serve as volunteers, particularly for those who are engaged in activities similar to the tasks of the employed worker.

A number of projects reported that the target community was involved in choosing nonprofessional personnel through the participation of residents in selection committees. In some instances these committees see all candidates; others see candidates who have been screened by the project's administration. Some committees make specific recommendations for hiring; others designate which candidates are acceptable, from among whom administration can then make their choice. Professional employees are not screened by selection committees, although in some cases their application forms are reviewed by these bodies. In these cases, local community residents are not a part of the personnel committee.

Identification. Recruitment practices are not unrelated to the question of whether the nonprofessional, particularly the indigenous nonprofessional, will identify with the project which employs him or the community from which he was recruited. When recruitment patterns select the upwardly mobile and job assignments encourage agency dependency, one can be reasonably certain that the project and the professionals will become the basic reference groups for these staff members. This is especially true for those whose desire for job security is strong.

The projects' experience confirms the numerous studies which describe the tendency of the less skilled and lower-class worker to favor security over a risky but real opportunity for advancement. Patterns of employment tenure among nonprofessionals indicate virtually no turnover, in contrast to the very high turnover rate among professionals in the same agency. The nonprofessional's general experience in the job market leads him to be conservative in his approach to employment. Realizing that his opportunities for employment are restricted, he will eschew conflict with the agency and seek rapport, both deliberately and unconsciously, by internalizing agency-professional norms.[14]

The experience of several projects with nonprofessional staff

---

[14] Cf. Charles Grosser, "Perceptions of Professionals, Indigenous Workers, and Lower-Class Clients," unpublished doctoral dissertation, Columbia University School of Social Work, 1965.

illustrates both their tendency to avoid certain nonprofessional, community-based activities and their tendency to emulate professional practice. In one of the projects nonprofessionals assigned to a service-provision program demanded regularly scheduled weekly supervisory conferences; offices equipped with desks, blotters, and lamps; and appointment books and office hours. These workers wished to avoid home visits to deteriorated buildings, baby-sitting, and homemaking assignments. However, nonprofessionals in the same agency who were assigned to community-organization tasks did not pursue a similar pattern. The success of this latter group depended on viable community ties. Thus they frequented the streets and the tenements, preferred storefront locations, dressed casually, and avoided any distinctions which would separate them from the neighborhood residents. This supports our earlier conclusion that choice of reference group is strongly influenced by job assignment, in part because job assignment may influence the pattern by which employment security is best established.

The role of the professional in the community organization program offers yet another affirmation of the potency of job assignment in this respect. In a number of ways the professionals in this division were more community-identified than the nonprofessionals in the other service divisions. They dressed casually, without tie or jacket, spoke the neighborhood argot, and did without desks, appointment books, and formal conferences.

Upward Mobility. Although some thought has been given to the problem of creating a career line through which the nonprofessional may be promoted and increase his earnings, no such plans are currently operational. Two patterns of advancement are discernible. The first brings the nonprofessional into common cause with professional, clerical, and maintenance personnel in a trade union organization. Advancement takes place collectively rather than individually, through negotiated agreements which include incremental salary increases and improved fringe benefits. Such benefits may include, as is the case in one project, the provision that current staff be given first option on all new job openings. This provision occasionally affords upward mobility for the nonprofessional.

In the second pattern, which is much more widespread,

the individual advances by moving from one program in the community to another, seeking a higher rate of pay, or to a more demanding and better paid position in the project in which he is employed. As a nonprofessional worker gains white-collar experience in a project job, he not only learns the skills that are required to do the work but also becomes aware of employment possibilities in other CAP and OEO programs. Thus he might move from an ancillary or unrelated assignment to a direct service assignment, either within the same project or across several antipoverty programs.

Professional-Nonprofessional Relations. Generally the professional worker accepts his untrained, noncredentialed colleague in ancillary, bridge, or unrelated assignments within the project. Although there are a few professionals who feel that even in these areas the nonprofessional is inappropriately involved, in the main the professional views the untrained worker, particularly the indigenous worker, positively. In fact, the professional often has a somewhat romanticized reaction. The vaunted virtues of the nonprofessional—spontaneity, ability to communicate, informality, style, and identification with clients—are often perceived in idealized fashion although they are frequently belied by performance. The tendency of nonprofessionals to exhibit quite different characteristics under certain circumstances is infrequently asknowledged. In addition to inflating the virtues of the untrained, the professional tends to assume—often erroneously—that he himself wholly lacks these qualities.

A survey conducted by one of the projects indicated that the attitudes and beliefs of nonprofessional staff tend to be highly judgmental and moralistic regarding the behavior of local target area residents. They often regard illegitimacy, unemployment, drinking, and even boisterous asocial behavior as evidence of moral turpitude. They also tend to be somewhat fatalistic about a person's ability to affect his life. These observations indicate that the services of the nonprofessional might be utilized best if assignments were made selectively. The professional's objectivity and dispassion might be more functional in serving low-income clients in certain circumstances than the nonprofessional's congeniality and judgmentalness. However, it appears that little discretion in assignment was exercised consciously. When the project's view of the use of the nonprofessional was positive, their attitude was you can't have too much of a good thing; when their set was negative, they tended to feel that it doesn't matter anyway. Either view resulted in indiscriminate assignments.

Even in the area of advocacy, it was found that under certain circumstances, nonprofessionals constituted an impediment to effective service. This was most striking where project staff had to negotiate on behalf of a trainee with a hostile community institution. Such institutions tend to be more favorably disposed when approached by a professional whose "style, language, and affect" are familiar. If what is being sought is immediate service for the trainee, the professional is obviously the best bridge between project and formal community institution. Several projects identified this phenomenon in its negative aspect, describing how staff members with a Spanish accent were summarily brushed aside when they phoned certain institutions for assistance, whereas these same institutions responded favorably when called by (English-speaking) staff with no accent.

The reactions of nonprofessionals to professional staff tend to follow the patterns of identification described earlier. Those who are project-identified tend to be less critical than those who are community-identified. The community-oriented group shares the residents' perception of the professional as an outsider, something of a cold fish, too formal, bureaucratic, and not sufficiently sympathetic to the neighborhood. One is struck, however, by the clear-cut distinction made by virtually all community residents as well as by the nonprofessional staff between project professionals and professionals employed in other community service organizations. The former group is accepted and viewed critically in the light of this acceptance; from the latter group, however, there is virtually complete estrangement. In assaying the consequences of the use of nonprofessionals later in this paper, we shall suggest that not the least of them is the effect they have on total project staff.

Strain between the formally certified and untrained staffs is most likely to appear when nonprofessionals are assigned to direct service responsibilities. In virtually every instance, responses indicated that the professional group reacted defensively, at least at first. They were unwilling to concede that there were significant portions of their jobs which could be given over to nonprofessionals. As a result, administrators were reluctant to experiment with direct assignments, anticipating that professional staff would object sharply.

Clearly, the professional in these instances saw the direct service assignment of the nonprofessional as an encroachment on his designated area of practice. It appears that this resistance owed more to the feeling that the use of untrained persons denigrated professional training than to any actual threat to job security. The problem was much more formidable in anticipation than in practice. Where nonprofessionals were actually given direct service assignments, accommodation soon resulted. Unfortunately, the timidity of administrators appears to have precluded many such assignments.

Personnel practices have proved to be a source of dissonance in the relationship of these two groups. As indicated, the problem of dismissing workers, particularly when the nonprofessionals call on community support, has created enmity between the staff groups, exacerbating feelings which may already have been present as a result of differential hiring practices, salaries, and working conditions. Personnel practices for nonprofessionals in a number of agencies are the same as those for maintenance and clerical staff rather than the more generous arrangements made with the professionals.

In some projects, direct assignments have evolved to the point where staff members from both groups are engaged in identical activities. In many cases, the only difference between them is a year or two of formal training, or training in a different area, with the result that the members of one group have professional certification. Yet the salary differential between such workers might be as much as 40 to 50 per cent. Typically it is in the neighborhood of 25 per cent, which may amount to several thousand dollars a year.

Training Programs

Before discussing problems of training nonprofessional personnel, we would do well to consider a few of the generic issues which underlie training. In a war troops are often forced into situations which they are unprepared to face, because the time, resources, or necessary personnel to conduct proper training programs are lacking. It appears that in the current effort to socialize welfare and other services, which we have euphemistically dubbed a war, the same circumstance prevails. Legislators, funding agencies, administrators, and beneficiaries prefer that funds be utilized to produce visible service programs. Statistics of persons served do not result from training programs. The qualitative differences which are produced are not sufficiently visible to meet the pressures being exerted. As a result, available resources are allocated to programs that produce quantitative results; training is not among these.

Some respondents indicated that the training programs for project nonprofessionals were generally a part of the training program offered the total project program staff. This means that there was no formal orientation period and that in-service training consisted of staff meetings, in some instances regularly scheduled, in others, sporadic. Administrators feel some discomfort with this situation though it is clear that they have resigned themselves to it. Only one project administrator was candid enough to acknowledge, without probing, that he had no training program worth mentioning.

What separate programs exist for nonprofessional staff sometimes have a strong doctrinaire character. They are designed to encourage agency loyalty and to interpret agency programs and policy. One respondent suggested that training served as a vehicle to handle the strong negative feelings that the nonprofessionals had toward such public agencies as the welfare department.

Nonprofessionals who had participated in new careers programs as clients or project beneficiaries did receive extensive training. This may be because the training itself is in this case service which can be cited statistically. The program was quite imaginative and creative. The training was distinct from that offered to any other staff group and unlike the conventional functions of job orientation and administrative information. It focused on correcting deficiencies in basic education skills and exposing the careerist nonprofessional to new experiences—trips around the state, attendance at meetings, participation in conferences and conventions, and visits to legislative bodies. Attention was also given to developing organizational, job-related, and general social skills.

Substantive training of both professional and nonprofessional staff often took place at the inception of the earliest evaluation and development projects (usually amalgams in which OMAT, OJD, and municipal and private funding sources participated). Because these projects were charged to produce knowledge rather than services, they were permitted the luxury of substantial training investments. One such program, which devoted 6 per cent (some $300,000) of its budget to training, was able to assign three staff members in addition to outside resource personnel to a full-time training program for one group of local nonprofessionals. Once the total program was in full swing, such an arrangement was not possible; as nonprofessionals were added they were placed in their jobs with little orientation or training.

In two of the projects observed, the MDTA project had turned over its training function to another agency. In both cases, nonprofessional staff received high-quality training experiences. In one case a citywide agency had undertaken responsibility for training nonprofessionals for all public programs in the city, and the project reluctantly complied. The administrator of the training program complained that she was hard-pressed by the groups she was serving to push trainees through quickly and avoid wasting time on nonessentials. The agencies made it clear that they regarded themselves as the proper training agents. They resented the central system and participated in it only to comply with the demands of the local CAP. In other cities, proposals to centralize training or negotiate training contracts with local academic institutions encountered similar resistance.

The centralized training program itself is quite comprehensive. Under the direction of a full-time training supervisor a functional syllabus has been prepared which outlines the goals and methods of the training unit. The training is directed to building a broad knowledge base encompassing the rationale behind the program as well as preparation for specific tasks. Relationships between nonprofessionals and professionals, clients and the community at large, are explored. The presentation of material takes into account educational, cultural, and ethnic differentials. Local historical and traditional materials as well as such topics as the culture of poverty, the role of the family, and economic and educational theories and institutions are covered in the syllabus. It appeared, on the basis of a brief site visit, that this material was effectively presented to the trainees.

There is much to commend this training arrangement. It relieves the service program of the burden of training and greatly increases the likelihood that training will take place. It raises the content level of training from concern with narrow operational issues to more creative exploitation of personnel and program.

In the second instance the training function was assumed by the National Committee for the Employment of Youth. In a sense this is a variant on the new careers model, except that it is specifically geared to meet the needs of manpower projects. In this regard it stands as perhaps the most effective, most relevant, and most sophisticated of those reviewed. It consists of twelve weeks of on-the-job and classroom training combined with discussion and field trips. Program content is geared to the general and the specific, attempting to elucidate the conditions underlying the problems that the nonprofessionals will be coping with as well as their own functions in the projects. The program is staffed by three full-time professionals and operated under independent funding from OMAT.[15]

Apart from the substantive knowledge it generates, this program also serves as a training institution for other projects which hire graduates. It represents a most viable approach to training, combining the advantages of locating this function outside the service agency with the resources of an experienced, highly sophisticated staff. Local academic institutions will also lend themselves to this approach.

The employment of nonprofessionals has important consequences for the agency's program, its target population, the nonprofessionals themselves, and the professional staff. Nonprofessionals have no influence on the substance of a policy program. In their capacity as project employees, they must limit themselves to furthering organizational purpose. Although a nonprofessional may offer program in a unique style, he is discouraged from trying to alter its substance, nor could he do so if he were encouraged to. Agencies see professionals and nonprofessionals in light of their own organi-

[15] See National Committee on the Employment of Youth, *A Demonstration On-the-Job Training Program for Semi-Professional Personnel in Youth Employment Programs: Final Report* (New York, 1966).

zational needs, as solutions to problems of service provision, not as vehicles of institutional change or program innovation.

Issues of job security support these tendencies. Programs become locked in place, much as they do in continuing institutions. Issues of funding, politics, organizational self-interest, and the like are among the operational imperatives which determine program. Neither professional nor nonprofessional staff can alter this pattern through programmatic strategies. The actual substance of program will be altered by strategies that are economic, political, or organizational, not programmatic.

In visiting projects, particularly in the community itself, where many nonprofessionals pursue their assignments, the observer is impressed with the extent to which the target population has been engaged. The presence of the nonprofessionals is very much felt. Often they are regarded as "the agency" by the neighborhood population. Professionals are less well known, and their presence is not felt to the same degree.

In areas like Hunters Point in San Francisco, Hough in Cleveland, and East Los Angeles, all of which reflect severe deprivation and urban blight, nonprofessional staff were among the few social welfare personnel who remained engaged with these communities through their recent crises. A stated goal of antipoverty programs in the use of nonprofessionals is to relieve tensions. To this end local persons of influence as well as residents of a troubled area are sought out for nonprofessional assignments. One program effectively emasculated a militant local civil rights organization by hiring virtually all its leadership as nonprofessional staff. However, the militant mantle of the first organization was promptly seized by another group.

Another project placed former activists ("hell-raisers") in program positions, where they were quickly immersed in diverse complex procedures which inhibited their ability to perform. These nonprofessionals then found themselves in the position of having to explain to their neighbors that their demands could not be met for reasons having to do with funding, legislation, jurisdiction, and so on.

In another context, the function of the local untrained nonprofessional was described as keeping the clients from "conning the professionals." It is being suggested here that the target community joins the project in an interacting continuum. At the point of juncture nonprofessional positions provide a number of residents with channels for upward mobility; however, the essential issues of discord (unemployment, housing, education, and so on) remain.

In this regard, it can be noted that project employment has profound consequences for the nonprofessionals themselves. Most striking, and not at all atypical, is the high school tutor group mentioned earlier. Welfare recipients, school dropouts, unwed mothers, and the chronically unemployed have also utilized the opportunities afforded through project employment to enormous personal advantage. In such instances, standards of living have risen, debts have been cleared, permanent employment maintained and school continued for the nonprofessional employee and his family. These results are perhaps the clearest and least ambiguous positive consequence of nonprofessional employment.

Professional staff has probably been affected more than is generally asknowledged by the employment of nonprofessionals. For one thing, they find in the office, on their own side of the desk, as it were, attitudes, life styles, and points of view which heretofore they saw only in clients and usually characterized as pathology. They are forced by their nonprofessional colleagues to justify their practice in client-related terms. The effect of the provision of services seems to be salutary, for professionals in these projects are markedly more effective with the poor than are their counterparts in ongoing agencies.

Experience in the use of nonprofessionals has suggested that some professional services can be effectively performed by untrained personnel. Although this issue has by no means been resolved, the fact that it has been clearly stated is of no small consequence.

It appears that the advantages sought through the utilization of nonprofessionals (particularly bridging gaps and fulfilling democratic ideology) will stem from three factors, one of which is nonprofessional indigenous status. Locating the nonprofessional in a decentralized, neighborhood-based, comprehensive setting appears to be required if his contribution is to come forth. In addition, the organization within which this program is located will determine the extent to which his qualities are utilized. Nonprofessional status is essentially instrumental; organizational policies and structural forms will determine in large measure the direction of this instrumentation. Perhaps the greatest disappointment in using this staff group has resulted from the expectation that their nonprofessional status in itself contained sufficient magic to transcend the limitations which plagued the rest of the project. We have tried to suggest that this is not the case.

Implications for Manpower Training. Certain trends are discernible in the use of nonprofessionals which may cause some concern. The patterns of service provision seem to cast the nonprofessional staff member with the lower-class minority-group client while the professional serves the middle-class, more highly motivated client. The former provides direct, concrete service while the latter provides therapeutic and rehabilitative services. Clients of family agencies, suburban schools, and private and voluntary hospitals will ordinarily find no occasion to have contact with the nonprofessional. Such contact is reserved for clients of welfare departments, city hospitals, slum schools, public nursing homes and antipoverty projects, which deal with the most disadvantaged segment of the population. The use of nonprofessionals in this way reinforces the dual standard which already characterizes the participation of the poor in society. It may also be offered as a substitute for more schools, reorganized employment services, or higher salaries for nurses.

Problems of training nonprofessional staff are related to the issue of how to use them most effectively in broad social terms rather than narrow organizational terms. To achieve such ends it is necessary to resist the pressures to produce visible results often before the projects are prepared to do so. Adequate training will take time and resources which have rarely been available. Succumbing to the blandishments and threats of the poverty war's armchair generals, professionals and administrators have too often utilized nonprofessionals as the shock troops. As a result administrators have squandered the potential of this vast resource of service personnel for a quick increase in the gross statistics of clients served. Perhaps the most striking aspect of this waste is the widespread failure to make the nonprofessional an integral part of the service offered. As we have suggested, this failure is particularly noticeable in manpower programs. That it is not an inevitable consequence, implicit in the nature of employment training, is demonstrated by the several outstanding experiences cited.

Generally, the problem of replicating experience in using nonprofessionals is formidable. Local programs administered through such continuing agencies as the state employment service and the Bureau of Apprenticeship Training are notably unresponsive to the potentials available to them. This lack of receptivity is a matter of public policy to be resolved in other quarters than the nonprofessional utilization programs.

We have cited negative factors first in the belief that experience has established the value and viability of using nonprofessional staff. The potential of this approach on all levels—meeting manpower needs, bridging the gap between service agency and the very poor, and creating new careers to alleviate chronic unemployment —has been demonstrated by the broad range of program undertaken by the Department of Labor, sponsored by the Office of Manpower Training.

This chapter has highlighted several issues in the experience of a handful of projects funded by the Department of Labor under the Manpower Development and Training Act. Because of the nature of these programs, considerable attention has been focused on the new careers–antipoverty models. Although the point that the use of nonprofessionals transcends this model has already been made, it bears reiteration. The many projects demonstrating the usefulness of working and middle-class nonprofessionals in educational, health, therapeutic, recreational, child care and other roles comprise a substantial part of the literature on the subject. Generalizations regarding manpower social-policy issues, which go beyond the observations of this paper, reflect these experiences, as well as those cited in this report.

This report has presented a number of issues judged to be salient and useful to agencies currently engaged in manpower-antipoverty programs. The provisions of the Scheuer Amendment have insured that areas of nonprofessional use will continue and expand. We would suggest the following priority considerations for agencies participating in programs of this general type:

Some Conditions. Nonprofessional employment is a complex,

differentially useful strategy, not a panacea which will solve problems of chronic unemployment or make up for the inadequacies of the service professions. Organizational malfunction, inadequacy of service, and other problems which stem from administrative or legislative policy will not be altered by the employment of nonprofessionals. The employment of the nonprofessional in the labor force will ultimately be justified on the basis of production, as is true of other workers. There is no particular "magic" associated with their employment.

Some Virtues. The only foreseeable solution to the chronic and pervasive manpower shortages in the service professions is in the vast resources of the nonprofessional. Differential usage of nonprofessionals acknowledges the unique contributions they can make in such distinctive roles as bridge, helper-therapist, and the like.

Some Issues. The training function, central to all productive employment, has been neglected in nonprofessional employment. As nonprofessionals move from special training, demonstration, and experimental projects into continuing public departments and institutions, as well as private industry, suitable training programs become critical. To be effective, nonprofessional positions will have to be located in a job continuum which provides open career lines. Any strategy which restricts the nonprofessional to entry-level positions will not benefit the nonprofessional, the service recipient, the agency, or the community. The relationship between professional and the nonprofessional ought to be supporting and complementary. However, strains often develop out of explicit issues. Such issues, particularly those which make invidious or marked distinctions between the two groups, must be anticipated and avoided.

As a final comment, we wish to make explicit what we believe to be the implicit conclusion of this brief report. We believe that recent programs have demonstrated the manpower resource nonprofessionals represent, the enrichment which this resource can provide to programs, and the direct and indirect benefits which may accrue to the total community. We do not believe that current programs have yet realized the potential available from this new manpower source. The conviction that the nonprofessional must not be exploited for short-range, superficial, relatively insignificant goals moves us to some of the critical suggestions embodied in this paper. Diligent appraisal of past experience and utilization of whatever insight such appraisal produces may provide us with clues as to how the use of nonprofessionals can ultimately solve substantial problems and meet significant long-range goals.

CHAPTER **IX**

Social Work Education

Beulah Rothman

For several years, social work has heard rumblings regarding the fact that more and more nonprofessionals are performing more and more services in social welfare. Whether one believes that too many or too few nonprofessionals are entering the field, that the tasks assigned to them are too demanding or too limiting, the arguments advanced in support of the employment of nonprofessionals in social welfare are sufficiently convincing to warrant the profession's approbation of this trend. The profession has been exhorted to admit to its ranks nonprofessional allies who supposedly possess propensities toward action and thus are capable of revitalizing outmoded practices and delivery systems. The profession has been challenged by a vision of expanding jobs in the human services offering new prospects of meaning-

149

ful employment to the indigent and disengaged. In addition, the profession has been admonished not to overlook the nonprofessional in its quest to relieve the oppressive manpower shortage in social welfare.

The validity of these arguments can scarcely be denied, despite the indignant reaction of many practitioners to "the hard sell" of the proponents of "new careers for the nonprofessional." Social workers understandably resist simplistic solutions to what experience has taught them are hard-core problems. The threats and conflicts elaborated upon by students and scholars of the professional-nonprofessional interchange further reinforce suspicion.

But those who support nonprofessionalism and those who oppose this trend may be approaching a new level of rapprochement, for there is nothing like actualization to quell the anticipatory fears of some and to curtail the excessive claims of others. Approximately 75,000 nonprofessional workers have already entered the human service field without producing the demise of the social work profession, as early skeptics feared. The circularity of the relationship between the professional and nonprofessional has become more evident. The increased utilization of nonprofessionals together with a concomitant demand for professionals leaves little doubt that each generates a need for the other. Furthermore, there has been a noticeable reduction in the defensiveness of the proponents of nonprofessionalism. A more dispassionate and realistic assessment of the problems, limitations, and potentials of the nonprofessional is coming to the fore.

However, the dialogue continues as to the relevant merits and contributions of the nonprofessional for the social work profession. Although the profession comprises a wide range of individual types, status groups, and institutions, most writers tend to ignore this diversity, treating the profession as a unitary system with a single homogeneous evaluation of the nonprofessional. Differential professional response patterns seem to be overlooked in such analyses. "The importance of really knowing what we think we know can hardly be overstated. Profile construction is a hazardous activity opening the door to stereotyping. . . . We run the risk of drawing imperfect or wrong conclusions . . . if we approach the data with built-in bias."[1]

Grosser, examining the role of nonprofessionals in nine manpower development programs, observes that the behaviors of nonprofessionals are functionally related to the organizational positions and tasks assigned to them.[2] In their study of neighborhood service centers, Perlman and Jones note that "some of the issues touched on in relation to indigenous workers are common to all center staff engaged in neighborhood organization . . . particularly of a conflict nature."[3] From these findings, we can hypothesize that the conditions which produce differences among nonprofessionals, or similarities between nonprofessionals and professionals, are just as likely to affect the professional community. Therefore, uniformity of professional assessment of the effectiveness of nonprofessionals seems most unlikely. The commissioner of a large welfare department and the executive of a small guidance clinic would hardly hold the same opinion on the value of the nonprofessional, and both would probably differ in their views from the executive of a community-action-oriented program. It may be more productive to recognize that segments of the professional community will affect different postures toward the nonprofessional depending upon their own positions in the social welfare system and the relative strength of the professional and bureaucratic forces acting upon them. In this context, social work education, because of its particular attributes and investments, can be examined with respect to its response to nonprofessionalism and its potential for advancing the cause of professional-nonprofessional collaboration.

Social work education, like the profession in general, is in a period of great change. Just as the profession cannot settle on its

---

[1] Vera Shlakman, "Mothers-at-Risk, Social Policy and Provision: Issues and Opportunities," in Florence Haselkorn, ed., *Mothers-at-Risk* (Garden City, N. Y.: Adelphi University School of Social Work, 1966).

[2] Charles Grosser, *The Role of the Nonprofessional in the Manpower Development Programs* (Washington, D.C.: U.S. Department of Labor, 1966).

[3] Robert Perlman and David Jones, *Neighborhood Service Centers* (Washington, D.C.: U.S. Department of Health, Education, and Welfare, 1967), p. 57.

major functions, so social work education has yet to evolve a hierarchy of educational objectives. The ferment in social work education is manifested in the increasing diversity of schools of social work, the emergence of factionalism within faculties, the increasing demands of students for participation in school affairs, and the sounds of alarm emanating from practitioners over the seemingly growing communication gap between education and practice. There is hardly an educational issue or a social problem that is untouched by inquiry. Presumably, this climate should predispose social work education toward the innovating aspects of nonprofessionalism.

Curiously, social work education has played a neutral role in the debate on the place and function of the nonprofessional in social welfare. As early as 1951, Hollis and Taylor, reporting on social work education in the United States, suggested the possibility of a semiprofessional social work position comparable to those in the health professions.[4] Throughout that decade, social work education paid scant attention to these recommendations. Although there have been some signs of interest of late, the situation has not altered drastically in the sixties. Several papers dealing with nonprofessionalism have been presented at national conferences of educators.[5] A recent article by Slavin is the first to address itself specifically to the relationship of social work education and the nonprofessional.[6] A statement issued by a Committee of the Deans of New York State called for "the extension of in-service and on-the-job training, as well as the development of a continuum of education to provide appropriate education for all persons in social welfare."[7] Nevertheless, no official policy statement has yet been issued by the Council on Social Work Education to provide guidance to constituent schools or faculties regarding their obligations to nonprofessionalism. Technical education, the level of education

[4] Ernest Hollis and Alice L. Taylor, *Social Work Education in the United States* (New York: Columbia University Press, 1951), p. 167.

[5] Some of these were recently published in a volume edited by Sherman Barr, *Personnel in Anti-Poverty Programs—Implications for Social Work Education* (New York: Council on Social Work Education, 1967).

[6] Simon Slavin, "The Role of Schools of Social Work in Educating Social Workers for Anti-Poverty Programs," in Barr, *op. cit.*, pp. 9–27.

[7] Committee of the Deans, *A Comprehensive Proposal to Relieve the Manpower Shortage in Social Welfare*, New York, October 2, 1967 (mimeo.).

most clearly related to nonprofessionals, still remains isolated from the mainstream of professional education.

The neutrality of the educational establishment, however, should not be interpreted as a lack of interest on the part of individual educators. Several social work educators have been at the forefront in stimulating professional interest in the nonprofessional, but they have been identified primarily with the antipoverty programs rather than with professional education, since their writings do not deal with substantive educational issues and they do not present themselves as representing social work education. Other educators have participated in conferences sponsored by governmental and voluntary agencies for the purpose of studying the optimal utilization of nonprofessional manpower. An even greater number have contributed to training programs for nonprofessionals through research, consultation, and direct teaching. Thus a substantial group of social work educators has been involved, in some capacity, with the nonprofessional movement. Why, then, has this not resulted in legitimation of the relationship between social work education and nonprofessionalism?

One answer may lie in the channels utilized by educators for their participation. Individual educators have tended to use extracurricular time for this purpose. Through this mechanism, a faculty member may contribute to the growth of nonprofessionalism, satisfy service ideals, pick up extra earnings, and still avoid tangling with his colleagues on the controversial issue of nonprofessional education within the context of professional or university-based education. Informal recognition has always been a convenient means of handling conflicting orientations. In this respect the "moonlighting" of social work educators has its counterpart in the behavior of administrators of schools of social work who are not only well aware of the arrangements entered into by their faculty but often direct faculty to such opportunities. The tradition of supplementing faculty salaries through outside activities is a strong one, but in this case it can be said that the tradition protects schools of social work from openly confronting and dealing with their responsibilities for the education of nonprofessionals. Faculty involvement with nonprofessionalism credits the school as innovative in the eyes of the profession, while preserving the academic image of the school on the university campus. It cannot be denied that the realities of competition among professional schools and academic departments for scarce university resources affects the stance of social work education toward the nonprofessional. Each unit of the university stakes its claim on the basis of scholarship and scientific pursuit of knowledge. Conceptions of service and of training for practice must be dealt with cautiously lest the denigrating cry of apprenticeship be raised.

Were it not for the emergence of new and compelling forces within the university and profession, an inquiry into the institutional relationship of social work education to nonprofessional personnel would be somewhat hypothetical. The expansion of schools of social work has bearing on this issue. During the past five years, nine new schools of social work have come into existence, and six more are expected to open before the end of 1968. Approximately twenty more new schools will be established within the next decade. These new schools can be expected to produce ten to twelve thousand graduate professionals over a ten-year period. But this additional output will hardly meet the manpower needs required to keep pace with the expanding health and welfare programs. Furthermore, the U. S. Bureau of the Census projects a population of 210 million by 1970 and a rise to 220 or 225 million by 1975. Thus the ratio of social workers to the population will steadily decline, even with the increased output of the schools. As Samuel Finestone has stated:

> It is almost certain that there is no practicable answer to the question, "By what means will professional social workers be obtained to fill all direct service positions in welfare agencies?" But if the more fundamental question is posed—"By what means can the purposes of public welfare be accomplished?"—it may well be that answer can be found, that program designs can be developed which will be more effective or more economical (or both) than our present operations. Put into this context, the problem of manpower is approachable through the questions: What kinds of functions are needed to accomplish the mission of social welfare? What kinds of people are needed to carry out these functions?[8]

[8] Samuel Finestone, *Summary of Conference on Experimentation in Differential Use of Personnel in Social Welfare,* Illinois, National Association of Social Workers, May 6, 1964 (mimeo.), p. 1.

Social work education is not the only institution to which these questions are being put. The university itself has been forced into the anomalous position of providing both the knowledge and the manpower necessary to keep the wheels grinding in contemporary society. Having derived power from its role as the major supplier of manpower, the university must keep faith with these expectations. The public university is most vulnerable in this respect. With few exceptions, the educational institutions in which the newer schools of social work are being established are either city- or state-funded, located either in heavily populated states with large urban concentrations or in less developed areas of the South and the Far West, where rapid social change is taking place.

Increasingly, the public university in these areas is looked to as an important instrument of positive social development, serving not only as a resource of needed educational manpower for new and changing professional and subprofessional roles, but as a source of needed knowledge for dealing with social problems, old and new, or for the realization of social potentials. As a general trend, universities and colleges with a serious commitment to the development of new schools of social work express their interest in terms of the development of "nontraditional" programs of social work education. Most universities begin with the concept of the school of social work as a center for social welfare education at all levels. Their interest is not only in a master's program but in finding the proper fit for professional education within the continuum of undergraduate to advanced education. Many universities are less interested in following a traditional model for social work education. They appear to be more interested in creating a model that reflects their particular purposes, resources, and the needs of the geographic areas they serve.[9]

To be sure, publicly funded schools of social work, as they increase in number, will have strong influence on social work education. They will reflect the greater emphasis on education for service of their parent universities. It can be expected that they will stimulate a broader approach to education and will themselves, over

[9] Bess Dana, *New Schools Project Progress Report* (New York: Council on Social Work Education, 1967, mimeo.).

time, relate to the entire continuum of social welfare education, including that of the nonprofessional.

Of equal importance to the subject at hand is the rapid growth of undergraduate programs in social welfare. Most undergraduate programs, although initially independent of graduate schools of social work, ultimately establish strong ties with graduate schools in their region or state. The relationship between undergraduate and graduate education was officially recognized by the Delegate Assembly of the Council on Social Work Education (CSWE) in 1966.[10] The assembly called for an integrated approach to social work education at all levels and suggested increased leadership by CSWE in undergraduate social welfare education. This statement clearly establishes that education for social welfare begins at the subprofessional level and extends to technical education. Interestingly, in 1967, the Council on Social Work Education engaged a staff member to survey the number, locations, and curriculum patterns of associate programs.

A third trend with relevance to the concern of this paper is the movement of graduate schools of social work toward a closer alliance with other professional schools on the campus. Prestige factors undoubtedly play a part in this, but there also appears to be a genuine compatibility of interest as all the professions review their interrelations in the context of professional preparation for more effective service delivery. In particular, social work education cannot fail to be impressed with the research and experimentation conducted by many professional schools to assess patterns of manpower utilization in light of available technologies. Several professional schools have already begun to alter their professional curricula in line with findings derived from such studies.

Thus the recognized need of the social welfare field and the precedents being established by older and higher-status professional educational institutions provide sanctions for similar activities in social work education.

It seems timely now to explicate several assumptions on which this paper is based. These assumptions are intended to con-

---

[10] Council on Social Work Education, *Minutes of Meeting of House of Delegates,* New York, January 25, 1966 (mimeo.).

vey my perspectives on various contentious issues regarding the contribution of social work education to nonprofessionalism.

First, social work education occupies a leadership position in the profession of social work. Therefore, its manifest interest in and involvement with nonprofessionals can exert considerable influence on professional acceptance of the nonprofessional. If it is true that the professional views the nonprofessional with skepticism, apprehension, or resistance, then social work education can help to change this attitude by conferring status on professional-nonprofessional relationships.

Second, social work education must retain leadership and guidance within its field of expertise—namely, education for social welfare—particularly during this period of exploding demands for human services. If it does otherwise, educational institutions not intrinsically related to social welfare may attempt to fill the gap.

Third, social work education, in its relationship to the nonprofessional, must adhere to the principle of professional determination of nonprofessional functioning, implemented through direct supervision of the nonprofessional or in collaboration with him.

Fourth, educational opportunities for all nonprofessionals, both in the new formal educational programs and in continued education, must be expanded regardless of the risk of cooptation of the nonprofessional or the threat to some sectors of the professional community.

There is not now, and perhaps there never can be, a clearcut prescription for the activities to be undertaken by social work education in enhancing the quality and quantity of nonprofessional functions. Even if the Council on Social Work Education were to issue a policy statement, it would undoubtedly provide only broad guidelines, leaving it to each school to develop its own approach and course of action. However, several areas within the field of social work education suggest themselves as targets for achieving the objectives stated above as assumptions: differential utilization of manpower, training of nonprofessionals, and education and preparation of professionals for collaborative practice with nonprofessionals.

Utilization of Manpower

Underlying the issue of the differential employment of manpower is the ability of a profession to identify the tasks that can and should be performed by different levels of technicians and professionals. The capacity of paraprofessionals to perform tasks must be distinguished from what the profession deems it appropriate to consign to them. This is obviously a value question which cannot be resolved by research. C. W. Gillman, a noted dental educator, recognizes the value dilemma in the following statement, referring, of course, to dentistry:

> The experimental programs completed or in progress have, in my mind, proven one very important fact. Given persons of reasonable intellect and reasonable ability, we have the "know-how" to teach them to perform almost any function we desire. The question now is, what do we desire?[11]

A somewhat different view is held by the Council on Dental Education. Their proposal for dealing with auxiliary personnel is "based upon the precept that it should not be necessary or desirable to establish formal definitions of procedures which can be delegated to auxiliary personnel, and that decisions to extend the duties and responsibilities of dental assistants and hygienists should be predicated upon the principle that such decisions should rest upon the professional knowledge and skills of a licensed dentist."[12] This statement places the value decision squarely up to the individual practitioner.

Unlike dentistry, social work would have difficulty in defining technically all aspects of its skill, and it does not as yet possess the know-how to transmit this to others through anything other than the established educational route. Moreover, Wilensky's hypothesis has special relevance to social work: "If the technical base of an occupation consists of a vocabulary that sounds familiar to everyone or if the base is scientific but so narrow that it can be learned as a set of rules by most people, then the occupation will

[11] C. W. Gillman, "The History and Challenge of Auxiliary Utilization," *The Journal of the Alabama Dental Association,* 51 (1967), p. 12.
[12] *Ibid.,* p. 29.

have difficulty claiming a monopoly of skill or even a roughly exclusive jurisdiction."[13] If this hypothesis is correct, we can hardly expect that social work will turn over such important decisions to individual practitioners. The profession has struggled for too long to carve out its jurisdictional domain and still is uncertain of recognition of its professional authority. In addition, most social workers do not practice privately but in bureaucratic organizations in which an idiosyncratic determination of job description or role expectation would be regarded as dysfunctional, if not intolerable. It appears, then, that the profession will have to face both problems, clarifying the tasks it wishes nonprofessionals to carry, and testing whether these tasks can in fact be learned and effectively performed by nonprofessionals. The former appears to be within the province of the professional association, whereas the latter may best be served through a consortium of educational institutions and service agencies.

Several characteristics generally ascribed to higher education seem to be particularly salient to the involvement of social work education in manpower research. First, social work education is heir to the mantle of objectivity and nonpartisanship usually attributed to higher education. It is not tainted with "management aims" nor with hidden motives of administrative economies. Unions and other employee groups are less apt to be suspicious of research conducted by university faculty. While employees may still fear that such research will result in the downgrading of jobs or other dire consequences, there is little likelihood that faculty-led research will be perceived as intentionally skewed to these purposes. In a field where research depends heavily on subjective data-gathering techniques, the cooperation of staff is imperative to the conduct of a study.

Second, universities have a monopoly of research talent and research interest, emanating from the desire of the university to preserve its function as the principal producer of knowledge. Schools of social work, where research faculty may be in short supply, have access to other departments and disciplines in the university and can more readily procure special expertise when required. This is

[13] Harold L. Wilensky, "The Professionalization of Everyone," *American Journal of Sociology,* 70 (September 1964).

particularly true of universities where schools of social work are already engaged in interdisciplinary research, a trend rapidly gaining favor across the country.

Finally, higher education is often in a better position to commandeer public and private funds for experimentation, demonstration, and research, than are practice agencies, especially the smaller ones. Granting agencies, although they do not always make their demands explicit, look favorably upon the involvement of a school of social work, particularly with regard to evaluating outcomes. The involvement of a school appears to offer greater assurance of accountability and standards of excellence. The pattern of collaboration between schools and agencies is likely to continue and can be fully exploited in extending study into the area of nonprofessional utilization.

The contribution of a school to research in manpower utilization, however, need not be limited to making faculty available to agencies for research endeavors. A school can also establish fieldwork units or teaching centers to provide general experiential learning for all students while at the same time experimenting with different patterns of manpower deployment. Or a school can establish research centers unrelated to field instruction, whose sole purpose is the conduct of studies in differential manpower utilization. Prototypes of both already exist in social work education.[14]

Apart from the organizational structures that can be devised, there is need to identify the problems requiring intensive study. Gertrude Goldberg's excellent overview of the issues confronting utilization of nonprofessionals in the human services points up several critical areas.[15] There is the overall problem of developing concepts for systematically classifying nonprofessionals, social welfare tasks, agency contexts, professionals, and so on. For example, dentistry has found the concept of "reversibility" useful for classifying the dental tasks that can be assigned to auxiliaries. This concept suggests that tasks be scaled by the degree to which they can be corrected, if necessary, by a dentist. In social work, Richan's

[14] The Midway Project of the Chicago University School of Social Work, and the Center for the Study of Unemployed Youth of the Graduate School of Social Work, New York University, respectively.

[15] See Chapter One, "Nonprofessionals in Human Services."

twin variables of "vulnerability of the client" and "autonomy of the worker" have been fruitfully employed in designing utilization studies.[16]

The organizational and service structures best suited to utilize nonprofessionals deserve further study. It would appear that large bureaucratic organizations such as welfare departments, hospitals, and correctional institutions offer the greatest opportunities for specification and differentiation of tasks. Employee behaviors are highly specialized and often ritualized, lending themselves to systematic examination of the competencies involved. But what of the less formalized agencies? It is possible that the nonprofessional can function best where there is either a high degree of structure or virtually none. Certainly we need to know more about criteria for selecting nonprofessionals in relation to different settings as well as different tasks.

What constitutes the best grouping of nonprofessionals? Most of us would regard an agency wholly staffed by nonprofessionals as inadequate to meet the realities of organizational survival. But there are many questions that still remain to be answered—What is the best ratio of nonprofessionals to professionals within an agency? What is the best mix on service teams for maximal efficiency and effectiveness?

Finally, we know little about how the nonprofessional is socialized to the social welfare system. Who are the role models for the nonprofessional? Which norms is he more likely to internalize— those of the profession or those of the bureaucracy? How long does it take for the indigenous nonprofessional to be coopted, if in fact he is? When faced with a value conflict, which orientation does he tend to fall back on? Which incentives are most powerful for the nonprofessional—money? Prestige? Recognition? Upward mobility? How do these interact and motivate the nonprofessional toward higher-quality performance? Clearly these and an infinite number of other challenging problems require solution if we are to plan rationally for maximal manpower utilization. The benefits social work education can derive from participation in the study of man-

[16] Willard C. Richan, "A Theoretical Scheme for Determining Roles of Professional and Nonprofessional Personnel," *Journal of Social Work*, 6 (October 1961).

power utilization are self-evident. Education for practice demands that we have clearer perspectives on the differential competencies required to carry out social welfare tasks.

Training

. . . when the OEO recently convened a conference on the "crisis in human services," training was identified as the most crucial and neglected variable in this crisis. Perhaps it was predictable in light of the speed with which that agency moved to create and implement so many of its programs. However, any review of a number of other national or local programs in human services confirms the fact that although training is invariably recognized as a critical element, it is developed with the least effectiveness.[17]

Without minimizing the difficulties imposed by lack of time, we cannot assume that this factor alone accounts for the almost universal failure of poverty programs to establish effective training arms. In those few agencies which have developed training programs, such programs have really been sustained. This fact appears to be related to the heavy emphasis given by these agencies to the development of entry positions for nonprofessionals. Agency resources have been largely committed to training, preparing, and supporting indigenous persons through initial work experiences. But the success of the nonprofessionals in bringing the impoverished community closer to the service agency has paradoxically created a demand for increased services and the diversion of training funds into service channels. If the benefits derived from "reaching out" are to be maximized for clients, service has to keep pace with demand. Under these circumstances, it is understandable that continuous training of the nonprofessional has been accorded low priority.

Perhaps a crucial element in the failure of antipoverty agencies to institute strong training programs is their basic distrust of training. Educational processes are often assumed to be antithetical to the "naturalness" of the nonprofessional. Since antipoverty agencies usually justify the employment of nonprofessionals on the

---

[17] Aron Schmais, *Implementing Nonprofessional Programs in Human Services* (New York: New York University, Graduate School of Social Work, Center for the Study of Unemployed Youth, 1967), p. 48.

basis of their "natural" attributes, training may indeed be regarded as a threat. It is evident that career training which implies life's work, progression, and transferability of skills has little place in an agency oriented to immediate opportunities for employment of the poor.

The older established agencies, mostly in the mental hospital, child welfare, and public assistance fields, similarly tend to concentrate efforts to train nonprofessionals at the initial entry level. Although many provide vertical career routes, in-service training is generally designed to enhance performance once a person has moved to a new level; it is rarely offered in preparation for promotion. The usual pattern in these agencies is to encourage the nonprofessional to utilize out-of-agency educational resources for such a purpose by providing incentives such as released time from work and scholarships.

All that has been said suggests that agencies may have neither the resources nor the motivation to mount full-time career training programs for nonprofessionals. The necessary conditions for stabilizing career training seem to be lacking in the service agency. Even if additional funds for training are made available through new legislation, such as the Scheuer Amendment or the Public Health Act, the future of nonprofessional careers buttressed by agency in-service training seems rather dismal. Additional funds will not necessarily affect the relative isolation of training personnel in the service agency, a factor which may be very much related to the demise of agency-based training programs. Trainers seldom find their professional colleagues interested in pedagogical problems. Colleagues enthusiastically applaud the trainer for turning out a good "product," but they are primarily interested in the results rather than the means by which these results were obtained. The professional trainer, on the other hand, if he is to maintain a critical approach to his job, must view himself as an educator rather than a practitioner; his reference group must be the educational community rather than the service system. Pride in one's role as an educator and continued motivation for improving curriculum design and contruction largely depend on communication with others in the educational enterprise. Whatever an agency's interest in or commitment to training, an educational climate soon gives way to service imperatives, and training personnel are left without the stimulation and reinforcement they require.

As should be obvious, our position in this paper is that career training for the nonprofessional should be linked to an educational institution. Realization of the careers concept envisioned by Pearl and Riessman[18] and others requires a long-range commitment to education for social welfare, which is currently institutionalized in schools of social work or undergraduate programs in social welfare. As long ago as the late 1800s, service agencies acknowledged the limitations of agency training as a foundation for building careers in social welfare. Thus they urged the establishment of schools of social work within the university. The assumptions made then seem no less applicable to technical education today and to its relationship to the promotion of nonprofessional careers.

Commonality of interest and shared obligations to the social welfare field suggest, moreover, that technical education should be related to schools or departments of social welfare rather than to more generalized units of the university. If the nonprofessional is to become an integral part of the social welfare system, then his training must also be part of the mainstream of education for social welfare.

A further rationale for closer interrelations between technical training and social work education lies in the essential ingredients found in all social welfare curricula. The importance of a sound mix of experiential and classroom learning, or providing individualized help during the learning process, of developing awareness of oneself as a helping instrument, of understanding organizational structures and roles—these elements are present at every level of social welfare education. The same can be said of many of the procedures and skills of social welfare practice. In other words, the content and skills which the technician acquires and the learning experiences necessary to impart them can borrow much from the experience and expertise of existing educational institutions.

Of course, the argument persists that closer ties between the nonprofessional and formal education will subvert his "natural-

[18] Arthur Pearl and Frank Riessman, *New Careers for the Poor* (New York: Free Press, 1965).

ness." The careers concept itself makes this a specious argument. If an individual is to make social welfare his life's career, then it seems obvious that whether he is trained or not, he will gradually be socialized to the welfare institution, and many former behaviors will be replaced by newer learned ones. Moreover, it is untenable to deny educational opportunity to the nonprofessional in the name of retaining his uncultivated qualities. And it should be noted, the differences and dissatisfactions abounding in the professional community suggest that excessive compliance does not inevitably result from training.

The need for closer alliance between training and education becomes even more compelling when we consider the question of credentials. Credentials can be defined in terms of a reward system attesting to the bearer's rights to confidence. Two types of credentials can be identified: those that certify competence, and those that designate social status as well. In social work, certificates for completing agency training illustrate the former, whereas the M.S.W. or B.S. degree exemplifies the latter. A service agency, no matter how well it does its job of training, will not be able to offer credentials that embody both competence and status. In our society that privilege is reserved to the college or university.

Bertram Beck's proposal for democratizing the profession by offering alternative routes for professional entry through certification of competence does not take account of the status dimension.[19] Put into practice, it could even introduce undemocratic elements. Why should there be two different classes of workers at each level of practice—those with partial credentials and those with full credentials? Furthermore, why should anyone embarking on a career in social welfare, which involves training, not prefer to earn the broadest possible credentials?

There is also an implicit assumption in Beck's proposal that certification of competence can be achieved in the near future. The working definition of social work practice which he suggests as a framework for determining competence has already been rejected as a useful tool for tackling this question.[20] It may be years before

[19] See Chapter Four, "Nonprofessional Social Work Personnel."
[20] In December 1967 the M.S.W. Commission on Practice expressed

competence can be rigorously tested. A better strategy, therefore, may lie in asking how career training can be dovetailed with the continuum of education in social welfare, and what alternatives there are for earning full credentials at various terminal points in the continuum. When the problem is seen in this light, the answer seems to lie not in creating a competitive agency-based training system which would be mediocre at best, but, rather, in expanding the educational delivery system and making it more effective in serving nonprofessional career objectives.

Within this frame, social work education must take the responsibility for expanding the number of undergraduate and associate programs in social welfare. This is especially important in states with few educational resources in social welfare, where a school of social work is looked to for leadership in all aspects of social welfare. Such a school may choose to work toward establishing an associate program within its own university or encouraging smaller colleges in the area to establish the program.

As a step toward achieving the expansion of associate programs, schools of social work will need to resist the urging of service agencies that they offer single or intermittent courses of training for nonprofessionals, unless these are formally related to some level of education for which academic credits can be earned. It may be hard to withstand the temptation of ad hoc involvement with nonprofessional training, but this will divert commitment and undermine the more important job of creating a stable educational program in support of nonprofessional careers. This does not mean that non-credit extension courses cannot be offered to persons in other fields. But the nonprofessional social welfare careerist needs to be dealt with more purposefully by both the service agency and the educational institution.

As a second approach to the training of nonprofessionals, schools of social work can explore alternative means of meeting degree requirements, perhaps by equating work and life experience with some components of a degree program. Required field work

---

its dissatisfaction with the working definition as too vague and so abstract that it did not provide a satisfactory base for inquiry into practice competence.

is an area in which such equivalence might be established. A plan of this nature has been proposed by VISTA and is under consideration by several schools of social work.[21] Similar directions can be encouraged in undergraduate professional education. Since mastery of practice is not a required outcome of undergraduate field training, it would seem that nonprofessional experience is more readily comparable to this level of field work. Even at the associate level there are probably opportunities for alternatives to some course requirements. Giving advanced credit for nonprofessional experience does not necessarily weaken the academic demands of social welfare education. Such demands can be built, instead, into the professional work experience. This depends to a large extent on early identification of the nonprofessional careerist. Here the service agency can play a significant role: it can direct the potential careerist to the appropriate training level and institution; it can serve as a bridge between the nonprofessional and the university or college. The model of close collaboration between agencies and schools of social work in the education of the professional student is applicable to the training of the nonprofessional technician. Obviously, associate programs must rely on full participation of service agencies both in the recruitment of students and in carrying out the training program.

Education of Professionals

Unless they are employed in agencies with a special interest in nonprofessionals, surprisingly few professionals are aware of the opportunities now open to nonprofessionals in social welfare. Professionals still tend to think of graduate education as the only route to a career in social welfare, and thus they define a career in social welfare as an unattainable goal for clients and other less advantaged persons. They therefore refrain from encouraging such persons to aspire to what appears to be a self-defeating goal. In earlier days, by contrast, social workers, heavily involved with middle- and

[21] In the VISTA proposal, a school will provide close supervision of the VISTA volunteer during his work experience to ensure a quality of experience similar to that offered to first-year graduate students in field-work practice. Academic seminars conducted by the school of social work are also included in the proposal.

working-class populations, saw every gifted youth as a potential recruit for social work. Often attachments between actual and aspiring young social workers extended over many years, with the worker offering encouragement and guidance at each step of the educational career route. Knowledge of different career possibilities and supporting educational programs designed to integrate the nonprofessional into the social welfare work community must be transmitted to today's professionals, particularly to students preparing to enter the profession. The social work curriculum must not only convey knowledge of existing opportunities; it must confront the barriers that deny the economically disadvantaged access to these opportunities.

It would seem, too, in this era of rising student demand for participation in the educational enterprise, that social work students can play a unique role in promoting the expansion of educational and vocational opportunities within their own field of endeavor. The newer career concept may provide an additional source of identification between the student and his youthful client, perhaps an important element in countering alienation. Some of the quality of the earlier relationship must be recaptured in present-day associations between social workers and disadvantaged youth, but this is possible only if professionals believe that opportunities exist within reach of their clients.

Earlier we mentioned that schools can develop field-work centers with special emphasis on research in manpower deployment. These centers can have great impact on the general development of field-work teaching and on professional practice oriented to the future. Such teaching centers would necessarily require the inclusion of nonprofessionals in the learning environment of the professional student, and could demonstrate the advantages of this provision for education and practice. There is the danger that teaching centers focused only on strengthening the educational components of field-work learning will tend to gravitate toward an exclusively professional staff. These schools may mistakenly interpret the presence of nonprofessionals in the learning environment as undermining sound professional education. This could result in further entrenchment of outmoded educational perceptions and practices. For example, it could perpetuate the concept of solo

practice, that is, social work practice executed by a single practitioner as the predominant modality of social work service, to which
social work education currently clings. Although this concept does
not preclude the collaboration of the social worker with other professions, it does imply that the social work aspects of interdisciplinary practice are the responsiblity of the individual social worker.
In such centers the concept of vertical team practice consisting of
different levels of social welfare practitioners may not be accepted so
readily as in centers where the nonprofessional is included in the
learning environment. The obsolescence of solo practice—for that
matter, its sheer absurdity—is readily apparent when we consider
the changes that are taking place in practice and the increased
demands that students incorporate a broad base of knowledge in
their understanding of social problems. Practice in child welfare,
the rehabilitation of the mentally ill, the care of the chronically ill
and the aging, and poverty programs are but a few examples of
service areas in which vertical practice teams are operating routinely.

Academically, students are being subjected to a widening
body of theory that increasingly strengthens their capacity to com-
prehend and analyze a network of interlocking systems that spawn
social problems. Sophistication in analytical thinking is not always
accompanied by confidence that one can effect change in these
systems. This is due in part to the lag between the output of basic
knowledge and the application of this knowledge into implementing
techniques. But in part it is due to the fact that a single practitioner
lacks the time, the energy, and the power to influence more than
a limited range of variables. One practitioner cannot work with a
child, his parents, his siblings, the school, the doctor, the peer group,
the department of welfare investigator, and the public health nurse,
all of whom may require intensive contact to change the child's
external conditions. "Partializing the problem," a venerated principle of social work practice, may have been a useful way to relieve the pressure on the social worker and the client, but it also
may have narrowed the professional's vision and, in fact, delayed
the acceptance of the "many helpers" concept. Without such a
concept, nothing but frustration and failure are possible as the end
product of increased understanding. Surely newer knowledge sug-

gests the necessity of revising traditional patterns of manpower utilization if more effective services are to be delivered to individuals, groups, and communities. This concept seems to be as crucial to clinical practice as it is to practice directed toward institutional change. For that matter, the current polarization of professional education and practice between clinical and institutional change tracts can be reconsidered in the light of nonprofessional allies. Such allies may offer new dimensions for incorporating the elements of each into the approach of the other.

Unless opportunities for direct interchange between non-professionals and professional students are available in the field-practice situation, it is doubtful that the professional student will be prepared for vertical team practice. Learning experiences should provide for gradual progression from a position of membership to a leadership role. Administrative skills in the organization and management of the team will need to be learned as intrinsically related to the internal operation of casework, group work, or community-organizational processes rather than as elements external to these primary methods. The student must acquire the understanding, skills, and attitudes to assess the strengths of other helpers in relation to his own and to blend these strengths into a workable unit interacting with the client.

The inclusion of the nonprofessional in the learning environment opens several other avenues of learning for the professional student. Grosser speaks of four modalities of action possible to a professional practitioner engaged in direct practice.[22] A professional may cast himself in the role of an enabler, a broker, an advocate, or an activist. Social work education has long been partial to the first of these roles and has only just begun to accept brokerage and advocacy as legitimate social work strategies. The activist role is still the subject of much debate. Such hierarchical preference deserves challenge, particularly at the point of preparation for professional practice. Because the nonprofessional is less subject to professional preferences, he has more freedom to question a student's predilections for one or another approach. The student may

[22] Charles F. Grosser, "Community Development Programs Serving the Urban Poor," *Journal of Social Work*, 3 (July 1965), pp. 15–21.

have difficulty justifying his position and in the attempt may discover that preconceptions rather than disciplined assessment of the realities have guided his choice. Or the student may reason that his choices are correctly deduced and that he is committed to carry them out despite differences of opinion. Internship is not a time to protect the professional student from conflicting views and pressures. His ability to maintain objectivity and to withstand intimidating or guilt-provoking forces needs to be strengthened if he is ultimately to practice with integrity.

There is something to be said, however, for the early exposure of the student to the advocate role. Advocacy is close to the initial commitments of the student and should be emphasized as a means of preventing the mutual alienation of the professional and the client. The greater emphasis on rationalism coupled with more intensive preparation for indirect service functions in social work education could result in early disassociation between the professional student and the client. Some counterforce may be necessary to guard against this possibility. Medical education is beginning to recognize this danger. Concerns are being expressed that exclusive stress on intellectual or scientific thinking is undermining the service ideal of the medical student. New educational experiences are being provided in an attempt to produce a doctor more committed to his patients and to his caretaking functions. Similarly, we cannot take it for granted that the humanitarian service ideal of social work will flourish even if we do not intentionally plan for its continuance. Kurt Lewin warned that unless a society provides practice opportunities for democratic decision-making, democratic ideology will not long survive. So in social welfare, the service ideal must be shored up by additional eyes and ears on the client world. In this respect the nonprofessional is our greatest ally. He will help the student stay close to the client as a real person and to the realities of the client's world. If the nonprofessional is a respected member of the team, he will understand that his contributions are necessary correctives to professional distortions of what is and fantasies of what ought to be.

Educating professionals for responsible participation with nonprofessionals implies much more than team collaboration. There is a broad spectrum of tasks for which professional students can be prepared. Courses in the methods sequences and in administration need to be expanded to include content in the supervision and training of nonprofessionals. Slavin suggests that "skills in curriculum planning for trainee programs often need to be imparted to professional workers who carry these educational responsibilities. Curriculum planning is a highly developed skill area and is buttressed by a substantial technical literature. Most of this material remains unknown to social work students, a circumstance that is anachronistic for potential trainees."[23] The professional curriculum also needs to take cognizance of the growing body of experience and knowledge developing from current training programs. Students could benefit from systematic examination of different curricular models used in various training programs for nonprofessionals.

New possibilities for field work become apparent as schools consider preparing students for the training, teaching, and supervision of nonprofessionals. It is possible to conceive of placing students for field work in training programs or even as teaching assistants in associate educational programs. The standards for sound education do not rule out such possibilities. When integrated with other field-training provisions, such placements may indeed offer exciting prospects.

The broader planning aspects for utilization of manpower deserve special attention in the social work curriculum. Courses in social welfare policy can be directed toward the analysis of current and proposed legislation aimed at providing better solutions to manpower utilization problems. The extent to which the profession is able to provide guidance to legislative bodies and public agencies on the priorities, needs, and planning designs for better distribution of manpower within social welfare depends upon the availability of relevant knowledge. A curriculum that does not provide the minimum technical base for leadership in the manpower area is highly questionable.

From all that has been said, it is clear that schools of social work need to be at the front line in combating obsolescence of knowledge and in animating new areas of professional interest. The immediate future of the professional-nonprofessional relationship is

[23] Slavin, *op. cit.*, p. 20.

hard to forecast. One thing seems certain: tasks, functions, and roles will become increasingly diverse in social welfare. If we are to avoid intense status conflict as a consequence of this diversity, the social work professional will have to assume leadership in building bridges between himself and all other social work personnel. Social work education must accept its obligation to supply professionals who are willing and able to carry out this task.

CHAPTER **X**

Training Psychologists

Louis Cohen

Some time ago, George Albee, writing for the Joint Commission on Mental Health and Illness regarding manpower developments in the mental health professions, forecast an inevitable shortage of professional psychologists to meet the needs of hospitals, clinics, and other agencies which had begun to expect psychological services. As Albee predicted, most of our Ph.D. graduates in psychology today are being absorbed by the educational institutions that produce new psychologists, leaving a very few available for employment in the agencies which were expecting them. Carl Bramlette, of the Southern Regional Education Board, recently reported on a study that he had conducted contrasting the availability of psychologists for Southern mental health institutions at the beginning and end of a ten-year period. He indicated that despite the increased production of Ph.D.'s in psychology in the region, the actual increment of psychologists on the staffs of Southern mental health institutions was in the order of zero.

Not only does the number of psychologists being produced today fail to meet the existing demand from the mental health institutions; the prospects for an increasing demand are most alarming. The new community mental health programs sponsored by the NIMH and endorsed by all the states could result in the establishment of more than two thousand centers throughout the country, each of which will require the services of one or more psychologists. There are many other forces leading to an increased demand: population growth throughout the United States; growing awareness of the psychological problems produced by social, educational, and cultural deprivation; enhanced attention to learning problems in our schools; increased sensitivity to the need for constructive programs for the emotionally disturbed and the mentally retarded; and growing acceptance of responsibility for helping with a host of problems in living experienced by children, adults, and the aged. All of this signals a demand for larger and larger numbers of psychologists, as well as many other groups of professionals, to meet service requirements.

There is obviously a need for more psychologists. But the present strictures on the production of psychologists are compelling. The journeyman level for the professional psychologist is still the Ph.D. This calls for hand-tooled education, which is expensive and time consuming, and will obviously produce, with our present model, only a limited number of graduates.

If we look closely at the marketplace, however, and consider what is happening in the mental health institutions and clinics, we will note that a considerable number of people not trained at the Ph.D. level are being employed—people with all sorts and combinations of degrees, experience, and training. These qualifications do not entitle them to the designation of psychologist in the official APA roster. On the other hand, these personnel carry out duties of distinctly psychological character, and they are often the only personnel available to carry out such duties. It may even be asserted that these officially nonqualified workers are employed in consequence of the psychological fraternity's inability to produce and make available the personnel for whom the job specifications have been written. Officially, the jobs call for the Ph.D. in psychology plus x years of experience. In fact, workers with a reasonable approximation of these qualifications will be employed in order to get someone to do the job.

Thus, examination of the marketplace reveals that many substitute workers have had to be employed by administrators to man their institutions. Generally, these substitute workers have an uneasy role to fill. They may feel apologetic about their lack of formal training. Or they may be defensive, insisting that they are as capable as other workers with officially appropriate training. Whether these substitute workers are in fact doing a less effective job than a fully qualified worker would do is a moot point. Nor is there much value in exploring their effectiveness unless an alternate solution is available.

Let us eliminate from our present discussion a concern with solutions involving an increase in the production of Ph.D.'s. That is an important matter, but not within the scope of this paper. Let us consider, rather, some other solutions: (1) we can develop new professions and professionals to handle parts of the job of existing professionals; or (2) we can develop new subprofessionals to help existing professionals do their current jobs; or (3) we can train professionals from other fields to do their jobs in such a way as to be helpful in preventing or alleviating mental health problems; or (4) we can develop mechanized and automated data-producing systems about people to save time for existing professionals; or (5) we can reexamine the functions of psychologists so as to provide for more efficient utilization of their skills.

The health professions have developed a variety of methods to meet manpower shortages in the face of a burgeoning and complex technology. Medicine and dentistry, for example, have evolved a group of collaborating professions which provide highly skilled help in specific areas. Thus the dentist employs a dental hygienist to clean teeth, thereby freeing the dentist for the more complex duties which his training has equipped him to handle. The radiologist has an X-ray technician, who not only takes the X-rays and gets them developed but also handles the patient contact arrangement, thus leaving the radiologist free to read the plates and confer with his medical colleagues about the implications of what he sees.

All through medicine the model of the highly specialized, collaborating person has emerged. More than a hundred different professions have been identified as essential to medical care, as part of the support system through which the physician provides his services.

This limited specialist model has heuristic value for us in psychology. There is no reason that we should not similarly articulate highly specialized functions within all our areas of activity and in each case develop specialists qualified to work in specific areas. Examples come readily to mind: the psychometrician as an expert in psychological evaluation; the behavior therapist as an expert in applying behavior therapy techniques; the psychological research assistant, who may be specialized in perception, learning, or a host of special subject areas; the group therapist; the community psychology consultant; the school psychological consultant. The range of functions come out of the present activities of psychologists. The specification of a field could come out of the development of a cohesive body of knowledge, activities, and roles that may be functional for specific vocational settings.

Many of these functions have already been articulated and are more or less operational, but without the sanction of the profession of psychology. Efforts to gain such sanction in the past have been seen as attempts to dilute the quality of psychological activity and its potential contribution in the specific applied setting. The problem may not be with the effectiveness of the proposed solution but, rather, with the inability and unwillingness of the profession of psychology to accept the model.

In contrast to the highly specific, functional division discussed above, a transitional solution that is now emerging is that of the "generalist" psychological assistant. This model assumes that the psychologist aided by an assistant will be free to spend more time on his unique professional input. The assistant, depending upon what the psychologist himself is doing, may do psychological testing, carry on individual or group therapy, collect research data, process these data, or teach. In general, the assistant helps the psychologist in whatever he does. He may be a jack-of-all-trades or may become especially skillful in one or two, depending upon the character of the psychologist's work load. The requirements for the psychologist in the situation is that he be a teacher, that he exercise quality control over the work of the assistant, and that he devote himself to those responsibilities that are germane to his training, such as being an innovator in either programs or research and a program developer within the field of psychology.

Consultation methods and practice have highlighted the value of the proposal to train professionals in other fields so their efforts will help alleviate or prevent mental health problems. It has been noted that people in trouble come to community caregivers (general practitioners, ministers, teachers, police). These caregivers, who serve as a first line of defense, are often in the best position to help and frequently can prevent minor problems from becoming major difficulties. Consultation with caregivers to enhance their knowledge and skill may serve the public better than referrals to professional resources.

Automation and other mechanical techniques also seem to be possible solutions. An example which comes to mind is the recent development of computer analysis for reporting on MMPIs. These are taken by patients and submitted to the computer. The resulting computerized statements are apparently as good as what many clinicians can produce, and used with appropriate caution and circumspection, can indeed facilitate a better allocation of the professional psychologist's time.

Another solution that comes to mind is to rethink the kinds of data and operations that psychologists undertake to do, to see whether their time and effort can be utilized more efficiently. For example, psychologists often spend their time doing psychological testing of clients for whom the test results will in no way influence decisions for action. A more hard-headed approach to data collection, requiring that it be used for reaching a decision, could cut down time wastage and make for a more effective use of the limited services that are available.

The nature of training depends very much on the kind of model one follows and the kind of person one is interested in producing. If our concern is with the production of psychometricians, behavior therapists, or perceptual research assistants, the job of training can be a very straightforward one, which large numbers of our universities and colleges can carry out very efficiently. It does not seem to be an extraordinary or complex problem to devise a curriculum for the production of any of the types of specific personnel described; nor would it be difficult to find large numbers of universities and colleges that could provide within their own staff sufficient technical skill to teach the courses and to direct the programs. Again, the major block is the resistance within the profession to acceptance of these collaborative roles.

One training problem that does require additional thought is the need to provide some practicum experience which involves prolonged individual supervision in the various roles. Whether the universities and colleges can provide the manpower for this supervision without additional help is questionable. It might be possible for existing community institutions and agencies to provide such supervision. There are a number of examples of fruitful collaboration of this nature. In general, the problem of practicum experience seems solvable without a major financial investment.

It has been noted that a sequence of levels of preparation and sophistication characterizes many professions. Nursing, for example, has the following levels: (1) professional, (2) technologist, (3) technician, and (4) aide. The application of these levels to psychology might result in the following table of skills and training:

Levels of Preparation

Level	Education	Function
Professional	Ph.D.	Quality control, teacher, innovator
Technologist	M.A.	Technical expert in a limited field
Technician	B.S. or B.A.	Assistant to a professional in varied duties
Aide	A.A.	Data collection, data processing, facilitating client movement

The existence of the professional level is now approved by the profession of psychology. The technologist level exists but is not recognized officially. The technician and aide levels are now being explored in a number of innovative training programs, but these have not as yet been implemented formally on the professional scene.

There are a number of examples in the mental health field in which a function has been articulated and its utility demonstrated but without inspiring imitation of the professional model that has been made available. I have in mind the mental health worker program developed in Florida more than ten years ago. The general idea is that in addition to a centrally located community mental health center, there would be field workers who would go to outlying communities to serve as liaison persons as well as a basic consulting resource. This role was described originally as a community consultant role. An M.A.-level person, trained in psychology, education, nursing, or social work, was to serve as a community resource, providing mental health consultation four days a week. One day a week would be spent in a centrally located community mental health center, which would have the resources to provide direct-care services for clients whose need was discovered in the course of the mental health worker's community activity. A similar model was used in New Mexico to provide a community consultation role. The Florida model is still functioning, but there has been very little carryover from either model.

There may be a lesson to be learned from this; it is not enough to articulate a model or even to demonstrate its utility. There must be some promotion of the model, some institutionalization of the specialty, if it is to develop and become viable on a large scale.

Many thoughts arise as we consider the "specific skill" solution proposed above in relation to the mental health worker experience we have described. What institutionalizing techniques would be necessary to ensure that the psychometrician, the behavior therapist, or the group therapist model would actually be incorporated into the working practices of clinics and hospitals? The necessity for approval by the appropriate professional organization is clear. The encouragement of a model by official professional groups could help to effect changes in civil service and merit system criteria. The American Psychological Association and its constituent groups have not encouraged such developments, although the need for some solution has long been recognized.

It may be in order to report some experiences in regard to this approval process. At the University of Florida for the past year and a half we have been conducting a study of the feasibility of the generalist psychological assistant model and have trained seven women in these roles. To this date we are delighted with progress and see much advantage in the model, although many problems in institutionalizing the role have emerged.

We felt that it was incumbent upon us to try to call the nature of this model to the attention of the profession and to have the profession consider its implications. Thus, at the Southeastern Psychological Association Meeting, at the Florida Psychological Association Meeting, and APA meetings, we have presented papers describing our program and participated in symposia which considered the salient issues about the function and future growth of this model. To many of these meetings we brought our own psychological assistants, so that they could speak and interact with the membership of the association.

It was fascinating to note the heated arguments offered by a number of psychologists about the validity of the procedures being followed. There was no question about the skill that the psychological assistants were able to demonstrate, or about their effectiveness in the roles to which they had been assigned, or about the value to the psychologist of having an assistant. What was at issue was whether the standards of the profession were being downgraded.

It was our hope and expectation that sober confrontation with these data and examination of the work that the women were doing would produce some lessening of resistance. On the whole we are delighted with some of the changes that seem to have taken place. A few participants announced their intention to institute a psychological-assistant training program in their own clinics.

If the profession of psychology will approve the undertaking, it would seem that a detailed analysis of the psychologist's job would make it possible to identify a number of cohesive functions involving special skills and requiring special training. If such roles can be identified and articulated, and if personnel can be trained to function in these limited psychological specialties, it is reasonable to expect that demand will grow for such personnel. (There is some evidence that this is already happening in the field, but without

official approval.)' Once such personnel are demanded, then the
universities and colleges can begin to train them, and it would be
expected that training would take a number of directions. For the
moment, it would seem reasonable to expect to produce psychometricians, behavior therapists, research assistants, and possibly community and school consultants. These various roles will appeal to
different people and to different universities and colleges, so that
any one setting might produce one or another of these specialties.

The very real problems of psychological manpower at the
community level highlight the need for psychological services and
the inadequacies of our current official solutions. The accommoda-
tions that are being made are unsatisfactory to the personnel involved, and in many cases to the institutions that employ them.
A forthright confrontation is proposed here, in which the official
psychology family faces up to its social responsibility and takes
action to meet social needs in an effective way.

Among the solutions suggested is the further development
of a group of subspecialties within professional psychology, with
authentic training, career opportunity, and social acceptance as
integral parts. Although we have not discussed these professional
characteristics in detail, and we have ignored many of the implications of developing new professional groups, it seems that, if we
are to have viable alternatives, job satisfaction must be built into
these solutions. Our own experience has indicated that there is
much talent available in the community, talent that cannot find
a job outlet because of restrictive credentials that may not be
functional for the work to be done. It is my belief that we must
examine these credential barriers and devise solutions that will
make it possible to get these talented people to help us do our work,
and that this task should have a higher priority than the attempt to
discover new sources of untapped talent.

I am delighted that the discussion seems to be opening up.
My hope is that we will not stop here but think through the next
steps—the inevitable steps that will be required so that talented
people will be made available to do the work they seem able to do
so well.

CHAPTER **XI**

Psychologist Views
the Helper

Theodore H. Blau

ᘳᘰᘳᘰᘳᘰᘳᘰᘳᘰᘳᘰᘳᘰᘳᘰᘳᘰᘳᘰᘳᘰᘳᘰᘳᘰ

Ha`aving practiced clinical psychology for over fifteen years in the same city, I have jealously held and I feel a special place in my community. I am strongly concerned about the quality as well as the quantity of psychological service given in my community to people in need. On the other hand, I have been sufficiently involved in professional manpower developments during the past decade to know that, with rare exception, the senior clinical psychologist is most needed in a variety of administrative and directive roles. I therefore have a dual position on the question, "Should nonprofessionals be used in clinical psychology?"

Interest in using nonprofessional psychological helpers has burgeoned with the decreasing availability of full professionals trained by our current programs in relation to the increasing demand for service. If the current trend continues, and there is no reason to believe that it will not, the bulk of face-to-face services for people in behavioral stress will inevitably be provided either by individuals whose training is limited to secondary school plus special on-the-job training or by mental health specialists who have been trained in relatively brief university-supervised programs. If large numbers of nonprofessional helpers are turned out in the next ten years, how will these people be regarded by the professional psychologist, who has struggled to attain his status, his prestige, his affluence? Will the professional use his power to support this new helper—or to oppose him?

A useful volume could probably be produced detailing the real and fancied objections to the training and performance of psychologically oriented nonprofessionals. For the time being, however, we must realize that the nonprofessional or subprofessional helper in mental health offers an unusual and useful opportunity to meet ever-increasing needs for service. Not only are the classic service requests increasing (guidance centers, individual psychotherapy, counseling, family crisis resolution, and so on), but we are facing new demands for professional behavioral science services in more contemporary settings (inner-city conflict resolution, crime and delinquency, community participation and cooperation, the understanding and deceleration of violence, and the like).

Who Can Meet Demands?

Today we are turning out psychologists, guidance counselors, social workers, psychiatrists, youth workers, and other "professional" workers after long, arduous, expensive, and often very restrictive training programs. There is a growing body of evidence to indicate that relatively large numbers of people can be brought to a level of service competence in programs less demanding and more time-limited than the classic professional programs.

Many universities produce the *terminal degree psychologist* with a master of arts or a master of science in psychology. Such persons, who served a secondary role in the past, have begun to play major professional roles in a variety of institutions and agencies. Many state hospitals are staffed by master's-level psychologists who in effect direct the department of clinical psychology. Although there is some question as to the quality of the services rendered by these semiprofessional workers, we nevertheless continue to produce people at the master's level. Their training program could be modified to provide them with broader and more effective tools for functioning in a variety of service and supervisory settings.

The *specialty worker* concept offers an opportunity for people trained at the bachelor's level or below to function in specific, supervised roles in psychological practice. The possessor of the bachelor's degree in psychology is often designated a "psychometrist" and given considerable responsibility for the operation of assessment and evaluation programs. In most settings such psychologists are encouraged to continue their training by taking workshops and graduate credit. They are sometimes called "counselors," with person-to-person guidance added to their assessment role. Although many who hold the bachelor's degree are used in this way, few programs are geared to produce such counselors.

Apart from these semiprofessionals, there are relatively few nonprofessionals working in the field of psychology. Isolated instances can be found, such as the housewives used in the Rioch Studies, mother-volunteers used to conduct forms of play therapy or to do intake in guidance centers, and clerical personnel trained to handle a variety of semiprofessional functions (test administration, test scoring, data tabulation). Increasing service demands geometrically exceed the output of our formal and informal training programs.

Volunteers are being used more frequently in psychological service settings—to handle intake procedures, administer and score tests, interview parents, keep records, help in research projects, do remedial reading, operate teaching machines, and, in some cases, make home visits. Ogden Lindsley at Kansas has pioneered in the training of nonprofessionals to work as operant-conditioning advisors to parents with child-rearing problems.

Despite some real question about quality control, there would seem to be a substantial pool of personnel that could be used for the provision of psychological services in the community.

Pitfalls

Professional psychologists are particularly concerned about the quality of services that might be rendered by subprofessional or nonprofessional workers. They would want very much to know the extent of the services and the interaction network for supervision, observation, and control. In person-to-person interaction in the behavioral sciences, complex decision-making is often a necessary part of the helper-needer interaction. The potential negative impact of these decisions on the individual's psychological or physical life is immense. Interaction between a nonprofessional helper and a parent, for example, can have deleterious effects on the children in the "helped" family. This is not to say that such dangers do not exist between individuals in need and the best-trained professionals. It simply says that professionals can probably expect a considerable increase in negative outcomes with the use of untrained people.

When and if such nonprofessionals are used, there are the questions of how they will be supervised, what will be the power structure of their organization, who will be in charge, and how will checks and balances be established. At the present time, professional psychologists are unprepared to deal with a large influx of nonprofessionals. They may desperately need such people, but their concern for quality, their personal response to threat, and the overwhelming amount of time needed to train and supervise these people will make for a cautious reception. If a large group of subprofessionals were brought into the community at the present time, it seems probable that professional psychologists would band together to discuss "the dangers" and end up opposing the use of such people in all but very limited roles. If we are to take effective advantage of this opportunity to meet current psychological service needs, considerable preparation and training of existing professionals will have to be designed and undertaken.

Logistical Solutions

The professional in the community would be more interested in the availability of nonprofessionals if such workers were graduated from a program in which community psychologists had some role and authority. Universities, of course, ordinarily prefer not to share the responsibility for curriculum development with non-university people. This classic town-and-gown controversy exists to a larger or lesser extent, depending on the issues. The most practical situation for the early development of nonprofessionals would be for the training program to take place in a university setting, where the facilities, the know-how, the personnel, the prestige, and the expertise in acquiring and using grants all exist.

It is unlikely that any university today is capable of producing a nonprofessional who could work adequately and comfortably in the community. In part the worth and effectiveness of such professionals will be in their identity with the community and their attachment to the neighborhoods in which they will work. It is for this reason that on-the-job training—work with professionals who are well indoctrinated into the community setting—is vital. Professional psychologists, who go through eight years of training plus internship, have a hard enough time being effective before they come to understand the community in which they work. The nonprofessional trained solely in the university setting will undoubtedly be ineffective to some degree when placed in a community, and perhaps will fail to serve.

It is possible that we can design special schools for the production of nonprofessional persons depending on the skills we seek to build. For instance, there is a considerable demand throughout the country for instruction to mothers as to how they might deal more effectively with their children's growth and behavior problems. A training program could be designed for nonprofessionals who would be such mother-child counselors, or for future testing specialists, information specialists, academic-retardation remedial specialists, and so on.

Professional psychologists will be concerned about the quality and currency of the skills which are taught to nonprofessionals on the job, in a university setting, or in a specialty school. With the rapid development of new techniques, the well-trained professional finds himself hard pressed to keep up with changes. The nonprofessional will have an even more difficult time. If some method of upgrading skills and continuing education can be worked out as part of the total program, professionals in the community will be reassured about the currency of the skills being applied by nonprofessionals. (Indeed, this may spur the community professional to up-grade his own skills.)

Controls

At this point, let us assume that we agree on the desirability of training large numbers of competent nonprofessional psychological workers. Let us further assume that these new workers are able to meet specific community and agency needs. If we are aware of the pitfalls and have created the logistic pathways and frameworks within which such nonprofessionals can be produced, the question still remains as to whether turning large numbers of minimally trained workers loose in the community will prove to be a benefit or a scourge. Assuming that we can reach the point where these workers are available, we must pay some attention to the kinds of controls that should and can be established. The primary aim of these controls would be to protect the service-recipient and to ensure that effective service is rendered.

Organizational Controls. Any developing body of workers, whether at the master, journeyman, or apprentice level, will eventually form some sort of organization where they can maintain standards, protect themselves, bargain, and socialize. Most professional groups have professional societies. Nonprofessional psychological workers will eventually be interested in such an affiliation, perhaps a union. This does not seem to be a professional issue but rather a social movement issue. Attempts by professionals to regulate the nonprofessionals' organizational pattern may result in strong opposition. It is likely that the nonprofessionals will tend to seek their own solutions.

Professional Liaison. Nonprofessional workers who perform psychological services will undoubtedly find support and interest from various organizations, ranging from the manufacturers of tests and other psychological materials to national professional organizations whose focus is promoting human welfare within a fairly cohesive scientific and professional framework. These liaisons will be determined to a large extent by the kinds of relationships the nonprofessional has in his training setting. If the trainers advocate strong professional liaisons, it is likely that these recommendations will be carried through in the field with supervisors, directors, and consultants. Existing professional organizations will probably seek strong involvement with the nonprofessionals who offer psychological services.

Legal Controls. Although there may be no statutory limitations on the practice of various mental health skills by nonprofessionals at the time such nonprofessionals appear on the scene, complaints, training conflicts, hiring policies, organizational pressures, and demands from professional psychologists will eventually result in the establishment of at least minimal local or state standards. Ancillary problems of considerable importance are likely to result from such standard-setting. To regulate the practice of any mental health specialty will be to jeopardize the creation of new and variant specialties, and there is apt to be a good deal of resistance to rapid or restrictive legislation.

Supervisory Controls. Initial supervision will be provided by the agencies, the institutions, and the individual specialists under whose direction psychological nonprofessionals will work. As the field develops, various levels of authority among the nonprofessionals will begin to emerge, and in-group supervision will be established. If the nonprofessional works in municipal, state, or federal agencies, civil service boards will probably establish the supervisory chain of command.

Longitudinal Evaluation. Psychologists have functioned for years with only limited attempts at long-range evaluation of the efficacy and appropriateness of their professional work. A massive production of nonprofessionals in the psychological field will probably produce both short- and long-range evaluation programs. The early efforts will probably evaluate the effectiveness of the worker at the end of one or more years of function. The studies are likely to evaluate the training programs in relation to field supervisors' ratings. Should the evaluation indicate that work being done by the nonprofessionals is of poor quality, a very strong modification of the in-training program can be expected. This type of control is very desirable and should be a strong consideration when training programs are developed and placements are made for graduates of such programs. Training and placement without careful follow-up could have a deleterious effect on the long-range potentialities for the use of nonprofessional psychological workers.

Unique Role of Nonprofessional

Although training programs, general standards, assignment, employment, and promotion may be controlled from outside the community, the use of nonprofessionals will at some point come under the opposition or approbation of the professional psychologists within that community. Even in communities in which no psychologist practices, the activities of nonprofessionals will soon be the subject of opinions by psychologists in surrounding communities. Just as psychologists can oppose the use of nonprofessionals, specifying the possible negative effects, so can they help in establishing the standards and guidelines within which the nonprofessional can render needed psychological services to the community. Positive approaches to this interaction would include the following activities:

Setting Community Standards. As of this time, there are no standards for the practice of community psychology. The role of the consulting psychologist in the community is becoming a matter of great interest within professional psychology. We are beginning to set standards of service for assessment, for crisis consultation, for consultation with the schools, for psychotherapy, for family therapy, and so on. Although there are no agreed-upon general standards, these could well come about in the near future. Psychologists within the community, assessing community needs, can establish standards for meeting these needs through their own skills and abilities, amplified and enhanced by nonprofessional psychological workers.

Participation and Quality Control. It would be folly to develop training programs for nonprofessional psychological workers without the active participation of knowledgeable, involved community psychologists. An adequate training program must have close awareness and recognition of specific kinds of community problems and the ways in which psychological services are or should be rendered. If this awareness is built into the training program, the nonprofessional will emerge readier to participate in the psychological work of the community—certainly more so than if he comes to the community as an externally produced "power-boosting accessory" to the already functioning community psychologist.

Since professional psychologists in the community are concerned about the quality of service rendered by nonprofessionals, they can help a great deal by participating in quality-evaluation programs, as part of a program for updating and upgrading the skills of nonprofessionals. Such programs should take place at the community level. Removing the nonprofessional from the community to return him to school is probably wasteful and perhaps ineffective. A continuing educational function should take place within the community and should involve professional psychologists.

Local Professional Group. In the past few years, there has been a tremendous burgeoning of local professional groups of psychologists throughout the United States, ranging in size from a dozen to several thousand members. Psychologists who are practicing within the community are directly concerned with the impact of the nonprofessional on the needs of the community and the quality of psychological services rendered. These local professional groups form a focus around which support (or opposition) for nonprofessionals in psychology is likely to be generated. They can be a good base for training programs, for spawning associations for the nonprofessional, and for consultation and supervision.

The network of local groups throughout the United States can see to it that creative activities tested in one locality are communicated to professional psychologists in other localities. Since local groups meet more frequently and are more community-oriented than state and regional groups, a communication and educational chain between local groups and national organizations, between federal agencies and groups of psychologists in the community, and among psychologists who practice in a variety of communities seems feasible.

"Undesirable Patient." Certain "needers" in the community toward whom many mental health professionals have reacted adversely (drug addicts, alcoholics, delinquents, sexual deviates, problem families) are more and more falling within the province of the community psychologist. Social workers have always dealt with this kind of needer who has, until recently, been considered hopeless. There is a considerable cultural barrier between the life space of such people and that of the highly trained professionals sometimes available to help them. A good deal of empirical evidence

indicates that nonprofessionals are more effective with these groups than professionals are. This poses one of the most exciting challenges for the use of the nonprofessional. The psychologist in the community should be aware of this possibility and serve as a focal point for the establishment of experimental programs to offer help to these obvious needers.

Implications for Psychology

Our present training programs in no way meet the growing need for psychological services. New opportunities for psychologists to be of service within their community are identified almost daily. New techniques, research, methods, and funding are more available today than ever before. Our society has come to a high level of acceptance of behavioral science as a source of help for those in need. Psychology has moved to the forefront in the behavioral sciences. The time is critical, the need is great. The challenge is to bridge the gap between the large available pool of nonprofessional manpower and their final commitment as members of a helper group in the community. This challenge falls squarely on the shoulders of psychologists in the areas of both training and community service. Neither the challenge nor the need can be met by hesitation or equivocation.

CHAPTER **XII**

Nonprofessionals
in Social Work

Mitchell I. Ginsberg, Bernard M. Shiffman,
Morton Rogers

Recently, in New York City, graduation exercises were held for the first group of public service careers recruits to complete a work-training program under the Scheuer Amendment, which established the Public Service Careers Program of the Office of Economic Opportunity. These graduates, approximately one hundred of them, recruited primarily from the welfare rolls, were taught to perform as assistants to professional staffs in welfare, health, and education. In addition to job training "on the work site," all students were enrolled in an educational program developed and operated by one of the New York colleges under a

193

special contract. The purpose of the educational program was to help the trainees obtain their high-school diplomas. To participate in this OEO employment program, the New York City Department of Social Services had to agree to develop a new entry position of aide, to institute a system of upward mobility for the aides so that they could continue their education and advance to their individual maximum potential, and finally to redefine the job of the case-worker so that the new worker could move from trainee to aide and on to the regular line positions in the agency.

It would be too painful to review the struggle and the frustrations involved in this first simple step of establishing the aide position. To redesign work tasks is not an easy job in any profession. The less secure and entrenched the profession is, the more difficult the job becomes. The more structured the field, whether through union organization or civil service regulation, the greater the resistance to redefining the duties and qualifications of practitioners.

The implications of this simple idea of employing the poor without formal qualifications in the field of social work are our first concern. But it is clear that even if we could handle our "in-house" social work professional problems, we would have to harmonize with the "out-of-house" educational, civil service, and employment systems to make it all work.

Even if the social work field were not facing a critical manpower shortage, we would be justified in investing the resources of the profession in order to accommodate the new manpower resources, to negotiate with unions and the Civil Service Commission, and the total educational-employment system. At the graduation exercises mentioned earlier, about a hundred people, primarily black and Puerto Rican, were inducted into the helping professions. Many of these men and women never dreamed of working, let alone becoming staff members, in the public service professions. Some nine hundred more will be graduating in the next four months. Thousands of men and women are in the wings, waiting to be designated as trainees. One member of the graduating class who spoke at the meeting was an ADC mother of nine children. She described in unmatchable eloquence what the opportunity of working for a salary and helping others meant to her, and to her children. The pride of being somebody who worked shone in her face. Her description of her children's interest in a mother who was studying and doing schoolwork stirred the most objective professional in the auditorium. And when she concluded with, "This is only the first step, I plan to go to college," everyone knew she meant it. If this woman, with all the real obstacles she faces, can see a chance to climb out of her frustrating existence and become a useful, productive person, a model to her children and neighbors, can we fail to join her and make it possible?

We have ideas about how we could redesign many of the tasks in law, education, and health in order to simplify the entry of new people into these professions. But for us to give advice to the other professions would be regarded as an intrusion; we would be told, with justification, that we had better clean up our own house before urging others to take on the task.

In the field of social work, we should be able to look at ourselves a little more critically. We should remind ourselves that most of the services in social work have been and are being performed by nonprofessionals. As a matter of fact, it has not been too long since these services were given exclusively by volunteers or nonprofessionals. The social work field was a mutation, born out of sociology, philanthropy, education, and psychology, searching for its own base, its own knowledge. As recently as 1921 an editorial in *The Compass* proclaimed, "The die has been cast. We are, and are to be, a professional organization of social workers." From summer institutes and seminars, a school of philanthropy or social work was established in New York in 1898, but social work education took root only during World War I. As late as the 1950s, Hollis and Taylor wrote that social work was in its "early adolescence" as a profession, and that only "the hard core of social work in the United States can be said to have attained a satisfactory professional status." Some of the educational analysts and social researchers in the late 1950s came to the conclusion that social work had finally attained the status of a profession, if we used the criteria developed for classical professions. Coincidentally, in the 1950s the social work organizations converged into one organization, the National Association of Social Workers, and began the process of defining professional practice and instituting licensing and certification for its practitioners.

The uneasiness which pervaded the professionalized field when "practice" was under scrutiny might have stemmed in part from the realization, which hit in the 1960s, that social work was becoming as irrelevant as the other professions in serving the economically and socially disadvantaged people of our communities. Social work professionals, if defined as those practitioners who held a master's degree in social work or better, had developed their skills in specialized settings with an emphasis on treatment and represented only a small part of those who were engaged in providing social services. The majority of practitioners in the field were, and remain, at best job-developed and staff-trained social service workers. The critical issues in social work are what academic or experience background should be required of recognized personnel in the field of social work, and what tasks can be performed at what levels of education and experience.

Because of the "adolescent" nature of the social work profession, it has equated educational accomplishment with qualification. Since World War II, recruitment has focused on those with the master's degree in social work, with a sharp step down to the college graduate and in limited areas to the high school graduate. But the total output of graduate schools of social work in the United States and Canada barely supplies the necessary replacements for those who are retiring. With the competition for college graduates becoming more and more desperate in other sectors of the economy, the social work profession no longer has free choice. In this decade it has become abundantly clear that we must reexamine the human and mechanical resources that are available to staff social services, and that we must consider the technological changes, such as cybernation, which might better meet the shortage of manpower. The professionals, whether in social work education or social work practice, have been slow in inventing alternatives to match the reality of the field of social work. But the trends are clear.

Bertram Beck, in his paper included in this volume, describes these trends. There is no question that personnel from allied professions and disciplines must be recruited to the field of social work. The professionally trained and qualified social worker is a rare bird and must be utilized more effectively to train, to administer, and to develop others who can work with people. The team concept, in which personnel with different levels of experience and skill are assigned to different levels of helping, has been successfully demonstrated in both industry and the professions. We need to develop criteria and procedures which foster the inclusion of all who can work, rather than the exclusion of the many who lack technical or educative background which is *not* related to the tasks to be performed.

We have been unwilling or unable to break down the functions which could be performed by others within the social services delivery system. A few years ago this task was a prerequisite if we were going to meet the manpower needs of the field of social work, and if the public was to have available to it the services which can and should be provided. Today the social work field, like education and many other city public services, can no longer control the pace of involvement of citizens, not only as recipients of service but as providers of service. In the world in which we now live, the professions and their fields of practice are no longer sacred cows.

Past performances in any of the helping professions cannot be utilized to justify continuation of the current system. All professions are being challenged to become relevant to the consumer by facing the real needs of the people, not to do for the consumer but to involve him in solving his problem. This is equally true on a policy level, in decision-making, and in serving as a worker-communicator between the expert and the consumer. If any factor galvanized this challenge, it was the professional biases which were developed into criteria to weed out those who were ineligible for the limited services available, instead of facing the community with the real issue: the underfinancing of public services, and the lack of availability of education, health, legal, and social services. Psychiatry, casework, employment, and housing all fell into this trap of excluding those who most needed the service. Even the Office of Economic Opportunity, the antipoverty federal agency, was almost involved, but was saved by the fact that community action groups, once launched, cannot be easily controlled.

The notion of maximum feasible participation in community

action may be the one lasting contribution of the antipoverty program. This idea not only uncovered an underutilized host of indigenous community leaders but created new neighborhood-based social services and new opportunities for the employment of nonprofessionals. While intended to influence the involvement of citizens in decision-making, it has had an equal, if not greater, impact in involving new people in the delivery of services. Thousands of people have been recruited from law offices, labor unions, welfare departments, schools, political clubs, libraries, and the welfare rolls. Since 1962 the number of these recruits has multiplied many times. Experience and skill have been acquired. This last year, the Scheuer Amendment to the OEO legislation made it possible to institutionalize the recruitment of poor people, for the program described earlier. This new blood will force the old institutions in the field of social work, not only to find legitimate positions and opportunities for the poor, but to redesign their service systems to utilize the unique contribution that can be made by experienced, mature people without the traditional educational requirements. The presence of these new workers will not mean an easier role for those who administer the program, but it may mean better service for people.

Various lay and business communities in our cities are interested for a variety of reasons in moving unemployed and underemployed employables into work assignments, rather than continuing free handouts. Any proposed program which promises to get people off the dole has a high level of support. Unfortunately this support falls away rapidly if the program proposes to pass the entry salary level or if there is the possibility that some poor people may enter in the middle of a career spectrum. In other words, even if the practitioners of social work were committed to the creative use of nonprofessionals—as they are not—they would be faced with the difficult task of developing a community-wide understanding of the problems and rationale for such development.

Unfortunately, in the past five years some of the enthusiasts who have been trying to overcome apathy to this new group and resistance to changing the professional mold have oversold the nonprofessional. They have defined the new role as an inexpensive substitute for a professional practitioner. This approach has contributed to the tendency of others to regard the introduction of the nonprofessional as a threat to standards. (The special programs with the most recently acquired standards are the most defensive—for example, day care.)

The field of social work must take on the task of refining the functions appropriate for variously qualified personnel in order to improve standards of performance. As a group worker expatriate, I remember how the Association of Group Workers went about defining worker roles. We were constantly engaged in the distillation of the roles, responsibilities, and duties of the governing board, the staff, and the members—and at another level, the responsibilities of the trained, untrained, and volunteer workers who were responsible for front-line service. Our professional association of social work, NASW, and the Council on Social Work Education are engaged in this same process today. Although their activity is laudatory, their timing is not. It is taking too long to get action. By the time the internal process of the two associations is completed, the external problem will have changed so much that the product will no longer be relevant.

The field of social work must move, at once, to redefine the tasks which can be accomplished by the new careerists and to establish an open system so that maximum upward mobility is assured. The professional association must act instead of reexamining its membership qualifications. If we look at the results of our practice as a profession rather than at our words, we turn out to resemble the building trades unions much more than our own self-image. It is true that we have had an open system, but strangely it has not produced significant numbers of black and Puerto Rican middle- and upper-management practitioners. In other words, if *we* accept the challenge of the Kerner Report and agree that the primary problem is white racism, let us not file complaints against our colleagues or picket the schools. Let us get on with our own business—and the employment of nonprofessionals is one obvious, ready-to-go opportunity.

The educational supportive arm to the field of social work—the Council on Social Work Education, the expanding community college educational system, the public and private universities, and the training centers—has an equal and not separate task. There is a definable body of knowledge that can be taught, knowledge which is useful if not essential in performing the tasks assigned to the field of social work. This information must be made available to the new careerists. The entire formal education system needs to develop continuity, which requires the same kind of redefinition of tasks and assignments as mentioned earlier for the practice area. Intake requirements, faculty, student involvement, teaching methods, testing, scores, content, even the very settings in which education takes place (that is, the modern "Seagram's type" of building versus the storefront college), need to be studied. The educational supportive services currently operate as instruments of exclusion rather than inclusion. If we are going to make any significant change in our lifetime, we will have to turn around our social institutions so that they welcome people in—for service, for employment opportunities, and for sharing in decisions—instead of keeping people out.

What we have written about the profession and the educational institutions is equally true of other types of allied organizations, such as the Civil Service Commission and its legislation and unions in the field of social work. There is no question that all these supportive units began with the desire to protect the service and its practitioners. But times have changed. The original inequities have been corrected by law and by civil service and union organizations. The solutions themselves have in many instances become the inequities which hinder the further development of the field of social work. It is indeed ironic when unions and civil service function in such a way as to become obstacles for the entry of the poor into public service careers.

Our American society believes that it is just to provide scholarships to people who have acquired a high school or bachelor's degree. In fact, in New York State, individuals who obtain a master's degree in social work are given a $1200 bonus if they accept employment in the public welfare system. Why not apply the same principle to the other end of the career ladder—the entry-level nonprofessional position? If subsidized mobility is acceptable, why not at the other end of the work spectrum? The high school dropout is in greater need of subsidized training than is the college graduate. Unless we are flexible enough to think in that fashion, and about all the systems which make up the field of social work, we will not be able to do much in the way of developing relevancy. Even the current totally inadequate ratio of one social worker per five thousand population will not be maintained if we continue our present system of recruitment, training, and employment of social service workers.

We are not knowledgeable about how this challenge is being met in other parts of the United States. We can report tentatively only for that little part of the social work field in which we have labored for the past two years, namely, public welfare.

In spite of extensive recruitment drives for university graduates, the New York City Department of Social Services could not fill the available staff positions. The shortage in personnel created hardships for clients, staff, and administration. An accelerated graduate school scholarship program exists, but today it is just a promise that there may be an upgrading impact on the quality of service in the 1970s. It should be remembered that we faced not only an expanding caseload and the consequent need to enlarge the staff, but a high rate of staff turnover at the lower level, created by the complexity of the work, its demands, its rules and regulations, and the mountains of bureaucratic paper work, aggravated by union and client organizational activity. It became obvious that recruitment and personnel management needed to be improved. It was equally important to reexamine the work tasks, reassign necessary functions, and eliminate degrading and unnecessary activities in connection with establishing and maintaining eligibility. Briefly, we were faced with the need to convert an investigatory system to a supportive service which people have as a social right. If we had failed to recognize this need on our own, the welfare clients organizations would have persuaded us. The implications for the Department of Social Services were obvious. Our ability to make the obvious operational is another matter.

The current administration of the Department of Social Services has listed these implications as a number of actions which should be taken, as follows: (1) separation of income assistance from social service support; (2) institution of the declaration or affidavit on a universal basis to establish eligibility; (3) reorganization of the manner in which income maintenance is made available to those who are eligible; (4) development of a system of providing appropriate social services to clients who want and can use the available social services; (5) design of a new social service unit which will include and use the range of skill currently existing in the department plus the skills of the new careerists who are being added; (6) establishment of new career positions within both the City Personnel Department and the State Department of Social Services; (7) institution of educational programs to retrain permanent personnel and develop relevant programs for the new careerists; and (8) application of the new computer-administrative technology to facilitate services to all those who are eligible.

This list of tasks, although designed for the New York City Department of Social Services, with a little manipulation could be equally valid for the entire field of social work in the years ahead.

No change can be accomplished without giving rise to unanticipated concerns. But the absence of change is death, and the field of social work is too young to die, and has too much to contribute. Throughout its history, the field has pledged itself to explore new ideas, new ways of solving new, old, and different problems. The manpower shortage is an old problem to be solved within a new set of circumstances. The use of nonprofessionals is not an implication; it is a must.

CHAPTER XIII

Congressional Actions

Russell A. Nixon

A new stage in the developing program for new career nonprofessional public service employment has been reached. Important statements of national policy and new legislative proposals in the Ninetieth Congress (1967–68) indicate that this program is now emerging as a major new element of national manpower policy and of the antipoverty program. This is not to say that the experimentation and demonstration phase of the new careers program is or should be ended, for many important problems remain to be solved. Nor is it to say that an adequately comprehensive and integrated national new careers program either exists or is in the works. But a healthy baby has been born, and the need now is to assure its full and healthy growth.

The initial vitality and the enormous potential of the new careers program is based on the confluence of the following powerful socioeconomic trends: (1) the shifting emphasis of our economy from the private to the public sector with education, health, and other public services becoming the fastest growing "industries"; (2) the great and increasing need for manpower and the concomitant desperate shortage of professionals in public service;[1] (3) the stubborn continuation of a large volume of unemployment with a hard core of jobless concentrated in the disadvantaged population, and the long-range problem of providing jobs for all in our changing economy; (4) the militancy of the civil rights movement, leading to increased demands for decent employment opportunities, dignity, and improved social service for Negroes, Puerto Ricans, Mexican-Americans, and other minorities; (5) a new appreciation, growing out of the philosophy and the experiences of manpower and anti-poverty programs of the 1960s, of the feasibility and great potential of the poor's participation and their constructive contribution in our society (this encompasses rejection of the idea that "dead end" menial jobs are suitable for the poor); and (6) a mood—and even necessity—to innovate and experiment with new methods of training and teaching, of manpower utilization, and of organization and development in our social and economic relations.

The use of nonprofessionals as auxiliary personnel assisting professionals is not new. There have been many precedents, especially during World War II, and more recently in scattered experimental and demonstration projects. But in 1964, with the enactment of the Economic Opportunity Act and its emphasis on participation of the poor, and on the provision of both services and jobs for the poverty population, the new careers program began to jell. In 1965 the publication of Arthur Pearl's and Frank Riessman's *New Careers for the Poor*[2] gave currency and direction to the program. Concurrently, experimental and demonstration projects for the use of nonprofessionals began to multiply under the sponsorship of the Office of Juvenile Delinquency and the Welfare

---

[1] The Report of the National Commission on Technology, Automation, and Economic Progress, *Technology and the American Economy*, February 1966, p. 36, estimates that there is a potential of 5.3 million new public service jobs.

[2] Arthur Pearl and Frank Riessman, *New Careers for the Poor: The Nonprofessional in Human Service* (New York: Free Press, 1965).

Division of the Department of Health, Education, and Welfare, the Office of Manpower Policy, Evaluation, and Research of the Labor Department, and in a variety of correctional and law enforcement agencies throughout the country. More than 25,000 nonprofessionals were employed by the Office of Economic Opportunity in its Community Action Program.[3]

Then, in the 1966 amendments to the Economic Opportunity Act, a new program was authorized (Title II, Section 205 [e]) to prepare unemployed or low-income persons to enter career jobs in public service as nonprofessional personnel. This program, sponsored by Congressman James H. Scheuer, and known as the Scheuer program, is now in its initial stage of implementation with approximately $30 million being allocated annually to fund new careers work-training and employment projects.

It is with this background that we now find significant recognition of the potential of nonprofessional employment in a variety of reports, messages and statements by the president, by various national commissions, and by major public officials. Paralleling these messages bills have been introduced in Congress and major legislation has been enacted which either specifically provides for nonprofessional programs, or clearly opens the door to executive implementation of such provisions. This paper outlines these legislative developments. It is presented to illustrate the possible dimensions of new congressional enactments, and the significantly widened role being assigned to the development of nonprofessional careers in public service.

In some still pending legislation, the new careers program will need to be added, as was the Scheuer amendment, to the originally proposed 1966 amendments to the Economic Opportunity

---

[3] A study of such programs in nine cities employing about five thousand nonprofessionals by Daniel Yankelovich, Inc., states: "The program is now operationally viable. . . . A large number of previously unemployed or underemployed poor people without background or training for the kind of work they are now doing, have been routinely hired, have received some training and are working hard and enthusiastically on their jobs. After some months of experience, supervisory personnel supervising professionals and agency personnel in the CAA feel that the nonprofessionals are filling an indispensable role rather well." *A Study of the Non-Professional in the CAP* (New York, 1966), p. 15.

Act. In other legislation the tentative and limited new career proposals need further definition and expansion. But these further legislative steps can be expected to confirm the enhanced status of the new careers program made clear by the legislative developments described in this paper.

Economic Opportunity Act

The 1966 amendments to the Economic Opportunity Act included the following addition to the section of Title II on "Community Action—Adult Work Training and Employment Programs":

> The Director is authorized to make grants or enter into agreements with any state or local agency or private organization to pay all or part of the costs of adult work training and employment programs for unemployed or low-income persons involving activities designed to improve the physical, social, economic or cultural condition of the community or areas served in fields including, but not limited to, health, education and welfare, neighborhood redevelopment, and public safety. Such programs shall (1) assist in developing entry level employment opportunities, (2) provide maximum prospects for advancement and continued employment without federal assistance, and (3) be combined with necessary educational, training, counseling, and transportation assistance, and such other supportive services as may be needed. Such work experience shall be combined, where needed, with educational and training assistance, including basic literacy and occupational training. Such programs shall be conducted in a manner consistent with policies applicable under this Act for the protection of employed workers and the maintenance of basic rates of pay and other suitable conditions of employment.

This amendment was sponsored by Congressman Scheuer who, on March 1, 1966, had introduced H.R. 13159, "The Career Opportunity Act," which proposed an amendment to the EOA "to provide employment opportunities for unemployed, low-income persons in subprofessional service careers." This original Scheuer bill emphasized the objectives of "providing new permanent jobs with career potential," and authorized $1,360 million to carry out the program during fiscal year 1967.

While this bill was not enacted, Congressman Scheuer, as

a member of the Antipoverty Subcommittee of the House Committee on Education and Labor, did succeed in having the committee add the new careers program to the amendments proposed by the administration. In the committee's report on the Economic Opportunity Amendments of 1966, the Scheuer new careers amendment was referred to jointly with the 1965 Nelson amendment (named after its sponsor, Senator Gaylord Nelson, and providing conservation and community beautification employment for elderly poor people) as part of the Public Service Employment Training Program. The report stated:

> The Nelson Amendment, as it now stands, is too limited in the scope of the activities it supports, and the size of the program it envisions to reduce substantially the many who are hard-core unemployed. The Committee has, therefore, recommended a new amendment specifically designed to enable chronically unemployed individuals to secure entry positions other than as professionals in the public service sector of the economy with built-in opportunities for training and experience. Hopefully, these opportunities will lead to promotion and advancement. The outlines of this program were first presented by Congressman James Scheuer.[4]

The Economic Opportunity Act amendments of 1966, including the Scheuer amendment, passed the House on September 29, 1966, and were accepted by the Senate on October 4, 1966. They became law on November 8, 1966, with the president's signature. Congress appropriated $73 million for the Nelson and the Scheuer programs and subsequently approximately $33 million was allocated to the new Scheuer program. In December, 1966, administration of the Scheuer program was delegated to the Department of Labor, Manpower Administration, Bureau of Work Programs by the director of the Office of Economic Opportunity.

Guidelines for the Scheuer new careers program were issued on Febraury 24, 1967, by the Secretary of Labor as part of the "Standards and Procedures for Work-Training Experience Programs under the Economic Opportunity Act of 1964, as

[4] United States Congress, House of Representatives Report No. 1568, Committee on Education and Labor, *Report on Economic Opportunity Amendments of 1966,* June 1, 1966, p. 10.

Amended."[5] The program is being implemented by the Manpower Administrator, Department of Labor, with the OEO Community Action Agencies as developers and sponsors of the resultant new careers projects.

The 1967 Economic Opportunity Act amendments continued the Scheuer new careers program until June 30, 1969. The new version separated the Nelson and Scheuer provisions and strengthened the new careers language. Whereas the 1966 program was limited to adults over twenty-one years of age, the new Scheuer program includes adults and youths age sixteen and over. In the 1967 amendment the OEO director is authorized to fund special work and training programs

> which provide unemployed or low-income persons with jobs leading to career opportunities, including new types of careers, in programs designed to improve the physical, social, economic, or cultural condition of the community or areas served in fields including without limitation health, education and welfare, neighborhood redevelopment, and public safety, which provide maximum prospects for advancement and continued employment without Federal assistance, which give promise of contributing to the broader adoption of new methods of structuring jobs and new methods of providing job ladder opportunities, and which provide opportunities for further occupational training to facilitate career advancement.

Both the House Committee on Education and Labor and the Senate Committee on Labor and Public Welfare in their reports on the Economic Opportunity Act amendments of 1967 reaffirmed and emphasized the special features of the new careers program. The House report stated:

> The need to create new careers with advancement opportunities was additionally stressed in the "new careers" program. The committee notes that "new careers" projects have been funded which provide only the most superficial attention to the career ladder concept or to the requirement that permanent jobs be available at the

[5] These guidelines also apply to the Neighborhood Youth Corps, the Kennedy-Javits Special Impact Program, and the Nelson Community Employment and Betterment Program. New guidelines which substantially tightened the quality controls and standards of the new careers program were issued on January 3, 1968, by the Labor Department.

end of training. The committee expects the Labor Department to act decisively in correcting these situations.[6]

The Senate report included the statement:

The new careers program is too new for evaluation. However, the committee notes that while the early emphasis is upon training, which is proper, it appears that not enough attention is being given to assuring that "new career" jobs, paid by other funds, will be available at the completion of training. It will not be easy to break down traditional barriers, such as civil service regulations and professional "standards," which block the disadvantaged from moving into public service occupations, but considerable effort must be made in this regard if the program is to succeed.[7]

In 1969, in the Ninety-first Congress, the Democratic majority in Congress proposes to continue the Economic Opportunity Act with its new careers provision. In his message on January 19, 1969, President Nixon called for reorganization and a continuation of the Economic Opportunity Act, but did not specify his position on the new careers program.

Education

In his February 28, 1967, message to Congress on education and health in America, President Johnson emphasized the critical shortage of educational manpower and said that "New kinds of school personnel—such as teacher aides—are needed to help in the schools." The president deplored the fact that "teacher aides . . . have not been eligible to participate" in federally sponsored "programs to improve and train teachers" and urged "a broader approach to training for the education professions [and that] at the state and local level, education authorities must have greater flexibility to plan for their educational manpower needs." President Johnson recommended passage of the Education Professions Act of 1967 to, in part, "Provide new authority for the training of

[6] United States Congress, House of Representatives Report No. 866, Committee on Education and Labor, *Economic Opportunity Amendments of 1967,* October 27, 1967, pp. 17–18.

[7] United States Congress, Senate Report No. 563, Committee on Labor and Public Welfare, *Economic Opportunity Amendments of 1967,* September 12, 1967, p. 25.

school administrators, teacher aides, and other education workers for schools and colleges."

Higher Education Act Amendments of 1967. Simultaneously with the president's message, on February 20, 1967, House Education and Labor Committee Chairman Perkins and Senate Education Subcommittee Chairman Wayne Morse introduced H.R. 6232 and S. 1126, the Higher Education Act Amendments of 1967. The legislation finally enacted on June 28, 1967 (P.L. 90–35—often referred to as the Education Professions Development Act), added to the Higher Education Act of 1965 a new "Part D—Improving Training Opportunities for Personnel Serving in Programs of Education other than Higher Education." The Commissioner of Education is authorized to make grants to appropriate public or private agencies "for carrying out programs or projects to improve the qualifications of persons who are serving or preparing to serve in education programs in elementary and secondary schools" and in vocational education programs. Included are "programs or projects to train teacher aides and other nonprofessional educational personnel," and to cover "the cost of (1) short-term or regular-session institutes (and) (2) . . . seminars, symposia, workshops, or conferences . . . [that are] part of a continuing program of in-service or pre-service training." The Commissioner of Education is authorized to pay those participating in the training programs "such stipends (including allowances for subsistence and other expenses for such persons and their dependents) as he may determine, which shall be consistent with prevailing practices under comparable federally supported programs."

Also a new section titled "Attracting and Qualifying Teachers to Meet Critical Teacher Shortages" was added which provided that state plans for grants under its provisions might include "Programs of such agencies to obtain the services of teacher aides and to provide them with the preservice or in-service training they need to perform their duties as teacher aides."

On June 20, 1967, the House Committee on Education and Labor reported favorably H.R. 10943 "Amending and Extending Title V of the Higher Education Act of 1965."[8] This report, as the

---

[8] U.S. Congress, House of Representatives Report No. 373. *Amend-*

following excerpts make clear, gave major emphasis to the development of auxiliary new career personnel in education:

The critical need for teachers continues. According to at least one nationwide survey, the need is more acute this year than it was last year. To meet this critical demand, many thousands of additional teachers and other educational personnel are needed at all levels. . . . [New programs are proposed for] grants to local educational agencies experiencing critical shortages of teachers to carry out programs to attract and qualify teachers and teacher aides. . . .

Under the provisions of the proposed new section 504, local school districts, state educational agencies, and colleges and universities will receive assistance to identify persons interested in the education profession, to encourage them to pursue an education career, whether such career would start at a professional or subprofessional level, and to publicize availability of opportunities in education.

The committee wishes to restate its interest in providing increased support of programs for the training of teacher aides. Under the proposed subpart (2) of part B of Title V up to one-third of the funds may be used for programs to attract and train teacher aides. In the new proposed part D programs or projects to train teacher aides are specifically mentioned as a type of undertaking which will qualify for support. The committee cannot overstate its interest in providing support for this type of program. Equally important, however, is the training of teachers to work with teacher aides. This committee is hopeful that other training programs supported by Title V funds, though designed for other purposes, will nevertheless include a component designed to prepare teachers to work with teacher aides, particularly to develop an awareness on the part of teachers and school administrators of the advantages of using such aides in positions of increasing responsibility commensurate with training and experience.

Similarly, the Senate Committee report on these amendments stressed the importance of teacher aides and of preparing teachers to work with such aides.[9]

Elementary and Secondary Education Act Amendments of

---

ing and Extending Title V of the Higher Education Act of 1965, June 20, 1967, pp. 2, 4, and 11.

[9] U.S. Congress, Senate Report No. 363, *Amending and Extending Title V of the Higher Education Act of 1965,* June 27, 1967, p. 9.

1967. It is estimated that in 1967, 125,000 education aides were employed under the terms of the Elementary and Secondary Education Act of 1965, Title I, "Assistance for the Education of Children of Low-Income Families," and Title V, "Grants to Strengthen State Departments of Education."

An important extension of this legislation is suggested in an amendment proposed by Senator Gaylord Nelson. This proposal would add a new Title VII, "Teacher Aide Programs," to the Elementary and Secondary Education Act of 1965. Senator Nelson was joined in 1967 by Senators Clark, Pell, Muskie, and Mondale in sponsoring this proposal.

While not finally acted on, the language of this proposed teacher aide program is indicative of congressional approach to new careers in education. Grants under this new Title VII would be granted only if:

> (1) the project is designed to provide a combined program of training and experience to prepare persons to serve as teacher aides in preschool and elementary and secondary education programs;
> (2) the project is part of a comprehensive program for improved utilization of educational personnel in schools where the teacher aides are to serve;
> (3) the project is designed to provide more individualized attention for students and to relieve teachers and other professional staff of functions which can be performed competently by teacher aides under the supervision of professional staff;
> (4) the institution of higher education participating in the project will undertake to provide preservice training programs to prepare persons to become teacher aides and to provide, to the extent practicable, preservice programs bringing together teacher aides and the teachers and other educational personnel who will be supervising them.

The proposed definition of "teacher aide" in this amendment "includes assistants to teachers and also includes library aides, school recreation aides, and other ancillary educational personnel who are under the supervision of professional members of the school staff, but the term does not include persons who are primarily responsible for the instruction of pupils."

Education experts testified before the House Education and Labor Committee, seeking to strengthen the teacher aide program, particularly to increase the prospects of guaranteeing employment and upward mobility for trainees.

The Education Subcommittee of an informal New Careers Legislative Task Force comprised of representatives from Bank Street College of Education, Howard University, and the National Education Association on January 27, 1967, recommended the following amendments: (1) an amendment of Title I of ESEA to require submission of a plan for training of auxiliary personnel and the professionals with whom they work by all school systems which request funds under this title; (2) an amendment to the Higher Education Act to provide funds for faculty workshops on the new role of the teacher in relation to auxiliary personnel; and (3) an amendment to the ESEA and Higher Education Act to provide funds for planning, research, demonstration and evaluation of the use of auxiliary personnel in education.

The Task Force also arranged for testimony supporting such amendments. On March 15, 1967, John H. Niemeyer, president of the Bank Street College of Education, and Gordon Klopf, dean of the college, appeared before the House Education and Labor Committee. They were accompanied by Verona Williams, an educational aide working in the New York City school system. On March 18, Garda W. Bowman, program coordinator of the Bank Street College of Education study of demonstration training programs for nonprofessionals and a leader of the Task Force, also testified. The House of Representatives on May 24, 1967, approved the 1967 amendments to ESEA with two new careers amendments which were approved by the Senate and signed by the president on January 2, 1968. These two ESEA new careers amendments added in 1967 were: (1) Proposed by Congressman Scheuer—local education agencies receiving federal funds for projects using education aides must "set forth well-developed plans providing for coordinated programs of training in which education aides and the professional staff whom they are assisting will participate together." (Section 205 [a] Title II as amended) and (2) Proposed by Congressman William A. Steiger—to the state education agency programs which may be funded under Title V, there is added a new Section 144,

"Encouragement of Use of Auxiliary Personnel," covering projects "specifically designed to encourage the full and adequate utilization and acceptance of auxiliary personnel (such as teacher aides) in elementary and secondary schools on a permanent basis."

The House Education and Labor Committee report on the ESEA amendments strongly endorsed the use of subprofessionals under the terms of the Act, stating that there is "a crucial shortage of trained personnel" and that "training programs for professional staff in the use of teacher aides, as added by these amendments, may also contribute greatly to the fullest usage of professional skills and training . . . the committee hopes that the extension of the Title I authorization through fiscal year 1969 will provide sufficient assurance of program continuity to encourage States and communities to solve their manpower shortages through special training, increased use of subprofessionals and new recruitment methods."[10]

Other provisions of the Elementary and Secondary Education Act amendments of 1967 strengthened the mandate for innovative educational methods and manpower development to meet the needs of poor children. In the new Title VII, titled the "Bilingual Education Act," grants are authorized for "providing preservice training designed to prepare persons to participate in bilingual education programs as teachers, teacher aides, or other ancillary education personnel such as counselors, and in-service training and development programs to continue to improve their qualifications. . . ."

Vocational Education Act Amendments of 1968. An especially significant advance in new careers legislation appeared in the congressional action to extend and modify the federal program of vocational education. With strong bipartisan support Congress, on October 3, 1968, completed action on the Vocational Education Act amendments of 1968. Besides gearing vocational education more clearly to modern job market conditions, in these amendments Congress authorized $3,180,050,000 for this program through fiscal year 1972—that is, up to June 30, 1972.

[10] United States Congress, House of Representatives Report No. 188, Committee on Education and Labor, *Elementary and Secondary Education Act Amendments of 1967*, April 11, 1967, p. 3.

Under the primary sponsorship of Senator Ralph W. Yarborough, now chairman of the Senate Committee on Labor and Public Welfare, Congress authorized grants and contracts with nonprofit agencies or institutions "to encourage research and training in vocational education programs designed to meet special vocational education needs of youths and to provide education for new and emerging careers and occupations." The specifications for such new careers projects were outlined in very clear terms as follows:

(A) research and experimental projects designed to identify new careers in such fields as mental and physical health, crime prevention and corrections, welfare, education, municipal services, child care, and recreation requiring less training than professional positions and to delineate within such careers roles with the potential for advancement from one level to another,

(B) training and development projects designed to demonstrate improved methods of securing the involvement, cooperation, and commitment of both the public and private sectors toward the end of achieving greater coordination and more effective implementation of programs for the employment of persons in the fields including programs to prepare professionals (including administrators) to work effectively with aides, and

(C) projects to evaluate the operation of programs for the training, development, and utilization of public service aides, particularly their effectiveness in providing satisfactory work experiences and in meeting public needs.

In addition, the Senate committee report emphasized its interest in the new careers amendment in these terms:

The committee feels that the expanding dimensions and responsibilities of vocational education should encompass research and training in new and emerging careers and occupations in public-service-connected areas. Examples of the kinds of projects which the committee feel should be funded are set forth in section 132 (6). . . .

Key to the concept set forth in the legislation is the training of students for jobs which truly are careers—employment opportunities which provide for upward mobility commensurate with training and experience. Implicit in this new careers concept, then, is not only the training of students in public service occupations such as those set forth in clause (A), but the awakening of understanding on the part of administrators and professionals in making use of the services of nonprofessional personnel. Thus, clause (B) provides for training and development projects designed to demonstrate improved methods of securing the involvement, cooperation, and commitment of the public and private sectors toward the end of achieving greater coordination and more effective implementation of programs for the employment of persons in less than professional positions in the public service sector.

Concomitant with its desire that the experience of the vocational education community in working in the areas of new and emerging careers and occupations be one of continual learning, the committee has included clause (C) which provides for the evaluation of the operation of programs for the training, development, and utilization of public service aides, particularly their effectiveness in providing satisfactory work experiences and in meeting public needs.[11]

These provisions stress not only development of new careers programs for nonprofessionals, but preparation of professionals to work in new careers programs, and the need to evaluate such programs.

Law Enforcement and Corrections

The serious shortage of manpower in the law enforcement and corrections field has been widely noted.[12] One of the major means of meeting this need is increasingly recognized to be the use of auxiliary personnel. President Johnson, for example, in his message to Congress recommending crime control and law enforcement legislation on February 6, 1967, suggested the police forces could be restructured "to provide for uniformed Community Service Officers . . . these officers might not meet conventional educational requirements. They might have even had minor encounters

[11] United States Congress, Senate Report No. 1386, Committee on Labor and Public Welfare, *Vocational Education Act Amendments of 1968,* July 11, 1968, p. 24.

[12] For example, Martin Arnold, writing about the New York City Police Department, reports: "The manpower pool from which the city's police recruits traditionally are drawn is shrinking so that police officials say the department's future effectiveness is jeopardized." *New York Times,* February 14, 1967.

with the law as teenagers. But they would know the areas and the people who live in them."

The President's Commission on Law Enforcement and Administration of Justice in its report, *The Challenge of Crime in a Free Society*, discusses juvenile delinquency and youth crime and deplores the fact that "the great hopes originally held for the juvenile court have not been fulfilled. It has not succeeded significantly in rehabilitating delinquent youth." A major reason for the failure, the commission says, is lack of personnel. Many juvenile courts have no probation services and where there is such service, lack of personnel is such that "counseling and supervision take the form of occasional phone calls and perfunctory visits. . . ."[13] In its recommendations to rehabilitate delinquent youth in the community, the commission urges intensified efforts to "train and employ youth as subprofessional aides."[14]

The president's commission recommends that "probation and parole services should make use of volunteers and subprofessional aides in demonstration projects and regular programs." The commission report states that nonprofessionals could "significantly reduce the need for fully trained officers [and] could provide positive benefits beyond that of meeting manpower shortages. People who have themselves experienced problems and come from backgrounds like those of offenders often can help them in ways professional caseworkers cannot."[15]

After long consideration, Congress passed and the president, on June 20, 1968, signed into law the Omnibus Crime Control and Safe Streets Act (P.L. 90–351). Included in this law were provisions aimed at recruitment and training of law enforcement officers, but no specific new careers or nonprofessional manpower language was adopted. However, the provision for community service officers offers a wide-open opportunity for the new careers type of auxiliary personnel development. Grants are authorized for "the recruiting, organization and training and education of community

---

[13] *The Challenge of Crime in a Free Society: A Report by the President's Commission on Law Enforcement and Administration of Justice* (Washington, D. C.: U.S. Government Printing Office, 1967), p. 69.

[14] *Ibid.*

[15] *Ibid.*, pp. 167–8.

service officers to serve with and assist in the . . . improvement of police community relations; grievance resolution mechanisms; community patrol activities; encouragement of neighborhood participation in crime prevention and public safety efforts . . ." (Title I, Part C, Section 301). The new careers potential is clear in the law's definition of community service officer as "any citizen with the capacity, motivation, integrity, and stability to assist in or perform police work but who may not meet ordinary standards for employment as a regular police officer selected from the immediate locality. . . ." Other possibilities exist for new careers development through the general manpower recruitment, training, education, research, and demonstration grants sections of the Omnibus Crime Control and Safe Streets Act of 1968.

Juvenile Delinquency Prevention and Control Act of 1968. On July 31, 1968, the president signed into law, P.L. 90–445, the 1968 amendments to the Juvenile Delinquency Prevention and Control Act. This new legislation contains specific language concerning the implementation of the new careers model in the area of juvenile delinquency. The legislation reads:

> The Secretary is authorized, with the concurrence of the Secretary of Labor, to make grants or contracts for projects for the training of personnel employed in or preparing for employment in fields related to the diagnosis, treatment, or rehabilitation of youths who are delinquent or in danger of becoming delinquent, or for the counseling or instruction of parents in the improving of parental instruction and supervision of youths who are delinquent or in danger of becoming delinquent. Such projects shall include special programs which provide youths and adults with training for career opportunities, including new types of careers, in such fields. Such projects may include, among other things, development of courses of study of interrelated curriculum in schools, colleges, and universities, establishment of short-term institutes for training at such schools, colleges and universities, in-service training, and traineeships with such stipends, including allowances for travel and subsistence expenses, as the Secretary may determine to be necessary.

The Senate Committee on Labor and Public Welfare, which added the new career section to the juvenile delinquency law, stated:

Numerous witnesses before the committee stressed the need for more and better trained personnel in the delinquency area. The committee amendment is the same as the House-passed provisions except that the Secretary of Labor would be required to concur in the making of grants or signing of contracts for training, and that special provision is made for the training of youths and adults for new careers in fields related to juvenile delinquency prevention and control.[16]

National Institute of Criminal Justice. On February 16, 1967, Senator Edward Kennedy and Congressman James Scheuer introduced S. 992 and H.R. 5652 to establish a National Institute of Criminal Justice. Referred to the House and Senate Judiciary Committees, these identical bills would authorize $10 million in fiscal year 1968, for research and development into new ways to meet the crime problem and rehabilitate offenders. Grants are authorized for such efforts including "developing new career opportunities in these fields." Although not passed and still pending in Congress, this proposal illustrates a possible further application of the new careers concept in the law enforcement area.

Health and Welfare

President Johnson dealt directly with health manpower in his message to Congress February 28, 1967, on education and health in America. He told Congress:

The United States is facing a serious shortage of health manpower. Within the next decade this nation will need one million more health workers. If we are to meet this need, we must develop new skills and new types of health workers. We need short-term training programs for medical aides and other health workers. . . .

Health Manpower Act of 1968. On August 2, 1968, Congress completed its package of health manpower legislation in response to the president's proposal. Existing health manpower laws, primarily concerned with health professions, nursing, allied health professions, and public health, were revised and extended in an omnibus Health Manpower Act. None of this legislation con-

---

[16] United States Congress, Senate Report No. 1332, *Juvenile Delinquency Prevention and Control Act of 1968,* June 28, 1968.

tains specific new careers or auxiliary personnel provisions, although several possibilities for such programs are created.

A major such possibility is in the section on special project grants authorized "to assist schools of medicine, dentistry, osteopathy, pharmacy, optometry, podiatry, and veterinary medicine," in addition to other activities, "to develop training for new levels or types of health professions personnel. . . ."

Allied Health Professions Personnel Training Act of 1966. On November 3, 1966, the President signed "The Allied Health Professions Training Act of 1966." This act, as Title III of the omnibus Health Manpower Act, was extended through fiscal 1970. Although aimed at better professional training, this act opens the way for grants related to "the training of new types of health technologists and technicians." The Senate Labor and Public Welfare Committee report on this bill in 1966 quotes approvingly the statement of the National Commission on Progress "deploring the retention of traditional and basic training programs in the various health and medical fields" and calling for "training new categories of manpower who can perform many of the functions now carried out by highly skilled and scarce professional personnel."[17]

The 1968 health service amendments to the Narcotic Addict Rehabilitation Act provide support for staff and staff training of both professionals and technical personnel, with nonprofessional new careers possibilities embedded in the technician training activities.

Vocational Rehabilitation Act Amendments of 1968. A major and specific addition to the new careers program is contained in the far-reaching amendments to the Vocational Rehabilitation Act unanimously approved by Congress on June 25, 1968. As the following language in the special projects section of these amendments makes clear, the VRA new careers program aims both at using nonprofessional new careerists in rehabilitation services and at creating new careers job opportunities for the handicapped being served by vocational rehabilitation agencies. The Secretary of Health, Education, and Welfare is authorized to

[17] U.S. Congress, Senate Report No. 1722, Committee on Labor and Public Welfare, *Allied Health Professions Personnel Training Act of 1966,* October 13, 1966, pp. 3–4.

make grants to state vocational rehabilitation agencies and other public and private nonprofit agencies to enable them to develop new programs to recruit and train individuals for new career opportunities in order to provide manpower in programs serving handicapped individuals and to upgrade or expand those services, [and specifically calls for such grants] to recruit and train handicapped individuals to provide them with new career opportunities in the fields of rehabilitation, health, welfare, public safety and law enforcement, and other appropriate public services employment.

The reports of both the Senate and the House Labor Committee discuss this new careers provision and significantly establish the legislative intent of the new careers amendment as follows:

New career opportunities. The committee recognizes the outstanding work being accomplished by the professionals in vocational rehabilitation. It also acknowledges that a disproportionate amount of their time is occupied by routine and clerical duties. In order to alleviate this condition and at the same time upgrade and expand existing services for nonprofessionals, funds have been authorized to be made available through grants to agencies working with the handicapped. In meeting their manpower needs, agencies should not be limited to employing handicapped individuals but should draw from the entire population of potential workers.

Furthermore, with this provision the committee seeks not only to fill manpower needs but to promote job development which offers new career opportunities and the promise of advancement. Grants should be allotted on the basis of the degree to which the new positions enhance an agency's capacity to improve services and the employee's potential for vertical progression.

The committee in recognizing the further needs of the handicapped has also included a new grant proposal for the recruitment and training of handicapped individuals in order to provide them with new career opportunities in the varied fields comprising public service employment.[18]

Social Security Amendments of 1967. A number of new careers development possibilities are to be found in the wide-ranging 1967 amendments to the Social Security Act. The most significant of these is contained in the Harris amendments to the

[18] United States Congress, House of Representatives Report No. 1346, *Vocational Rehabilitation Amendments of 1968*, May 2, 1968, p. 9. The Senate committee report repeated this statement.

public assistance sections of the law. Sponsored by Senator Fred R. Harris, a new section, entitled "Use of Subprofessional Staff and Volunteers in Providing Services to Individuals Applying for and Receiving Assistance," requires that state plans be amended by July 1, 1969 to provide "for the training and effective use of paid subprofessional staff, with particular emphasis on the full-time or part-time employment of recipients and other persons of low income, as community service aides, in the administration of the plan. . . ." This language is now inserted as a part of the Public Welfare Title of the Social Security Act in six separate sections of the law.

The congressional rationale for this new career opening was well stated by Senator Harris when he introduced his amendment on October 16, 1967:

> I feel, Mr. President, that this country cannot begin to meet the health, education, welfare and other social needs of our people in the years ahead unless we provide for greatly expanded use of sub-professionals. We have made a bare beginning in this respect in some areas, such as health and education. These beginnings must be expanded and the concept of subprofessional staff must be broadened, not only in the welfare system, as my amendment attempts to do, but in many other agencies as well. . . . In no other way will we be able to meet the manpower needs in these fields. In no other way can we help make these programs as responsive as they must be to the needs of the people they serve.[19]

A number of other sections of the Social Security Act as amended in 1967 provide less specific but nonetheless potential openings for new careers projects and programs. These include sections on maternal and child health services, crippled children services and trainees, and child welfare services and training grants. Special project grants for the dental health of children provide for research and "demonstration of the utilization of dental personnel with various levels of training." After describing the serious problems of inadequate dental care for poor children, the official analysis of this legislation states that "The critical shortage of dentists makes it impossible to establish a full-scale program immediately.

[19] *Congressional Record,* October 16, 1967, p. S14819.

To meet the need, the nation will need to develop new systems of dental care and to train large numbers of auxiliary dental personnel to assist dentists. . . . An important aspect of the program will be the provision of opportunities to train dental auxiliaries of all types and to develop improved training methods."[20]

Even the much disputed Work Incentive Program for Recipients of Aid has some potential new careers implications. Aimed at requiring all "appropriate" adults on welfare to either take jobs or work training or lose their payments, the WINS program directs that "to the extent practicable" the program should provide basic education, training, work experience, the job development and placement services necessary to "assist participants in securing and retaining employment and security possibilities for advancement."

Other Health Legislation. A number of other bills introduced in the Ninetieth Congress dealt with various aspects of health manpower and open possibilities for new careers amendment and emphasis. For example: H.R. 6430, introduced by Congressman Harley O. Staggers, Chairman of the Committee on Interstate and Foreign Commerce (to which such bills are referred), would amend the Mental Retardation Facilities Act by authorizing "grants for the cost of professional and technical personnel. . . ." Another bill Staggers introduced jointly with Senate Labor Committee Chairman Lister Hill, H.R. 6431 and S. 1132, amends the Community Mental Health Centers Act and includes sections on staffing of such centers; another Staggers-Hill bill (H.R. 6418 and S. 1131) amends the Public Health Service Act in a number of ways; and S. 679 by Senator Norris Cotton would "encourage individuals to pursue the career of nursing." These are only illustrative of possible new careers applications and do not specifically contain new careers provisions.

Government Employment

Government employment presents the largest potential for new careers in the United States labor market. At the beginning of

[20] U.S. Congress, House of Representatives, Committee on Ways and Means, *Section-by-Section Analysis and Explanation of Provisions of H.R. 5710, the "Social Security Amendments of 1967."* February 20, 1967, pp. 40–41.

1967 there were 11,222,000 persons employed by federal, state, and local governments—2,639,000 were federal employees, not including the armed forces, and 8,583,000 were state and local employees. This reflects a strong and continuing upward trend in the absolute and relative importance of government employment.[21] Presumably such public employment is—or could become—particularly susceptible to public manpower policy seeking to develop new career opportunities for both unemployed and underemployed workers. Practically, however, to realize this potential will require widespread changes in civil service personnel policies and practices. These problems are beyond the scope of this paper, but it is very important to record that new legislative approaches to the civil service are under way and new career adjustments are on the agenda.

In a special message to Congress March 20, 1967, on the quality of American government, President Johnson stressed the manpower problems of the public service with emphasis on the needs of state and local governments. The president asked for the enactment of two bills—the Public Service Education Act and the Intergovernmental Manpower Act. These bills are directed primarily at the problem of professional shortages and the need to upgrade existing government personnel. No specific new careers features were indicated. These bills were introduced and assigned to the Senate Committee on Government Operations and the House Education and Labor Committee. They illustrate an especially important area of potential new career programming.

Intergovernmental Manpower Act of 1967. This administration bill was introduced in the House on April 6 by Congressman John Brademas and in the Senate on April 11 by Senator Edmund S. Muskie (H.R. 8234 and S. 1485). Its principal provisions, as described by Brademas, are:

> This bill would provide federal financial and other assistance to State and local governments to train and improve administrative personnel. . . . Federal agencies would be authorized to admit

[21] "Between 1955 and 1965, state and local government employment increased from 4.7 to 7.7 million persons. This is a 6 per cent increase—a rate of growth four times that of the U.S. economy as a whole and seven times that for federal employment." *Congressional Record,* April 11, 1967, p. S4810, statement by Senator Muskie.

State and local employees to training programs for federal grant programs. The Civil Service Commission would be authorized to make grants covering up to 75 per cent of the cost to assist State and local governments to establish and carry out comprehensive in-service training programs and to strengthen personnel administration. . . .[22]

The standards established to govern the granting of federal funds include the requirements of "clear and practicable actions" to improve "the recruitment, selection, assignment, and development of handicapped persons, women, and members of disadvantaged groups whose capacities are not being utilized fully" (Title II, Section 203).

Education for the Public Service Act of 1967. Congressman Brademas introduced this administration bill—H.R. 8175—on April 6, 1967. It would authorize $10 million in institutional grants and graduate fellowships aimed at improving the quality of professional entry and service in government employment. As written, it has no specific new careers features.

Federal Government Employment Opportunity Act of 1967. Senator Joseph Tydings, on March 22, 1967, introduced S. 1361 "to authorize a federal government employment opportunity program for unskilled and semiskilled individuals." A similar companion bill, S. 1360, would establish the same program in the District of Columbia. Eight other Senators sponsored these bills, which were referred to the Committee on Post Office and Civil Service and to the Committee on the District of Columbia.

Senator Tydings' bill makes the declaration that it is "the policy of Congress that all departments and agencies of the federal government shall, to the maximum degree practicable, conduct programs of recruitment and develop training programs for unskilled or low-skilled workers to meet shortages in skilled, semi-skilled, subprofessional, and subtechnical job categories within the government employment structure, and to develop and utilize fully the skill potentials of unskilled and low-skilled government employees. . . ." The Civil Service Commission is directed to identify job classifications "where functions performed . . . could appropriately be per-

[22] *Congressional Record,* April 6, 1967, p. H3677.

formed by subprofessionals or subtechnical personnel [and] establish new subprofessional or subtechnical job classifications. . . ." Programs for recruitment and training of unskilled or low-skilled workers "for specific classified civil service employment" would be required.

Public Service Employment Opportunity Act. Following the 1967 Senate hearings on the federal role in urban affairs, Senator Ribicoff introduced a series of bills including S. 585 "to provide meaningful public service employment opportunities to unemployed individuals with serious competitive disadvantages." The bill is aimed at job creation and would authorize $2 billion to provide jobs for hard-core unemployed to meet "public service needs in parks, streets, slums, countryside, schools and colleges, hospitals, nursing homes and rest homes. . . ." Although not a civil service nor a new careers measure, this bill is relevant to the new careers program in government employment.

Other Legislative Areas

Every piece of legislation proposed in Congress which deals with manpower and personnel has the potentiality of being related to new careers purposes. For many subjects the proposed legislation has not yet been formalized. In particular all manpower legislation, whether relating to training, placement, job development, or overall program coordination is subject to adjustment for new careers purposes.

Senator Ribicoff's bill S. 584, the Manpower Services and Educational Opportunity Act, is an example. This bill would establish centers for occupational education and consolidate manpower services in the Labor Department. Senator Percy's bill would extend this training beyond the Title VIII and Ribicoff proposal to cover "capable men and women who, although they might not have the formal credentials to qualify as technical and professional people, nonetheless could with the proper training develop into top-notch housing and community development specialists." Both bills are pending before the Senate Committee on Banking and Currency.

Other principal areas of potential new careers interest include legislation affecting welfare, farm extension services, and recreational services. Special attention might also be given to post-war economic planning to put an adequate new careers program into effect to offset the loss of employment following reduction of military spending.

Obviously, legislative opportunities for advancing the new careers are numerous and great. The variety of the legislative areas to which the new careers program relates gives a great opportunity for increased appreciation and application of the program. This diversity also presents a problem if the standards of a new careers program—opportunities for advancement, no dead-end jobs, structural integration into the total manpower organization, adequate training, maintenance of decent pay and work standards, avoidance of "ghettoization" of jobs and public services, and job opportunities for the poor—are not to be undermined. To maintain these standards while advancing the magnitude of the new careers program will require vigilance on many fronts. But properly used, these diverse new careers programs can help pave the way to a comprehensive national new careers program in which growth and the integrity of the program are both achieved.

CHAPTER **XIV**

Programs in the Federal Government

Joseph Kadish

ᘓᘓᘓᘓᘓᘓᘓᘓᘓᘓᘓᘓᘓᘓᘓᘓᘓᘓᘓᘓ

The increasing need for health manpower in the United States is an outgrowth of several developments, including the total population growth, the increasing concentration in urban areas, and the increasing percentage of the population aged under fifteen and over sixty-five; the greater dissemination of health information, particularly through the mass media; the proliferation of new knowledge stemming from medical research; the mounting impact of technological advances on health care, services, and facilities; and the increasing availability of health services as a result of national legislation, the growing national affluence, and the growing acceptance of the concept that health services are a right of all rather than a privilege for few.

228

The consequent need for manpower in all health occupations is impressive. The U.S. Department of Labor estimates that the employment requirements of hospitals, nursing homes, private physicians' offices, and other establishments in the health "industry" will rise from the 1966 level of 3.7 million to 5.35 million by 1975 —an increase of about 45 per cent.[1]

One approach to meeting health manpower needs has been to try to increase the number of persons trained in medicine, dentistry, and nursing. Although there has been some progress in this direction, the supply of these professional persons has not been able to meet current needs. Shortages are so acute that if every state were to be brought up to the current national average without lowering the supply in those states that are now above average, we would still need 35,879 more physicians, 14,223 more dentists, and 65,570 more nurses.[2]

In addition to the effort to increase the number of physicians, dentists, and nurses, there has been an acceleration of the proportion of allied health workers who are being utilized. (The term *allied health manpower* includes all those in the fields of medical care, community health, public health, and environmental health services who engage in activities that support, complement, or supplement the professional functions of the physician, dentist, or professional nurse. It is estimated that there are between 85 and 125 occupations which fall under this definition.) In 1900 there were only 35 trained allied health workers for every hundred physicians; by 1960 there were 371 per hundred physicians.[3]

Persons with less than full professional training are needed in the health industry if we are to meet current and future manpower demands. According to William H. Stewart, Surgeon General of the U.S. Public Health Service,

Year by year, our top professional personnel are being trained to perform still more complex tasks. How long can each profession

---

[1] U. S. Department of Labor, *Health Manpower 1966–75,* Report No. 323, Bureau of Labor Statistics, p. 1.

[2] "Manpower in the 1960's," *Health Manpower Source Book* (Washington, D. C.: U.S. Department of Health, Education, and Welfare, U.S. Public Health Service, 1964).

[3] *Ibid.*

afford to hang on to its simpler functions—the routine filling of a tooth, for example, or the several easily automated steps in a medical examination? How can we train the physician or dentist to make full use of the skills available in other people, freeing himself to perform only those duties for which he is uniquely qualified?[4]

The magnitude of the training challenge is enormous in quantitative terms. Today in medicine, dentistry, nursing, and other health professions there are perceived needs for over 500,000 additional workers—numbers far greater than the national training capacity. This means that two things must be done. First, we must augment and make the best possible use of programs and facilities for training professional health workers. Second, we must give greatly increased effort to the analysis of health-service functions, to the development of meaningful technicians and assistant groups, and to the development and support of training programs which will prepare people to work together more effectively.[5]

The role that is being assumed by allied health workers is acknowledged by Robert E. Kinsinger:

The lone practitioner of medicine is an anachronism, as is his counterpart in other professions. The knowledge explosion has overwhelmed the professional and escalated his responsibilities. Increasingly he analyzes, plans, and administers services which are provided by others—others to whom he delegates in large measure routines carried out under his direction. The "others" are technicians and assistants.[6]

These technicians and assistants are part of a large group of persons in allied health occupations who work with and support health professionals. The optimal utilization of these workers and their incorporation into a coordinated, effective effort produce the

---

[4] William H. Stewart, "Education for the Health Professions," paper given at the White House Conference on Health, Washington, D. C., November 3–4, 1965 (mimeo.).

[5] William H. Stewart, "Mobilizing Our Resources for Health Services," in *Training Health Service Workers*, Proceedings of the Conference on Job Development and Training for Workers in Health Services, 1966.

[6] Robert E. Kinsinger, "Education for Health Technicians—An Overview," Report to the American Association of Junior Colleges, February 1966, p. 11.

"health team," a concept which is becoming increasingly accepted in attempts to improve health care services.

Programs for Education

A variety of federal programs provide assistance in the education of allied health service personnel. The programs described here are representative. Further details are available from the governmental agencies which administer the programs. Programs within the Public Health Service are presented in relative detail because they are new and because the Bureau of Health Manpower was recently formed in PHS to focus on health manpower.

Public Health Service. Until very recently, the concern for health manpower in the Public Health Service was centered primarily on physicians, dentists, and nurses. With the passage of the Allied Health Professions Personnel Training Act of 1966, the service committed itself to further the health team concept, and consequently to pay greater attention to allied health occupations personnel. The purpose of this act is to improve the opportunities for training allied health personnel and the educational quality of the schools which train them. This legislation is directed to the technician and technologist level, with attention to the enhanced role of the junior college, college, and university. The technician is generally a person who has completed a two-year junior college curriculum. The technologist is trained to at least a four-year baccalaureate level. Those with less than two years of college training are generally designated aides.

The Allied Health Professions Personnel Training Act of 1966 authorizes construction grants for teaching facilities; grants to improve curricula; project grants for the development of new teaching methods; special improvement grants to help maintain, improve, or provide specialized functions in training allied health workers; advanced traineeship grants to provide more teachers, specialists, supervisors, and administrators in the allied health occupations; and project grants to spur the development of new types of health personnel. The act is administered by the Division of Allied Health Manpower, which was established January 1, 1967.

Grants are provided for the construction of new facilities or for the replacement or rehabilitation of existing facilities for junior colleges, colleges, and universities which meet eligibility requirements. Federal support may not exceed two-thirds of the cost of construction for new facilities and one-half for other kinds of construction.

Basic improvement grants are provided to increase the output and improve the quality of educational programs for allied health personnel through the development of improved curriculums, the expansion of training, and the support of additional faculty. The basic-improvement grant is essentially an entitlement of eligible training centers and is based on a formula which provides $5,000 for each of the designated curriculums in which training is provided, plus $500 for each full-time student receiving training in such curriculums.

Traineeship grants are made to colleges and universities to provide support for personnel who are pursuing advanced training to prepare them to teach health services technicians or allied health professions personnel, serve in administrative or supervisory capacities in the allied health professions, or provide services in those allied health professions specialties which require advanced training.

Grants are authorized to junior colleges, colleges, and universities for projects to develop, demonstrate, or evaluate curriculums for training new types of health technologists. Projects to develop curriculums for expanding the functions of existing allied health personnel, as well as for regrouping selected duties currently performed by allied health personnel, are within the scope of the development grant program.

In 1967 grants were made for the development of training curriculums in a variety of allied health occupations. These are described in the section on "New Types of Health Workers," below.

Office of Education. Through the Office of Education, ongoing programs in vocational and technical education have been carried on for several years. Through provisions of Title II of the Vocational Education Act of 1956, and the Vocational Education Act of 1963, thousands of persons are trained annually as practical nurses, dental assistants, dental technicians, dispensing opticians, medical assistants, medical laboratory assistants, nursing unit management assistants, nurse's aides, and operating room assistants.

Funds for these programs are provided on a fifty-fifty matching basis through grants to state departments of education. These grants cover the costs of vocational training, counseling, training of teachers and supervisors, and instructional supplies and equipment. Construction costs are provided under the Vocational Education Act of 1963. Eligibility for aid is extended to community and junior colleges, in addition to high school and post-secondary vocational and technical schools.

The Office of Education has responsibility for approving project grants for and conducting training in educational institutions at the vocational, technical, or junior-college level under the Manpower Development and Training Act of 1962. The administrative component of these programs is in the Department of Labor.

The MDTA program offers training and retraining programs to unemployed or underemployed youth and adults and underwrites programs to upgrade the skills of workers facing displacement due to technological and economic changes. The program provides teaching costs and allowances to trainees. Training may be provided either through public agencies or through arrangements with private educational and training institutions. Since 1962, MDTA has trained practical nurses, nurse's aides, professional nurses in refresher courses, psychiatric aides, dental assistants, surgical assistants, medical laboratory assistants, and home health aides.

Students in the allied health fields are eligible for financial assistance under programs administered by the Office of Education. These are National Defense student loans under the National Defense Education Act; guaranteed loans and educational opportunity grants, both under the Higher Education Act of 1965; and college work-study aid under the Economic Opportunity Act of 1964.

The college and university community service program authorized by Title I of the Higher Education Act of 1965 enables colleges and universities to provide community service and continuing education programs to upgrade training for professional or technical health personnel. As part of its program of training teachers of the handicapped, the Office of Education provides aid for the training of selected allied health professions.

Social Rehabilitation Service.[7] The Social Rehabilitation Service, in administering the Vocational Rehabilitation Act, has supported the training of personnel who provide rehabilitation services to disabled persons. Grants are made in medicine, nursing, occupational therapy, physical therapy, prosthetics and orthotics, psychology, public health, rehabilitation counseling, social work, speech pathology and audiology, recreation for the ill and disabled, sociology, and dentistry. Support is provided for both long- and short-term training through grants to or contracts with educational institutions and agencies. Support has been extended to all levels of education, from technical education to graduate or professional education.

Through Title V of the Economic Opportunity Act, the Social Rehabilitation Service provides aid for basic training of health personnel, primarily through the work experience program of the Bureau of Family Services. This program funds experimental, pilot, and demonstration projects that help needy persons to become capable of self-support. Many projects have included training for such health service occupations as practical nurse, nurse's aide, dental assistant, and hospital orderly and attendant.

The Children's Bureau provides project grants for training professional personnel in maternal and child health care and crippled children's services. In general, the training is offered to persons who have already completed basic professional education. Grants under the 1960 amendments to the Social Security Act have supported the training of physicians and nurses, audiologists and speech pathologists, medical social workers, and members of other allied health professions.

Department of Labor. Under the Manpower Development and Training Act, financial assistance is provided to employers and institutions for on-the-job training of workers. Grants have been made to hospitals, nursing and old-age homes, dental laboratories, and rehabilitation centers for training in nearly forty health

[7] The Social Rehabilitation Service was established on August 15, 1967, to carry out the functions of the Welfare Administration, the Vocational Rehabilitation Administration, the Administration of Aging, and the Mental Retardation Division of the Bureau of Health Services of the Public Health Service.

care occupations. With regard to programs in educational institutions which are administered by the Office of Education, the Department of Labor determines needs in cooperation with state employment agencies. New techniques have been sought for providing needed basic education, work orientation, and other pre-vocational remedial services, and new job-instruction methods and settings have been tested. Some projects have trained new types of aides in health, education, and welfare fields.

Office of Economic Opportunity. Many persons are being trained for allied health occupations under various programs of the Economic Opportunity Act of 1964. A pilot program administered cooperatively by the Community Action Program and the Public Health Service aims at recruiting and training the poor, aged forty-five and over, as home health aides. In the initial phase of this project, three thousand were trained in conformity with standards for home health service under Medicare. Neighborhood Health Centers employ neighborhood residents who receive training on the job or in other institutions and agencies. Among the programs of VISTA (Volunteers in Service to America) are intensive six-week training courses to qualify persons to work in hospitals and with the mentally ill and retarded. The Job Corps program of the Office of Economic Opportunity is a resident program of vocational training, remedial education, and work experience, designed to equip youth from impoverished homes with the skills and attitudes needed to find and hold suitable employment in a wide variety of occupations, including the health field.

Where Personnel Are Trained

Educational programs for the allied health occupations are located in a wide variety of academic settings, including colleges and universities, at least sixteen of which have schools of allied health professions, medical and dental schools, technical and vocational schools, junior colleges and hospitals. The trend is away from hospital-based programs and toward a shared relationship with educational institutions.

Schools of Allied Health Professions. An approach which is gaining increasing attention is the grouping of several health curriculums in a college or school, generally within a university medical center. Through this approach individual curriculums gain status and strength. Programs which are related to one another are placed in an environment which facilitates interaction. Duplications in administration, faculty, and facilities are minimized by combining several curriculums in one college or unit. This arrangement also encourages students to learn more about other related occupations, and ultimately to work together more effectively.

At least sixteen medical centers currently have or are developing formal structures for interdisciplinary programs in the allied health professions. The organization of health professions education in these universities varies considerably. In some, programs are administered in a single organizational unit. In others, the health programs are located in several departments and are coordinated through a dean of health affairs. In still others, some of the programs are located in a school of allied health professions and others in the dental school, the school of arts and sciences, or the university hospital center, with little coordination. In each case, however, there is some university organization to ensure program quality and flexibility.

Programs in Other Universities and Colleges. In addition to the universities with schools of allied health professions, about fifty universities offer three or more programs for the education of allied health professions in their medical and dental schools. Close to six hundred other universities and colleges offer specialization in one or more of the allied health occupations at the baccalaureate and graduate level. These programs are designed to permit students to combine curriculums for preparation in the allied health professions, liberal arts, and basic sciences.

The Community or Junior College. The two-year college (commonly called the community college in the Midwest and East and the junior college in the West and South) is growing at an exceptional rate and is regarded as the most promising development in recent years for the training of allied health personnel. In the past few years, as many as fifty new community colleges or junior colleges have been established annually. The associate degree programs offered by these institutions train enrollees as nurses, radiological technologists, dental hygienists, dental assistants, medical assistants, medical laboratory assistants, and environmental health technicians.

Vocational Schools. Vocational schools have been preparing students for entry-level jobs in the health field for many years. Since 1950, they have prepared some five thousand practical nurses annually. Today, these schools prepare students for at least a dozen health occupations, including dental assistant, medical assistant, medical laboratory assistant, surgical technician, physical therapy assistant, practical nurse, and inhalation therapist.

Educational Programs in Hospitals. Hospitals are continuing to train large numbers of persons for many health occupations. In recent years, however, hospitals are placing greater emphasis on providing the clinical training while educational institutions are providing the basic educational functions for allied personnel in a wide variety of occupations.

Hospital training activities related to the allied health occupations can be categorized in three areas: they provide basic education for students enrolled in the hospital's own programs, they provide clinical experience for students of health-related occupations in affiliated educational institutions, and they provide in-service training for their own staff and for new employees.

New Types of Health Workers

Many of the duties and responsibilities which were considered to be solely within the province of physicians, dentists, nurses, and related professional workers are now being carried out by persons with less training. Some health occupations which were not known twenty years ago are now well established—for example, the inhalation therapist, who is in charge of the technical details of oxygen administration; the prosthetist, who works as a fitter of artificial limbs; and the cytotechnologist, who is trained in special laboratory techniques for detecting body cell changes which are particularly important in the early diagnosis of cancer.

Through the Allied Health Professions Personnel Training Act, specifically through its provision for developmental grants, several projects have been funded for the development of new types of health technologists. For example, at the College of Medicine of

Ohio State University, a training program is producing personnel capable of operating all types of extracorporeal circulatory systems and commonly used medical electronic instrumentation, such as cardiopulmonary bypass, renal dialysis, organ storage and transplantion, and related activities.

The University of Kentucky Medical Center is formulating an electroencephalography technician training program which will provide a defined curriculum for this occupation, in which personnel are currently trained on the job.

At the School of Industrial Engineering of the Georgia Institute of Technology, a program is under way with persons expert in industrial engineering, operations research, management sciences, and systems analysis and design to teach them to apply their expertise to the delivery of health services.

St. Petersburg Junior College in Florida is engaged in developing a training program for administrators of extended care facilities, such as nursing homes.

Additional programs for training new types of allied health manpower are stimulated through contracts administered by the Division of Allied Health Manpower in the Bureau of Health Manpower of the U. S. Public Health Service. One contract provides for the training of an orthopedic assistant to work under the supervision of the orthopedic specialist in applying and removing casts, placing patients in traction beds, and otherwise helping the physician in the operating room, on the ward, in clinics, and in private practice.

In another contract, young women college graduates are being trained on the job to serve as psychological assistants. Trainees conduct, score, and participate in the interpretation of psychological tests; prepare data for computers; prepare charts and assist with library research and manuscript preparation. After one year of training these psychological assistants are considered indispensable by the staff psychologists who are their teachers and supervisors.

In addition to these developmental programs, experiments are being carried out under various auspices to develop new types of health workers. For example, the "pediatric nurse practitioner" is being trained to assume an expanded role in child health. In one of these programs, nurses with the regular nursing Bachelor of

Science degree receive four months of intensive training at a medical center, followed by twenty months of field experience, which prepares them to furnish comprehensive well-child care to children of all ages, to identify and appraise acute and chronic conditions and refer them to other facilities as indicated, and to evaluate and temporarily manage emergency situations until medical assistance is available. Similarly trained nurses are also joining the offices of private pediatricians to act as the doctor's associate.

A two-year program is under way for ex-medical corpsmen and others with comparable experience to develop highly skilled, career-oriented assistants for physicians who will assume responsibility for repetitious and technical tasks classically performed by physicians.

The training of men as "medical emergency technicians" and ambulance technicians is conducted at a few universities. Since physicians no longer ride ambulances, there is a need for well-trained ambulance attendants to direct emergency operations and to provide emergency care on the scene and en route to the hospital. New York State has recently enacted legislation requiring training for ambulance technicians.

Experiments in the training and use of dental auxiliaries with expanded functions have been conducted by the Divisions of Dental Health and of Indian Health of the Public Health Service. In evaluating the work performed by these auxiliary workers, no significant difference has been found in the quality of fillings placed by the dentist or by the auxiliary, in cavities first prepared by the dentist.

Directly related to the problem of developing new occupations is that of properly utilizing people whose training is outside the generally accepted and established academic patterns. Methods of providing additional training must be devised to enable these individuals to meet with the educational and licensing requirements of their occupations. Every year more than ten thousand corpsmen and other health technicians are released from the armed services. These men have effectively performed many functions in medical, dental, optical, operating room, physical therapy, and radiology sciences. However, there have been no mechanisms for finding these men, attracting them to civilian medical services, and utilizing their valuable skills. Project REMED, sponsored by the Office of Education in cooperation with the Department of Labor, Public Health Service and their counterparts at State and local government levels, seeks to correct this deficiency.

Implications

It is increasingly recognized that the vast health needs of our country cannot be met by traditional methods. New approaches to meeting manpower needs are being considered along with the application of newer technology in health care services, new methods of financing health care, and experiments in systems of delivery of services.

When demands for health care were less acute, little attention was paid to the professional person who carried out activities below the level for which he was trained. Today such wasteful practices are considered among the reasons that some people are not getting needed care.

The health-care field does not have to look far to find examples of lesser trained persons or differently trained persons who are assuming responsibilities formerly carried out solely by the professional. At one time registered nurses spent a major part of their time performing elementary chores associated with bedside nursing; today these services are performed by licensed practical nurses and nurse's aides. Dental prophylaxis was once the function of the dentist alone, whereas now this function is often carried out by the dental hygienist. Not only are professional persons delegating many of their duties and functions to allied health personnel on the technologist level, but the technologist is now passing on duties and functions to technicians. Work requiring even less training and skill is being performed by aides. This division of labor is not only economical but serves the purpose of enhancing job satisfactions.

Professionals and other high level personnel are sometimes reluctant to relinquish some of their duties and responsibilities. They seem to be concerned that the lower-level persons will infringe on their professional roles. Although some of these less trained persons may insist that they can perform on the professional level, this seems to be an unrealistic concern. On the other hand, the development of allied health personnel frees the professional to work on a higher level, the level for which he has been trained. It provides the professional with the opportunity to use his unique skills to the utmost.

The development of new allied health personnel will require the professional to work closely with persons whose education and training have been in the same field but at a lower level. Effective interpersonal contacts will therefore be a challenge to the professional, and the new staff person will need to be recognized as a member of the health team. The professional worker also will be in a position to further the development of the new allied health worker. Efforts may need to be exerted individually and through their professional organizations to provide opportunities for allied health workers to advance to higher level jobs and in other ways attain job satisfactions.

The significance of allied and auxiliary health workers in total efforts to meet community health needs has been stated by the National Commission on Community Health Services:

> The most promising single measure for assuring an adequate supply of health manpower is optimal use of large numbers of allied and auxiliary personnel. Adequate numbers of such workers can permit the efficient use of highly educated and specialized personnel. Many allied health workers have a unique competence in specific segments of health service. With adequate supervision and effective liaison among related professional and occupational groups, allied health workers in different specialties and with varying levels of education and training can make an enormous contribution to enlarging the provisions of community health services. Their participation in the health team can enhance the quality of services and implement the principle that health personnel should not normally be used for tasks below the level for which they are prepared.
>
> Educational institutions, health agencies, and health workers —individually and through their associations—should give high priority to increasing the numbers of both existing and new kinds of allied and auxiliary personnel.
>
> The health team should function with each member contributing his most highly developed skills. Innovation and experimentation should be undertaken to expand and develop the roles of allied and auxiliary personnel.

In order to develop fully the roles of allied and auxiliary workers, health agencies and professional and occupational associations should undertake continuing assessment and evaluation of the character of allied and auxiliary personnel required to provide them.[8]

[8] National Commission on Community Health Services, *Health Manpower, Action to Meet Community Needs* (Washington, D. C.: Public Affairs Press, 1967), p. 22.

Conference on the Use of Nonprofessionals in Mental Health Work

᭦᭦᭦᭦᭦᭦᭦᭦᭦᭦᭦᭦᭦᭦᭦᭦᭦᭦

MELVIN E. ALLERHAND, Director, Division of General Studies, Case Western Reserve University, Cleveland, Ohio

FRANKLYN ARNHOFF, Manpower Analytic Studies Branch, Division of Manpower and Training Programs, National Institute of Mental Health, Bethesda, Maryland

LENIN A. BALER, Associate Professor Community Mental Health, School of Public Health, University of Michigan, Ann Arbor, Michigan

RAYMOND J. BALESTER, Deputy Director, Division of Manpower and Training Programs, National Institute of Mental Health, Bethesda, Maryland

ROBERT S. BARTLETT, Sociology Instructor, University of Bridgeport, Bridgeport, Connecticut

ARTHUR BRAYFIELD, Executive Officer, American Psychological Association, Washington, D. C.

THOMAS L. BRIGGS, Research Director, Utilization of Social Work

Personnel Project, National Association of Social Workers, New York, New York

MAXINE BROWN, Family and Child Service Agency, Washington, D. C.

SARGENT CARLTON, Administrative Assistant to James H. Scheuer, Congressman, Twenty-first District, New York, New York

LOUIS D. COHEN, Professor and Chairman, Department of Clinical Psychology, University of Florida, Gainesville, Florida

WILLIAM COLLINS, Occupational Specialist, Standards Division, United States Civil Service Commission, Washington, D. C.

MARY E. DUREN, Executive Director, Action for Appalachian Youth, Inc., Charleston, West Virginia

JOHN L. ERLICH, Assistant Professor, School of Social Work, University of Michigan, Ann Arbor, Michigan

EUNICE EVANS, Pennsylvania Department of Public Welfare, Harrisburg, Pennsylvania

JOHN R. FERGUSON, Associate Director, Department of Social Work Practice, National Association of Social Workers, New York, New York

MURIEL FLYNN, Staff Associate in Charge of Newark Teacher Aide Training, Scientific Resources, Inc., Newark, New Jersey

ELIZABETH FULLERTON, Bureau of Work Programs, United States Department of Labor, Washington, D. C.

CHARLES D. GARVIN, Assistant Professor, School of Social Work, University of Michigan, Ann Arbor, Michigan

ELLIOTT GODOFF, Vice President and Director of the Hospital Division, Local 1199, Drug and Hospital Employees Union, AFL-CIO, New York, New York

STUART GOLANN, Associate Administrative Officer, State and Professional Affairs, American Psychological Association, Washington, D. C.

GERTRUDE S. GOLDBERG, Research Associate, Information Retrieval Center on the Disadvantaged, Yeshiva University, New York, New York

CHARLES GROSSER,* Associate Professor, School of Social Work, Columbia University, New York, New York

WILLIAM E. HENRY,* Professor of Psychology and Human Development and Chairman, Committee on Human Development, University of Chicago, Chicago, Illinois

PAUL E. JARVIS, Psychology; affiliated with Metropolitan State College and Ft. Logan Mental Health Center, Denver, Colorado

JOAN JENKINS, Manpower Analytic Studies Branch, Division of Man-

* Conference co-director

power and Training Programs, National Institute of Mental Health, Bethesda, Maryland

KENNETH JOHNSON, Executive Secretary, American Speech and Hearing Association, Washington, D. C.

ANNE JONES, Training Director, Training Center of the Mayor's Committee on Human Resources, Pittsburgh, Pennsylvania

OPAL C. JONES, Executive Director, Neighborhood Adult Participation Project, Los Angeles, California

JOSEPH KADISH, Education Specialist, Educational Program Development Branch, Division of Allied Health Manpower, Bureau of Health Manpower, United States Public Health Service, Washington, D. C.

JAMES G. KELLY,* Associate Professor, Department of Psychology, University of Michigan, Ann Arbor, Michigan

ALVIN KOGUT, Assistant Professor, School of Social Work, Adelphi University, Garden City, New York

TOM LEVIN, Assistant Professor of Psychiatry, Albert Einstein College of Medicine, Lincoln Hospital Mental Health Services, Bronx, New York

HARRY LIEBERMAN, Manpower Analyst, Office of Program Design and Standards, United States Department of Labor, Washington, D. C.

JUDITH MAGE, President, Social Service Employees Union, New York, New York

ALBERT MASLOW, Chief of the Personnel Research Center, United States Civil Service Commission, Washington, D. C.

JAMES C. MCDONALD, Associate Director, New York University New Careers Development Center, New York, New York

JOHN J. MCMILLAN, Administrative Officer, State and Professional Affairs, American Psychological Association, Washington, D. C.

SAMUEL J. MEER, Associate Professor and Director, Educational Clinic, School of Education, the City College of the City University of New York, New York, New York

HENRY R. MEYER, Professor of Social Work and Sociology, University of Michigan, Ann Arbor, Michigan

HOWARD E. MITCHELL, Professor and Director, Human Resources Program, Department of City and Regional Planning, University of Pennsylvania, Philadelphia, Pennsylvania

LONNIE E. MITCHELL, Clinical Psychologist, Howard University, Washington, D. C.

PHOEBE NICHOLAS, Office of Manpower Policy, Evaluation, and Research, Manpower Administration, Department of Labor, Washington, D. C.

JOSEPHINE NIEVES, Regional Director, Northeast Regional Office of Economic Opportunity, New York, New York

JOSEPH NOEL, Doctoral Candidate, Committee on Human Development, University of Chicago, Chicago, Illinois

VICTORIA OLDS, Professor of Social Work, Howard University, Washington, D. C.

ROBERT REIFF, Associate Professor and Director, Division of Psychology, Albert Einstein College of Medicine, Lincoln Hospital Mental Health Services, Bronx, New York

RICHARD SANDERS, Director of Psychological Services, Philadelphia State Hospital, Philadelphia, Pennsylvania

MAXWELL J. SCHLEIFER, Project Coordinator of the Newton-Baker Project, Boston, Massachusetts

AARON SCHMAIS, Associate Director, Neighborhood Service Center Program; Instructor, Department of Psychology, Albert Einstein College of Medicine, Lincoln Hospital Mental Health Services, Bronx, New York

EDWARD E. SCHWARTZ, Professor, School of Social Service Administration, University of Chicago, Chicago, Illinois

JOSEPH SEILER, Manpower Analyst, Office of Manpower Policy, Evaluation, and Research, United States Department of Labor, Washington, D. C.

JEFFREY SHAPIRO, Arkansas Rehabilitation Research and Training Center, Little Rock, Arkansas

AUDREY SHEPARD, Assistant Director, Neighborhood Services Project of Family and Child Service Agency, Washington, D. C.

HARRY SPECHT, Acting Associate Professor, School of Social Welfare, University of California, Berkeley, California

WRAY STROWIG, Professor, Department of Counseling and Behavioral Studies; Chairman, APGA Professional Preparation and Standards Commission, University of Wisconsin, Madison, Wisconsin

JOHN E. TRUE, Associate Professor of Psychology and Associate Program Director, Associate Degree Program in Mental Health, Purdue University, Lafayette, Indiana

ROSE WHEELER, Mental Health Consultant, Mental Health Division, Chicago Board of Health, Chicago, Illinois

C. L. WINDER, Chairman, Department of Psychology, Michigan State University, East Lansing, Michigan

LIVINGSTON WINGATE, Director, New York Urban League, New York, New York

MILTON WITTMAN, Chief, Social Work Training Branch, National Institute of Mental Health, Bethesda, Maryland

APPENDIX **B**

Recent Legislation

EDUCATION

Legislation	Program	Eligible Agency
Handicapped Children Early Education Act of 1968, Section 2	Provides for the training and career advancement of paraprofessionals in the provision of early education services for the handicapped	Public and private nonprofit organizations
Higher Education Act Amendments, 1968, Sec. 408, ". . . Special services for (Low-income) students in Institutions of Higher Education"	Special supportive services for disadvantaged college students	Institutions of higher education
Higher Education Act Amendments of 1968, Title I, Sec. 453, "Grants and Contracts for Training and Research"	Provides funds for research into new methods of cooperative education and the training of administrative staff for such programs	Institutions of higher education, public and private nonprofit organizations
Higher Education Act Amendments, 1968, Title IX, "Education for Public Service"	Supports college education programs for part-time students for careers in the public sector	Institutions of higher education
Vocational Education Act Amendments, Sec. 122, Part D, "State Vocational Education Programs"	Provides funds for programs of vocational education include the training of subprofessionals	States

Vocational Education Act Amendments, Sec. 131, Part C, "Research and Training in Vocational Education"	Funds available for support of training of paraprofessionals; in the utilization of paraprofessionals; and the evaluation of public service aid programs	Public and private nonprofit organizations
Vocational Education Act Amendments, 1968, Part D, "Exemplary Programs"	Funds available for experimental projects to bridge the gap between school and employment	Local public and private nonprofit organizations

Contact Agency: U.S. Office of Education
Department of Health, Education, and Welfare
Washington, D.C. 20202

H E A L T H

Health Manpower Act, 1968, Title I, Health Professions Training, Part B, Sec. 772, "Special Project Grants"	Supports programs for the training of new levels of personnel in the health professions of dentistry, medicine, osteopathy, optometry, pharmacy, podiatry, and veterinary medicine	Schools of medicine, podiatry, and other health professions
Health Manpower Act, 1968, Title II, "Nurse Training" Part B, "Special Project and Institutional Grants to Schools of Nursing"	Funds available for experimental and special projects to expand nursing education programs	Schools of nursing, public and private nonprofit organizations
Health Manpower Act, 1968, Title III, "Allied Health Professions and Public Health Training"	Provides funds for programs demonstrating curricula for the training of health technologists	Public and private nonprofit organizations and institutions
Health Services Amendments, 1968, Alcoholic and Narcotic Addict Rehabilitation Amendments, Sec. 252, "Training and Evaluation"	Provides support for staffing as well as the training of professional and technical (nonprofessional) personnel of narcotic addict treatment and prevention projects	Public and private nonprofit organizations and agencies

RECENT LEGISLATION (*cont'd*)

HEALTH (*cont'd*)

Legislation	Program	Eligible Agency
Health Services Amendments, 1968, Alcoholic and Narcotic Addict Rehabilitation Amendments, Part C, Sec. 240, "Alcoholism"	Supplies funds to support professional and technical (nonprofessional) personnel in programs and centers for the prevention and treatment of alcoholism	Public and private nonprofit organizations and agencies

Contact Agency: U.S. Public Health Service
Department of Health, Education and Welfare
9000 Rockville Pike
Bethesda, Maryland 20014

HOUSING

Legislation	Program	Eligible Agency
Housing Act 1964, 1968 Amendments, Title VIII, "Training and Fellowship Programs for Community Development"	Provides funds for the training of paraprofessional and professional staff of government agencies	States, local governments

Contact Agency: Director, Urban Manpower and Development
Department of Housing and Urban Development
1626 K Street, N.W.
Washington, D.C.

MUNICIPAL SERVICES

Legislation	Program	Eligible Agency
Fire Research and Safety Act, 1968, Title I, Sec. 16(a) 5	Authorizes funds for research, demonstration, experimental, education, and training programs that improve the delivery of fire prevention and control services	States, local governments, public and private nonprofit organizations

Legislation	Purpose	Eligible Recipients
Omnibus Crime Control and Safe Streets Act, 1968, Part C, "Grants for Law Enforcement Purposes"	Provides for the training and education of "community service officers" (a local resident who may not meet the ordinary entrance standards) to assist in the improvement of police-community relations	States, local governments
Part D, "Training, Education Research Demonstration and Special Grants," Sec. 406	Supports programs demonstrating the value of new techniques or methods in the provision of police services	Nonprofit private and public organizations
	Authorizes funds for tuition for part-time academic education for all types of police personnel	Individuals

Contact Agency: Office of the Secretary
Department of Health, Education, and Welfare
330 Independence Avenue
Washington, D.C. 20201

WELFARE

Legislation	Purpose	Eligible Recipients
Juvenile Delinquency Prevention and Control Act, 1968, Title I, "Planning, Preventive and Rehabilitation Services," Title II, "Training," Title III, "Improving Techniques and Practices"	Provides funds for support of direct services, demonstration, and experimental programs of diagnosis, treatment, and rehabilitation of delinquent youth	States, local government, public and private nonprofit organizations and agencies
Vocational Rehabilitation Amendment, 1968, Sec. 7(a) (2) c & d, "Special Projects"	Provides for the use of paraprofessionals as a vehicle for training the handicapped and in the provision of vocational rehabilitation services	Public and private nonprofit organizations

Contact Agency: Social and Rehabilitation Service
Department of Health, Education, and Welfare
Washington, D.C. 20201

Index

A

Act (legislative): Allied Health Professions Personnel Training, 220, 231, 237; Community Mental Health Centers, 223; Community Mental Health Services, 58; Delinquency Prevention, 100; Economic Opportunity, 58, 94, 101, 110, 121, 123, 204, 205–209, 233, 234, 235; Education Professions Development, 209–210; Elementary and Secondary Education, 100, 211–214; Federal Government Employment Opportunity, 225; Health Manpower, 219–220; Higher Education, 210–211, 213, 233; Intergovernmental Manpower, 224–225; Juvenile Delinquency and Youth Offenses, 118, 218–219; Law Enforcement Assistance, 100; Manpower Training and Development, 116, 118, 128, 134n, 141, 233, 234–235; Mental Health, 80; Mental Retardation Facilities, 223; Model Cities, 100; Narcotic Addict Rehabilitation, 220; National Defense Education, 223; Omnibus Crime Control and Safe Streets, 100, 217–218; Public Health, 163, 223; Public Service Education, 224, 225; Public Service Employment Opportunity, 226; Scheuer-Nelson Subprofessional Ca-

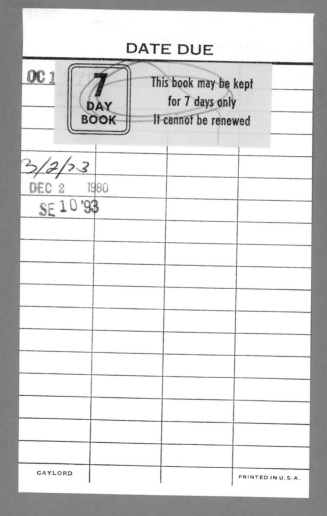